A YEAR WITH
ASLAN

Daily Reflections from
The Chronicles of Narnia

C. S. LEWIS

Edited by Julia L. Roller

HarperOne
An Imprint of HarperCollinsPublishers

HarperOne

HarperCollins books may be purchased for educational, business, or sales promo-
tional use. For information please write: Special Markets Department, HarperCollins
Publishers, 10 East 53rd Street, New York, NY 10022.

HarperCollins Web site: http://www.harpercollins.com

HarperCollins®, 📖®, and HarperOne™ are trademarks of HarperCollins Publishers

Illustrations by Pauline Baynes. Copyright © C. S. Lewis Pte. Ltd. 1950–1956.

The Chronicles of Narnia®, Narnia®, and all book titles, characters, and locales
original to The Chronicles of Narnia are trademarks of C. S. Lewis Pte. Ltd. Use
without permission is strictly prohibited.

Narnia.com

NARNIA®

FIRST EDITION

Library of Congress Cataloging-in-Publication Data

Lewis, C. S. (Clive Staples), 1898–1963.
    A year with Aslan : daily reflections from The chronicles of Narnia / C. S. Lewis ;
edited by Julia L. Roller. — 1st ed.
        p.   cm.
    ISBN 978-0-06-198551-5
    1. Lewis, C. S. (Clive Staples), 1898–1963—Calendars.   2. Lewis, C. S. (Clive
Staples), 1898–1963—Quotations.   3. Conduct of life—Quotations, maxims,
etc.   4. Lewis, C. S. (Clive Staples), 1898–1963. Chronicles of Narnia.   I. Roller,
Julia L.   II. Title.
    PR6023.E926A6   2010
    823'.912—dc22   2010012439

10   11   12   13   14   RRD(H)   10 9 8 7 6 5 4 3 2 1

Preface

Some books are fun to read. Rarer are those volumes that still delight us upon rereading. And then there are those rarefied species of books, those that we read, read again, and again, and keep reading. In fact, a part of us never really leaves the story. They become part of the geography of our souls, the landmarks by which we map and measure our lives. At least that has been my experience with C. S. Lewis's Narnia books. Unlike most, I missed them completely when I was the right age to begin and only discovered them in college. And so my cycle of reading began. Especially helpful was the cover I was given by having two daughters who pleaded with me each night to read the books to them. "Well, if you insist." Still, forever after, unbidden, and at all the right moments in my life, I saw Eustace struggle with his dragon skin, Digory debating obedience to Aslan versus saving his mother, Lucy chastising herself for sticking with the group even after she saw Aslan, Edmund facing his shame after his rescue from the White Witch, or Tirian and Jewel racing up Aslan's mountain laughing while the dwarves think they are still in a dark hut.

We have created this volume for all those similarly haunted. Each day for a whole year brings an episode from anywhere in the seven volumes of the chronicles, an isolated story or scene that provides both delight and nourishment, an opportunity to reflect and deepen our experience of this landscape of wonder (with questions at the bottom of each selection for those who appreciate a nudge in a particular direction). I grew up in a tradition that encouraged a daily practice of reading and reflection as a spiritual workout, and we often heard admonishments for why we had to will it earnestly and overcome our natural resistance to this vital practice. (In other words, it was presented as the spiritual equivalent of "eat your vegetables.") Yet this led me to the unexpected query, *But what if I enjoyed it?* Follow that line of thought and you will arrive at the very logic and purpose of this book.

We need to pause and thank Julia Roller, who selected the readings and drafted the questions; Cynthia DiTiberio, the editor at HarperOne who captained the project as well as Drinian guided the *Dawn Treader;* and, finally, to the C. S. Lewis Company, who graciously allowed us to play in this field. And now, for everyone else, "Further up and further in!"

—Michael G. Maudlin
Editorial Director
HarperOne

JANUARY

The Creation of Narnia

F̲AR AWAY, and down near the horizon, the sky began to turn grey. A light wind, very fresh, began to stir. The sky, in that one place, grew slowly and steadily paler. You could see shapes of hills standing up dark against it. All the time the Voice went on singing. . . .

The eastern sky changed from white to pink and from pink to gold. The Voice rose and rose, till all the air was shaking with it. And just as it swelled to the mightiest and most glorious sound it had yet produced, the sun arose.

Digory had never seen such a sun. The suns above the ruins of Charn had looked older than ours: this looked younger. You could imagine that it laughed for joy as it came up. And as its beams shot across the land the travelers could see for the first time what sort of place they were in. It was a valley through which a broad, swift river wound its way, flowing eastward toward the sun. Southward there were mountains, northward there were lower hills. But it was a valley of mere earth, rock and water; there was not a tree, not a bush, not a blade of grass to be seen. The earth was of many colors; they were fresh and hot and vivid. They made you feel excited; until you saw the Singer himself, and then you forgot everything else.

It was a Lion. Huge, shaggy, and bright, it stood facing the risen sun. Its mouth was wide open in song and it was about three hundred yards away.

—*The Magician's Nephew*

What do you think it is like for Digory, Polly, and the others to stumble upon such a scene? Have you ever stumbled upon a scene of such wonder that it was hard to fathom? How did you react?

Their Own Secret Country

THE STORY BEGINS on an afternoon when Edmund and Lucy were stealing a few precious minutes alone together. And of course they were talking about Narnia, which was the name of their own private and secret country. Most of us, I suppose, have a secret country but for most of us it is only an imaginary country. Edmund and Lucy were luckier than other people in that respect. Their secret country was real. They had already visited it twice; not in a game or a dream but in reality. They had got there of course by Magic, which is the only way of getting to Narnia. And a promise, or very nearly a promise, had been made them in Narnia itself that they would some day get back. You may imagine that they talked about it a good deal, when they got the chance.

—*The Voyage of the* **Dawn Treader**

What does having a place that you dream about, whether real or imagined, do for you? Have you been able to retain that sense of imagination and dreams in your adulthood?

Into the Wardrobe

A ND SHORTLY AFTER THAT they looked into a room that was quite empty except for one big wardrobe; the sort that has a looking-glass in the door. There was nothing else in the room at all except a dead blue-bottle on the window-sill.

"Nothing there!" said Peter, and they all trooped out again—all except Lucy. She stayed behind because she thought it would be worth while trying the door of the wardrobe, even though she felt almost sure that it would be locked. To her surprise it opened quite easily, and two moth-balls dropped out.

Looking into the inside, she saw several coats hanging up—mostly long fur coats. There was nothing Lucy liked so much as the smell and feel of fur. She immediately stepped into the wardrobe and got in among the coats and rubbed her face against them, leaving the door open, of course, because she knew that it is very foolish to shut oneself into any wardrobe. Soon she went further in and found that there was a second row of coats hanging up behind the first one. It was almost quite dark in there and she kept her arms stretched out in front of her so as not to bump her face into the back of the wardrobe. She took a step further in—then two or three steps—always expecting to feel woodwork against the tips of her fingers. But she could not feel it.

"This must be a simply enormous wardrobe!" thought Lucy, going still further in and pushing the soft folds of the coats aside to make room for her. Then she noticed that there was something crunching under her feet. "I wonder is that more moth-balls?" she thought, stooping down to feel it with her hand. But instead of feeling the hard, smooth wood of the floor of the wardrobe, she felt something soft and powdery and extremely cold. "This is very queer," she said, and went on a step or two further.

Next moment she found that what was rubbing against her face and hands was no longer soft fur but something hard and rough and even prickly. "Why, it is just like branches of trees!" exclaimed Lucy. And then she saw that there was a light ahead of her; not a few inches away where the back of the wardrobe ought to have been, but a long way off. Something cold and soft was falling on her. A moment later she found that she was standing in the middle of a wood at night-time with snow under her feet and snowflakes falling through the air.

Lucy felt a little frightened, but she felt very inquisitive and excited as well. She looked back over her shoulder and there, between the dark tree-trunks, she could still see the open doorway of the wardrobe and even catch a glimpse of the empty room from which she had set out. (She had, of course, left the door open, for she knew that it is a very silly thing to shut oneself into a wardrobe.) It seemed to be still daylight there. "I can always get back if anything goes wrong," thought Lucy. She began to walk forward, crunch-crunch over the snow and through the wood toward the other light.

—*The Lion, the Witch, and the Wardrobe*

What does it tell us about Lucy that she continues alone into the wardrobe even after finding something so unexpected there? Do you have this kind of curiosity? If so, how has it affected your life? If not, what would it mean for your life?

A Sense of Wonder

"THEY SAY ASLAN is on the move—perhaps has already landed."

And now a very curious thing happened. None of the children knew who Aslan was any more than you do; but the moment the Beaver had spoken these words everyone felt quite different. Perhaps it has sometimes happened to you in a dream that someone says something which you don't understand but in the dream it feels as if it had some enormous meaning—either a terrifying one which turns the whole dream into a nightmare or else a lovely meaning too lovely to put into words, which makes the dream so beautiful that you remember it all your life and are always wishing you could get into that dream again. It was like that now. At the name of Aslan each one of the children felt something jump in its inside. Edmund felt a sensation of mysterious horror. Peter felt suddenly brave and adventurous. Susan felt as if some delicious smell or some delightful strain of music had just floated by her. And Lucy got the feeling you have when you wake up in the morning and realize that it is the beginning of the holidays or the beginning of summer.

—The Lion, the Witch, and the Wardrobe

When was the last time you felt the sense of anticipation and wonder that the four children feel upon hearing Aslan's name?

Who Is Aslan?

O H, YES! Tell us about Aslan!" said several voices at once; for once again that strange feeling—like the first signs of spring, like good news, had come over them.

"Who is Aslan?" asked Susan.

"Aslan?" said Mr. Beaver. "Why, don't you know? He's the King. He's the Lord of the whole wood, but not often here, you understand. Never in my time or my father's time. But the word has reached us that he has come back. He is in Narnia at this moment. He'll settle the White Queen all right. It is he, not you, that will save Mr. Tumnus."

"She won't turn him into stone too?" said Edmund.

"Lord love you, Son of Adam, what a simple thing to say!" answered Mr. Beaver with a great laugh. "Turn *him* into stone? If she can stand on her two feet and look him in the face it'll be the most she can do and more than I expect of her. No, no. He'll put all to rights as it says in an old rhyme in these parts:

Wrong will be right, when Aslan comes in sight,
At the sound of his roar, sorrows will be no more,
When he bares his teeth, winter meets its death,
And when he shakes his mane, we shall have
spring again.

—The Lion, the Witch, and the Wardrobe

What might the children be picturing from Mr. Beaver's description of Aslan? What would your reaction be if someone you knew told you there was someone in the world right now who will right all your wrongs?

The Door to Narnia

I F ONLY THE DOOR WAS OPEN AGAIN!" said Scrubb as they went on, and Jill nodded. For at the top of the shrubbery was a high stone wall and in that wall a door by which you could get out on to open moor. This door was nearly always locked. But there had been times when people had found it open; or perhaps there had been only one time. But you may imagine how the memory of even one time kept people hoping, and trying the door; for if it should happen to be unlocked it would be a splendid way of getting outside the school grounds without being seen.

Jill and Eustace, now both very hot and very grubby from going along bent almost double under the laurels, panted up to the wall. And there was the door, shut as usual.

"It's sure to be no good," said Eustace with his hand on the handle; and then, "O-o-oh. By Gum!!" For the handle turned and the door opened.

A moment before, both of them had meant to get through that doorway in double quick time, if by any chance the door was not locked. But when the door actually opened, they both stood stock still. For what they saw was quite different from what they had expected.

They had expected to see the grey, heathery slope of the moor going up and up to join the dull autumn sky. Instead, a blaze of sunshine met them. It poured through the doorway as the light of a June day pours into a garage when you open the door. It made the drops of water on the grass glitter like beads and showed up the dirtiness of Jill's tear-stained face. And the sunlight was coming from what certainly did look like a different world—what they could see of it. They saw smooth turf, smoother and brighter than Jill had ever seen before, and blue sky, and, darting to and fro, things so bright that they might have been jewels or huge butterflies.

Although she had been longing for something like this, Jill felt frightened. She looked at Scrubb's face and saw that he was frightened too.

"Come on, Pole," he said in a breathless voice.

"Can we get back? Is it safe?" asked Jill.

At that moment a voice shouted from behind, a mean, spiteful little voice. "Now then, Pole," it squeaked. "Everyone knows you're there. Down you come." It was the voice of Edith Jackle, not one of Them herself but one of their hangers-on and tale-bearers.

"Quick!" said Scrubb. "Here. Hold hands. We mustn't get separated." And before she quite knew what was happening, he had grabbed her hand and pulled her through the door, out of the school grounds, out of England, out of our whole world into That Place.

—The Silver Chair

Why do you think that upon seeing something amazing she has always longed for, Jill feels frightened and hesitates? Have you ever felt like Jill, drawn toward something that seems wonderful but afraid at the same time? Would you be angry with Eustace, or relieved that he took charge of the situation?

Trust

"Are you not thirsty?" said the Lion.

"I'm *dying* of thirst," said Jill.

"Then drink," said the Lion.

"May I—could I—would you mind going away while I do?" said Jill.

The Lion answered this only by a look and a very low growl. And as Jill gazed at its motionless bulk, she realized that she might as well have asked the whole mountain to move aside for her convenience.

The delicious rippling noise of the stream was driving her nearly frantic.

"Will you promise not to—do anything to me, if I do come?" said Jill.

"I make no promise," said the Lion.

Jill was so thirsty now that, without noticing it, she had come a step nearer.

"*Do* you eat girls?" she said.

"I have swallowed up girls and boys, women and men, kings and emperors, cities and realms," said the Lion. It didn't say this as if it were boasting, nor as if it were sorry, nor as if it were angry. It just said it.

"I daren't come and drink," said Jill.

"Then you will die of thirst," said the Lion.

"Oh dear!" said Jill, coming another step nearer. "I suppose I must go and look for another stream then."

"There is no other stream," said the Lion.

It never occurred to Jill to disbelieve the Lion—no one who had seen his stern face could do that—and her mind suddenly made itself up. It was the worst thing she had ever had to do, but she went forward to the stream, knelt down, and began scooping up water in her hand. It was the coldest, most refreshing water she had ever tasted. You didn't need to drink much of it, for it quenched your thirst at once.

—*The Silver Chair*

Why won't Aslan put Jill's fears to rest?

Too Beautiful to Believe

I CANNOT SET MYSELF to any work or sport today, Jewel," said the King. "I can think of nothing but this wonderful news. Think you we shall hear more of it today?"

"They are the most wonderful tidings ever heard in our days or our fathers' or our grandfathers' days, Sire," said Jewel, "if they are true."

"How can they choose but be true?" said the King. "It is more than a week ago that the first birds came flying over us saying, Aslan is here, Aslan has come to Narnia again. And after that it was the squirrels. They had not seen him, but they said it was certain he was in the woods. Then came the Stag. He said he had seen him with his own eyes, a great way off, by moonlight, in Lantern Waste. Then came that dark Man with the beard, the merchant from Calormen. The Calormenes care nothing for Aslan as we do; but the man spoke of it as a thing beyond doubt. And there was the Badger last night; he too had seen Aslan."

"Indeed, Sire," answered Jewel, "I believe it all. If I seem not to, it is only that my joy is too great to let my belief settle itself. It is almost too beautiful to believe."

"Yes," said the King with a great sigh, almost a shiver, of delight. "It is beyond all that I ever hoped for in all my life."

—*The Last Battle*

What does Jewel mean by saying that his joy is too great to let his belief settle itself? Has any news ever struck you this way? What, deep down, have you hoped for all your life?

The Call

ASLAN THREW UP HIS SHAGGY HEAD, opened his mouth, and uttered a long, single note; not very loud, but full of power. Polly's heart jumped in her body when she heard it. She felt sure that it was a call, and that anyone who heard that call would want to obey it and (what's more) would be able to obey it, however many worlds and ages lay between. And so, though she was filled with wonder, she was not really astonished or shocked when all of a sudden a young woman, with a kind, honest face stepped out of nowhere and stood beside her. Polly knew at once that it was the Cabby's wife, fetched out of our world not by any tiresome magic rings, but quickly, simply and sweetly as a bird flies to its nest. The young woman had apparently been in the middle of a washing day, for she wore an apron, her sleeves were rolled up to the elbows and there were soapsuds on her hands. If she had had time to put on her good clothes (her best hat had imitation cherries on it) she would have looked dreadful; as it was, she looked rather nice.

Of course she thought she was dreaming. That was why she didn't rush across to her husband and ask him what on earth had happened to them both. But when she looked at the Lion she didn't feel quite so sure it was a dream, yet for some reason she did not appear to be very frightened. Then she dropped a little half curtsey, as some country girls still knew how to do in those days. After that, she went and put her hand in the Cabby's and stood there looking round her a little shyly.

—*The Magician's Nephew*

Why do you think Aslan chose a Cabby and his wife as the first king and queen of Narnia? She doesn't know what she's been called to do, yet she seems to trust that all is as it should be. Though this situation is extreme, have you ever found yourself in an unexpected place but where, deep down, you knew you were supposed to be?

Picking Sides

THEY WERE ALL STILL WONDERING what to do next, when Lucy said, "Look! There's a robin, with such a red breast. It's the first bird I've seen here. I say!—I wonder can birds talk in Narnia? It almost looks as if it wanted to say something to us." Then she turned to the Robin and said, "Please, can you tell us where Tumnus the Faun has been taken to?" As she said this she took a step toward the bird. It at once flew away but only as far as to the next tree. There it perched and looked at them very hard as if it understood all they had been saying. Almost without noticing that they had done so, the four children went a step or two nearer to it. At this the Robin flew away again to the next tree and once more looked at them very hard. . . .

"Do you know," said Lucy, "I really believe he means us to follow him."

"I've an idea he does," said Susan. "What do you think, Peter?"

"Well, we might as well try it," answered Peter.

. . . They had been traveling in this way for about half an hour . . . when Edmund said to Peter, "if you're not still too high and mighty to talk to me, I've something to say which you'd better listen to. . . . [H]ave you realized what we're doing? . . . We're following a guide we know nothing about. How do we know which side that bird is on? Why shouldn't it be leading us into a trap?"

"That's a nasty idea. Still—a robin, you know. They're good birds in all the stories I've ever read. I'm sure a robin wouldn't be on the wrong side."

"If it comes to that, which *is* the right side? How do we know that the Fauns are in the right and the Queen (yes, I know we've been *told* she's a witch) is in the wrong? We don't really know anything about either."

"The Faun saved Lucy."

"He *said* he did. But how do we know?"

—*The Lion, the Witch, and the Wardrobe*

If you were Peter, how would you determine which is the right side? When have you been unsure whether someone was trustworthy or not? How did you decide?

The Source of Wisdom

AFTER THIS, Caspian and his tutor had many more secret conversations on the top of the Great Tower, and at each conversation Caspian learned more about Old Narnia, so that thinking and dreaming about the old days, and longing that they might come back, filled nearly all his spare hours. But of course he had not many hours to spare, for now his education was beginning in earnest. He learned sword-fighting and riding, swimming and diving, how to shoot with the bow and play on the recorder and the theorbo, how to hunt the stag and cut him up when he was dead, besides Cosmography, Rhetoric, Heraldry, Versification, and of course History, with a little Law, Physic, Alchemy, and Astronomy. Of Magic he learned only the theory, for Doctor Cornelius said the practical part was not proper study for princes. "And I myself," he added, "am only a very imperfect magician and can do only the smallest experiments." Of Navigation ("Which is a noble and heroical art," said the Doctor) he was taught nothing, because King Miraz disapproved of ships and the sea.

He also learned a great deal by using his own eyes and ears. As a little boy he had often wondered why he disliked his aunt, Queen Prunaprismia; he now saw that it was because she disliked him. He also began to see that Narnia was an unhappy country. The taxes were high and the laws were stern and Miraz was a cruel man.

—Prince Caspian

What is the difference between what Caspian's tutor taught him and what he learned using his own resources? Have you learned your most significant lessons from the instruction of others or from your own observations?

A Perfectly Ordinary Wardrobe

LUCY RAN OUT of the empty room into the passage and found the other three.

"It's all right," she repeated, "I've come back."

"What on earth are you talking about, Lucy?" asked Susan.

"Why," said Lucy in amazement, "haven't you all been wondering where I was?"

"So you've been hiding, have you?" said Peter. "Poor old Lu, hiding and nobody noticed! You'll have to hide longer than that if you want people to start looking for you."

"But I've been away for hours and hours," said Lucy.

The others all stared at one another.

"Batty!" said Edmund, tapping his head. "Quite batty."

"What do you mean, Lu?" asked Peter.

"What I said," answered Lucy. "It was just after breakfast when I went into the wardrobe, and I've been away for hours and hours, and had tea, and all sorts of things have happened."

"Don't be silly, Lucy," said Susan. "We've only just come out of that room a moment ago, and you were there then."

"She's not being silly at all," said Peter, "she's just making up a story for fun, aren't you, Lu? And why shouldn't she?"

"No, Peter, I'm not," she said. "It's—it's a magic wardrobe. There's a wood inside it, and it's snowing, and there's a Faun and a Witch and it's called Narnia; come and see."

The others did not know what to think, but Lucy was so excited that they all went back with her into the room. She rushed ahead of them, flung open the door of the wardrobe and cried, "Now! go in and see for yourselves."

"Why, you goose," said Susan, putting her head inside and pulling the fur coats apart, "it's just an ordinary wardrobe; look! there's the back of it."

Then everyone looked in and pulled the coats apart; and they all saw— Lucy herself saw—a perfectly ordinary wardrobe. There was no wood and no snow, only the back of the wardrobe, with hooks on it. Peter went in and rapped his knuckles on it to make sure that it was solid.

"A jolly good hoax, Lu," he said as he came out again; "you have really taken us in, I must admit. We half-believed you."

"But it wasn't a hoax at all," said Lucy, "really and truly. It was all different a moment ago. Honestly it was. I promise."

"Come, Lu," said Peter, "that's going a bit far. You've had your joke. Hadn't you better drop it now?"

Lucy grew very red in the face and tried to say something, though she hardly knew what she was trying to say, and burst into tears.

For the next few days she was very miserable. She could have made it up with the others quite easily at any moment if she could have brought herself to say that the whole thing was only a story made up for fun. But Lucy was a very truthful girl and she knew that she was really in the right; and she could not bring herself to say this. The others who thought she was telling a lie, and a silly lie too, made her very unhappy. The two elder ones did this without meaning to do it, but Edmund could be spiteful, and on this occasion he was spiteful. He sneered and jeered at Lucy and kept on asking her if she'd found any other new countries in other cupboards all over the house. What made it worse was that these days ought to have been delightful. The weather was fine and they were out of doors from morning to night, bathing, fishing, climbing trees, and lying in the heather. But Lucy could not properly enjoy any of it.

—*The Lion, the Witch, and the Wardrobe*

Why is it so hard for Lucy to say she's made up her story about the wardrobe? Should she have done so to make things easier? Why do you think not being believed on this one point could ruin her enjoyment of everything she does with her brothers and sister? Have you ever experienced something so strange that people didn't believe it was true? How did their disbelief make you feel?

The Voice

IN THE DARKNESS something was happening at last. A voice had begun to sing. It was very far away and Digory found it hard to decide from what direction it was coming. Sometimes it seemed to come from all directions at once. Sometimes he almost thought it was coming out of the earth beneath them. Its lower notes were deep enough to be the voice of the earth herself. There were no words. There was hardly even a tune. But it was, beyond comparison, the most beautiful noise he had ever heard. It was so beautiful he could hardly bear it.

—*The Magician's Nephew*

What does it mean for something to be so beautiful you can hardly bear it? What's the closest experience you've had to that feeling?

Reacting to the Voice

THERE WAS SOON LIGHT ENOUGH for them to see one another's faces. The Cabby and the two children had open mouths and shining eyes; they were drinking in the sound, and they looked as if it reminded them of something. Uncle Andrew's mouth was open too, but not open with joy. He looked more as if his chin had simply dropped away from the rest of his face. His shoulders were stooped and his knees shook. He was not liking the Voice. If he could have got away from it by creeping into a rat's hole, he would have done so. But the Witch looked as if, in a way, she understood the music better than any of them. Her mouth was shut, her lips were pressed together, and her fists were clenched. Ever since the song began she had felt that this whole world was filled with a Magic different from hers and stronger. She hated it. She would have smashed that whole world, or all worlds, to pieces, if it would only stop the singing.

—*The Magician's Nephew*

Why do you think each person reacted so differently? How do you think hearing such a powerful Voice would affect you?

I Just Know

L OOK! LOOK! LOOK!" cried Lucy.
"Where? What?" said everyone.

"The Lion," said Lucy. "Aslan himself. Didn't you see?" Her face had changed completely and her eyes shone.

"Do you really mean—?" began Peter.

"Where did you think you saw him?" asked Susan.

"Don't talk like a grown-up," said Lucy, stamping her foot. "I didn't *think* I saw him. I saw him. . . . Right up there between those mountain ashes. . . . Just the opposite of the way you want to go. And he wanted us to go where he was—up there."

"How do you know that was what he wanted?" asked Edmund.

"He—I—I just know," said Lucy, "by his face.". . .

"Her Majesty may well have seen a lion," put in Trumpkin. "There are lions in these woods, I've been told. But it needn't have been a friendly and talking lion any more than the bear was a friendly and talking bear."

"Oh, don't be so stupid," said Lucy. "Do you think I don't know Aslan when I see him?"

"He'd be a pretty elderly lion by now," said Trumpkin, "if he's one you knew when you were here before! And if it could be the same one, what's to prevent him having gone wild and witless like so many others?"

Lucy turned crimson and I think she would have flown at Trumpkin, if Peter had not laid his hand on her arm. "The D.L.F. doesn't understand. How could he? You must just take it, Trumpkin, that we do really know about Aslan; a little bit about him, I mean. And you mustn't talk about him like that again. It isn't lucky for one thing: and it's all nonsense for another. The only question is whether Aslan was really there."

"But I know he was," said Lucy, her eyes filling with tears.

"Yes, Lu, but we don't, you see," said Peter.

—*Prince Caspian*

Why are the others having such a hard time believing Lucy? Do you often have to see with your own eyes to believe something?

The Vote

"THERE'S NOTHING FOR IT BUT A VOTE," said Edmund.
"All right," replied Peter. "You're the eldest, D.L.F. What do you vote for? Up or down?"

"Down," said the Dwarf. "I know nothing about Aslan. But I do know that if we turn left and follow the gorge up, it might lead us all day before we found a place where we could cross it. Whereas if we turn right and go down, we're bound to reach the Great River in about a couple of hours. And if there *are* any real lions about, we want to go away from them, not toward them."

"What do you say, Susan?"

"Don't be angry, Lu," said Susan, "but I do think we should go down. I'm dead tired. Do let's get out of this wretched wood into the open as quick as we can. And none of us except you saw *anything*."

"Edmund?" said Peter.

"Well, there's just this," said Edmund, speaking quickly and turning a little red. "When we first discovered Narnia a year ago—or a thousand years ago, whichever it is—it was Lucy who discovered it first and none of us would believe her. I was the worst of the lot, I know. Yet she was right after all. Wouldn't it be fair to believe her this time? I vote for going up."

"Oh, Ed!" said Lucy and seized his hand.

"And now it's your turn, Peter," said Susan, "and I do hope—"

"Oh, shut up, shut up and let a chap think," interrupted Peter. "I'd much rather not have to vote."

"You're the High King," said Trumpkin sternly.

"Down," said Peter after a long pause. "I know Lucy may be right after all, but I can't help it. We must do one or the other."

—Prince Caspian

Why is Edmund the only one to believe Lucy this time? Why do you think Peter makes the decision he does?

Lu, You're a Hero

"I OUGHT TO HAVE MY HEAD SMACKED for bringing us this way at all," said Peter.

"On the contrary, your Majesty," said the Dwarf. "For one thing it wasn't you, it was your royal brother, King Edmund, who first suggested going by Glasswater."

"I'm afraid the D.L.F.'s right," said Edmund, who had quite honestly forgotten this ever since things began going wrong.

"And for another," continued Trumpkin, "if we'd gone my way, we'd have walked straight into that new outpost, most likely; or at least had just the same trouble avoiding it. I think this Glasswater route has turned out for the best."

"A blessing in disguise," said Susan.

"Some disguise!" said Edmund.

"I suppose we'll have to go right up the gorge again now," said Lucy.

"Lu, you're a hero," said Peter. "That's the nearest you've got today to saying *I told you so*. Let's get on."

—*Prince Caspian*

Would you be able to resist the temptation to say "I told you so"? How is this heroic?

Are You Good at Believing Things?

LOOK HERE, POLE, you and I hate this place about as much as anybody can hate anything, don't we?"

"I know I do," said Jill [Pole].

"Then I really think I can trust you."

"Dam' good of you," said Jill.

"Yes, but this is a really terrific secret. Pole, I say, are you good at believing things? I mean things that everyone here would laugh at?"

"I've never had the chance," said Jill, "but I think I would be."

"Could you believe me if I said I'd been right out of the world—outside this world—last hols?"

"I wouldn't know what you meant."

"Well, don't let's bother about worlds then. Supposing I told you I'd been in a place where animals can talk and where there are—er—enchantments and dragons—and—well, all the sorts of things you have in fairy-tales." [Eustace] Scrubb felt terribly awkward as he said this and got red in the face.

"How did you get there?" said Jill. She also felt curiously shy.

"The only way you can—by Magic," said Eustace almost in a whisper. "I was with two cousins of mine. We were just—whisked away. They'd been there before."

Now that they were talking in whispers Jill somehow felt it easier to believe. Then suddenly a horrible suspicion came over her and she said (so fiercely that for the moment she looked like a tigress):

"If I find you've been pulling my leg I'll never speak to you again; never, never, never."

"I'm not," said Eustace. "I swear I'm not. I swear by—by everything.". . .

"All right," said Jill, "I'll believe you."

—*The Silver Chair*

Why do you think Eustace chooses to share his secret? Are you good at believing things? What's the hardest thing anyone's ever asked you to believe?

Nobody Special

BREE TURNED ROUND AT LAST, his face mournful as only a horse's can be.

"I shall go back to Calormen," he said.

"What?" said Aravis. "Back to slavery!"

"Yes," said Bree. "Slavery is all I'm fit for. How can I ever show my face among the free Horses of Narnia?—I who left a mare and a girl and a boy to be eaten by lions while I galloped all I could to save my own wretched skin!"

"We all ran as hard as we could," said Hwin.

"Shasta didn't!" snorted Bree. "At least he ran in the right direction: ran *back*. And that is what shames me most of all. I, who called myself a war horse and boasted of a hundred fights, to be beaten by a little human boy—a child, a mere foal, who had never held a sword nor had any good nurture or example in his life!"

"I know," said Aravis. "I felt just the same. Shasta was marvelous. I'm just as bad as you, Bree. I've been snubbing him and looking down on him ever since you met us and now he turns out to be the best of us all. . . ."

"It's all very well for you," said Bree. "You haven't disgraced yourself. But I've lost everything."

"My good Horse," said the Hermit, who had approached them unnoticed because his bare feet made so little noise on that sweet, dewy grass. "My good Horse, you've lost nothing but your self-conceit. No, no, cousin. Don't put back your ears and shake your mane at me. If you are really so humbled as you sounded a minute ago, you must learn to listen to sense. You're not quite the great Horse you had come to think, from living among poor dumb horses. Of course you were braver and cleverer than *them*. You could hardly help being that. It doesn't follow that you'll be anyone very special in Narnia. But as long as you know you're nobody very special, you'll be a very decent sort of Horse, on the whole."

—*The Horse and His Boy*

Why is it helpful for Bree to think of himself as nobody special? Do you think of yourself that way? What are the benefits and limits of such a philosophy?

Awakening Evil

THE THING IN THE MIDDLE of the room was not exactly a table. It was a square pillar about four feet high and on it there rose a little golden arch from which there hung a little golden bell; and beside this there lay a little golden hammer to hit the bell with.

"I wonder . . . I wonder . . . I wonder," said Digory.

"There seems to be something written here," said Polly, stooping down and looking at the side of the pillar. . . .

What it said was something like this—at least this is the sense of it though the poetry, when you read it there, was better:

Make your choice, adventurous Stranger;
Strike the bell and bide the danger,
Or wonder, till it drives you mad,
What would have followed if you had.

"No fear!" said Polly. "We don't want any danger."

"Oh, but don't you see it's no good?" said Digory. "We can't get out of it now. We shall always be wondering what else would have happened if we had struck the bell. I'm not going home to be driven mad by always thinking of that. No fear!"

"Don't be so silly," said Polly. "As if anyone would! What does it matter what would have happened?"

"I expect anyone who's come as far as this is bound to go on wondering till it sends him dotty. That's the Magic of it, you see. I can feel it beginning to work on me already."

"Well, I don't," said Polly crossly. "And I don't believe you do either. You're just putting it on."

"That's all *you* know," said Digory. "It's because you're a girl. Girls never want to know anything but gossip and rot about people getting engaged.". . .

[Polly said,] "I'm off. I've had enough of this place. And I've had enough of you too—you beastly, stuck-up, obstinate pig!"

"None of that!" said Digory in a voice even nastier than he meant it to be; for he saw Polly's hand moving to her pocket to get hold of her yellow ring. I can't excuse what he did next except by saying that he was very sorry afterward (and so were a good many other people). Before Polly's hand reached her pocket, he grabbed her wrist, leaning across with his back against her chest. Then, keeping her other arm out of the way with his other elbow, he leaned forward, picked up the hammer, and struck the golden bell a light, smart tap.

—*The Magician's Nephew*

Whom do you most sympathize with in this situation? Why?

How Do You Know It's Not True?

THE TWO OLDER ONES were really beginning to think that Lucy was out of her mind. They stood in the passage talking about it in whispers long after she had gone to bed.

The result was the next morning they decided that they really would go and tell the whole thing to the Professor. "He'll write to Father if he thinks there is really something wrong with Lu," said Peter; "it's getting beyond us." So they went and knocked at the study door, and the Professor said "Come in," and got up and found chairs for them and said he was quite at their disposal. Then he sat listening to them with the tips of his fingers pressed together and never interrupting, till they had finished the whole story. After that he said nothing for quite a long time. Then he cleared his throat and said the last thing either of them expected:

"How do you know," he asked, "that your sister's story is not true?"

"Oh, but—" began Susan, and then stopped. Anyone could see from the old man's face that he was perfectly serious. Then Susan pulled herself together and said, "But Edmund said they had only been pretending."

"That is a point," said the Professor, "which certainly deserves consideration; very careful consideration. For instance—if you will excuse me for asking the question—does your experience lead you to regard your brother or your sister as the more reliable? I mean, which is the more truthful?"

"That's just the funny thing about it, sir," said Peter. "Up till now, I'd have said Lucy every time."

"And what do you think, my dear?" said the Professor, turning to Susan.

"Well," said Susan, "in general, I'd say the same as Peter, but this couldn't be true—all this about the wood and the Faun."

"That is more than I know," said the Professor, "and a charge of lying against someone whom you have always found truthful is a very serious thing; a very serious thing indeed."

"We were afraid it mightn't even be lying," said Susan; "we thought there might be something wrong with Lucy."

"Madness, you mean?" said the Professor quite coolly. "Oh, you can make your minds easy about that. One has only to look at her and talk to her to see that she is not mad."

"But then," said Susan, and stopped. She had never dreamed that a grown-up would talk like the Professor and didn't know what to think.

"Logic!" said the Professor half to himself. "Why don't they teach logic at these schools? There are only three possibilities. Either your sister is telling lies, or she is mad, or she is telling the truth. You know she doesn't tell lies and it is obvious that she is not mad. For the moment then and unless any further evidence turns up, we must assume that she is telling the truth."

—*The Lion, the Witch, and the Wardrobe*

Why are Susan and Peter so surprised at the Professor's opinion? Why do you think their first instinct is not to believe Lucy? When in your life have you had trouble reconciling belief with logic?

Minding Our Own Business

"B UT HOW COULD IT BE TRUE, SIR?" said Peter.
"Why do you say that?" asked the Professor.

"Well, for one thing," said Peter, "if it was real why doesn't everyone find this country every time they go to the wardrobe? I mean, there was nothing there when we looked; even Lucy didn't pretend there was."

"What has that to do with it?" said the Professor.

"Well, sir, if things are real, they're there all the time."

"Are they?" said the Professor; and Peter did not know quite what to say.

"But there was no time," said Susan. "Lucy had had no time to have gone anywhere, even if there was such a place. She came running after us the very moment we were out of the room. It was less than a minute, and she pretended to have been away for hours."

"That is the very thing that makes her story so likely to be true," said the Professor. "If there really is a door in this house that leads to some other world (and I should warn you that this is a very strange house, and even I know very little about it)—if, I say, she had got into another world, I should not be at all surprised to find that the other world had a separate time of its own; so that however long you stayed there it would never take up any of *our* time. On the other hand, I don't think many girls of her age would invent that idea for themselves. If she had been pretending, she would have hidden for a reasonable time before coming out and telling her story."

"But do you really mean, sir," said Peter, "that there could be other worlds—all over the place, just round the corner—like that?"

"Nothing is more probable," said the Professor, taking off his spectacles and beginning to polish them, while he muttered to himself, "I wonder what they *do* teach them at these schools."

"But what are we to do?" said Susan. She felt that the conversation was beginning to get off the point.

"My dear young lady," said the Professor, suddenly looking up with a very sharp expression at both of them, "there is one plan which no one has yet suggested and which is well worth trying."

"What's that?" said Susan.

"We might all try minding our own business," said he. And that was the end of that conversation.

—*The Lion, the Witch, and the Wardrobe*

Why does the Professor advise them to mind their own business? When does our concern for the well-being of others become problematic?

Pleased with Nothing

THE NAME OF THE SHIP was *Dawn Treader.* She was only a little bit of a thing compared with one of our ships, or even with the cogs, dromonds, carracks and galleons which Narnia had owned when Lucy and Edmund had reigned there under Peter as the High King, for nearly all navigation had died out in the reigns of Caspian's ancestors. When his uncle, Miraz the usurper, had sent the seven lords to sea, they had had to buy a Galmian ship and man it with hired Galmian sailors. But now Caspian had begun to teach the Narnians to be sea-faring folk once more, and the *Dawn Treader* was the finest ship he had built yet. She was so small that, forward of the mast, there was hardly any deck room between the central hatch and the ship's boat on one side and the hen-coop (Lucy fed the hens) on the other. But she was a beauty of her kind, a "lady" as sailors say, her lines perfect, her colors pure, and every spar and rope and pin lovingly made. Eustace of course would be pleased with nothing, and kept on boasting about liners and motorboats and aeroplanes and submarines ("As if *he* knew anything about them," muttered Edmund), but the other two were delighted with the *Dawn Treader,* and when they returned aft to the cabin and supper, and saw the whole western sky lit up with an immense crimson sunset, and felt the quiver of the ship, and tasted the salt on their lips, and thought of unknown lands on the Eastern rim of the world, Lucy felt that she was almost too happy to speak.

—*The Voyage of the* **Dawn Treader**

Why do some people fight magic and adventure, while others thrive in the unexpected? Which do you tend toward?

Puddleglum

I'M TRYING TO CATCH A FEW EELS to make an eel stew for our dinner," said Puddleglum. "Though I shouldn't wonder if I didn't get any. And you won't like them much if I do."

"Why not?" asked Scrubb.

"Why, it's not in reason that you should like our sort of victuals, though I've no doubt you'll put a bold face on it. All the same, while I am a catching them, if you two could try to light the fire—no harm trying—! The wood's behind the wigwam. It may be wet. You could light it inside the wigwam, and then we'd get all the smoke in our eyes. Or you could light it outside, and then the rain would come and put it out. Here's my tinder-box. You wouldn't know how to use it, I expect."

But Scrubb had learnt that sort of thing on his last adventure. The children ran back together to the wigwam, found the wood (which was perfectly dry) and succeeded in lighting a fire with rather less than the usual difficulty. . . .

"Now," said Puddleglum. "Those eels will take a mortal long time to cook, and either of you might faint with hunger before they're done. I knew a little girl—but I'd better not tell you that story. It might lower your spirits, and that's a thing I never do. So, to keep your minds off your hunger, we may as well talk about our plans."

"Yes, do, let's," said Jill. "Can you help us to find Prince Rilian?"

The Marsh-wiggle sucked in his cheeks till they were hollower than you would have thought possible. "Well, I don't know that you'd call it *help*," he said. "I don't know that anyone can exactly *help*. It stands to reason we're not likely to get very far on a journey to the North, not at this time of the year, with the winter coming on soon and all. And an early winter too, by the look of things. But you mustn't let that make you down-hearted. Very likely, what with enemies, and mountains, and rivers to cross, and losing our way, and next to nothing to eat, and sore feet, we'll hardly notice the weather. And if we don't get far enough to do any good, we may get far enough not to get back in a hurry."

Both children noticed that he said "we," not "you," and both exclaimed at the same moment, "Are you coming with us?"

"Oh yes, I'm coming of course. Might as well, you see. I don't suppose we shall ever see the King back in Narnia, now that he's once set off for foreign parts; and he had a nasty cough when he left. Then there's Trumpkin. He's failing fast. And you'll find there'll have been a bad harvest after this terrible dry summer. And I shouldn't wonder if some enemy attacked us. Mark my words.". . .

"Look here!" said Scrubb, suddenly losing his temper, as people so easily do when they have been frightened. "I don't believe the whole thing can be half as bad as you're making out; any more than the beds in the wigwam were hard or the wood was wet. I don't think Aslan would ever have sent us if there was so little chance as all that."

—*The Silver Chair*

Why might Puddleglum always think about the worst-case scenario? Why is his outlook so frustrating to Scrubb? Who have you known who seems to always look on the dark side? Do you have any tendencies in that direction?

The Narnian Lords

W AY! WAY! WAY!" came the voice. "Way for the White Barbarian King, the guest of the Tisroc (may he live forever)! Way for the Narnian lords.". . .

It was quite unlike any other party they had seen that day. The crier who went before it shouting, "Way, way!" was the only Calormene in it. And there was no litter; everyone was on foot. There were about half a dozen men and Shasta had never seen anyone like them before. For one thing, they were all as fair-skinned as himself, and most of them had fair hair. And they were not dressed like men of Calormen. Most of them had legs bare to the knee. Their tunics were of fine, bright, hardy colors— woodland green, or gay yellow, or fresh blue. Instead of turbans they wore steel or silver caps, some of them set with jewels, and one with little wings on each side. A few were bare-headed. The swords at their sides were long and straight, not curved like Calormene scimitars. And instead of being grave and mysterious like most Calormenes, they walked with a swing and let their arms and shoulders go free, and chatted and laughed. One was whistling. You could see that they were ready to be friends with anyone who was friendly, and didn't give a fig for anyone who wasn't. Shasta thought he had never seen anything so lovely in his life.

—*The Horse and His Boy*

Why do the Narnian lords make such a favorable impression on Shasta? What do they represent to him? What might people notice about you if they saw you walking by?

Aslan Roars

THE LIGHT WAS CHANGING. Low down in the east, Aravir, the morning star of Narnia, gleamed like a little moon. Aslan, who seemed larger than before, lifted his head, shook his mane, and roared.

The sound, deep and throbbing at first like an organ beginning on a low note, rose and became louder, and then far louder again, till the earth and air were shaking with it. It rose up from that hill and floated across all Narnia. Down in Miraz's camp men woke, stared palely in one another's faces, and grasped their weapons. Down below that in the Great River, now at its coldest hour, the heads and shoulders of the nymphs, and the great weedy-bearded head of the river-god, rose from the water. Beyond it, in every field and wood, the alert ears of rabbits rose from their holes, the sleepy heads of birds came out from under wings, owls hooted, vixens barked, hedgehogs grunted, the trees stirred. In towns and villages mothers pressed babies close to their breasts, staring with wild eyes, dogs whimpered, and men leaped up groping for lights. Far away on the northern frontier the mountain giants peered from the dark gateways of their castles.

—*Prince Caspian*

What kind of emotions would you say Aslan's roar stirs in those who hear it? How can one sound represent different things to different people? Where do you see that in our world today?

Real Magic

YOU?" SAID THE QUEEN in a still more terrible voice. Then, in one stride, she crossed the room, seized a great handful of Uncle Andrew's grey hair and pulled his head back so that his face looked up into hers. Then she studied his face just as she had studied Digory's face in the palace of Charn. He blinked and licked his lips nervously all the time. At last she let him go: so suddenly that he reeled back against the wall.

"I see," she said scornfully, "you are a Magician—of a sort. Stand up, dog, and don't sprawl there as if you were speaking to your equals. How do you come to know Magic? *You* are not of royal blood, I'll swear."

"Well—ah—not perhaps in the strict sense," stammered Uncle Andrew. "Not exactly royal, Ma'am. The Ketterleys are, however, a very old family. An old Dorsetshire family, Ma'am."

"Peace," said the Witch. "I see what you are. You are a little, peddling Magician who works by rules and books. There is no real Magic in your blood and heart. Your kind was made an end of in my world a thousand years ago. But here I shall allow you to be my servant."

—The Magician's Nephew

What might the Queen mean about having Magic in your blood and heart, as compared to Uncle Andrew's type of Magic? What have you learned by closely studying someone's face?

Strawberry Speaks

A LL THIS TIME THE CABBY had been trying to catch Strawberry's eye. Now he did. "Now, Strawberry, old boy," he said. "You know me. You ain't going to stand there and say as you don't know me."

"What's the Thing talking about, Horse?" said several voices.

"Well," said Strawberry very slowly, "I don't exactly know, I think most of us don't know much about anything yet. But I've a sort of idea I've seen a thing like this before. I've a feeling I lived somewhere else—or was something else—before Aslan woke us all up a few minutes ago. It's all very muddled. Like a dream. But there were things like these three in the dream."

"What?" said the Cabby. "Not know me? Me what used to bring you a hot mash of an evening when you was out of sorts? Me what rubbed you down proper? Me what never forgot to put your cloth on you if you was standing in the cold? I wouldn't 'ave thought it of you, Strawberry."

"It *does* begin to come back," said the Horse thoughtfully. "Yes. Let me think now, let me think. Yes, you used to tie a horrid black thing behind me and then hit me to make me run, and however far I ran this black thing would always be coming rattle-rattle behind me."

"We 'ad our living to earn, see," said the Cabby. "Yours the same as mine. And if there 'adn't been no work and no whip there'd 'ave been no stable, no hay, no mash, and no oats. For you did get a taste of oats when I could afford 'em, which no one can deny."

"Oats?" said the Horse, pricking up his ears. "Yes, I remember something about that. Yes, I remember more and more. You were always sitting up somewhere behind, and I was always running in front, pulling you and the black thing. I know I did all the work."

—The Magician's Nephew

Aslan has just made Strawberry a Talking Horse. How do you think the Cabby feels to hear Strawberry's depiction of their life together? When have you been surprised by another's point of view? How often do you try to see life from others' perspectives?

Asking for Help

ASLAN— and children from another world," thought Tirian. "They have always come in when things were at their worst. Oh, if only they could now."

And he called out "Aslan! Aslan! Aslan! Come and help us now."

But the darkness and the cold and the quietness went on just the same.

"Let *me* be killed," cried the King. "I ask nothing for myself. But come and save all Narnia."

And still there was no change in the night or the wood, but there began to be a kind of change inside Tirian. Without knowing why, he began to feel a faint hope. And he felt somehow stronger. "Oh Aslan, Aslan," he whispered. "If you will not come yourself, at least send me the helpers from beyond the world. Or let me call them. Let my voice carry beyond the world." Then, hardly knowing that he was doing it, he suddenly cried out in a great voice:

"Children! Children! Friends of Narnia! Quick. Come to me. Across the worlds I call you; I, Tirian, King of Narnia, Lord of Cair Paravel, and Emperor of the Lone Islands!"

—The Last Battle

Why do you think Tirian feels stronger after he asks for help, even before there is any sign that his pleas will be answered?

Trust Me

CASPIAN was unexpectedly wakened by Doctor Cornelius after he had been only a few hours in bed.

"Are we going to do a little Astronomy, Doctor?" said Caspian.

"Hush!" said the Doctor. "Trust me and do exactly as I tell you. Put on all your clothes; you have a long journey before you."

Caspian was very surprised, but he had learned to have confidence in his Tutor and he began doing what he was told at once. When he was dressed, the Doctor said, "I have a wallet for you. We must go into the next room and fill it with victuals from your Highness's supper table."

"My gentlemen-in-waiting will be there," said Caspian.

"They are fast asleep and will not wake," said the Doctor. "I am a very minor magician but I *can* at least contrive a charmed sleep."

They went into the antechamber and there, sure enough, the two gentlemen-in-waiting were, sprawling on chairs and snoring hard. . . .

"Have you your sword?" asked the Doctor.

"Yes," said Caspian.

"Then put this mantle over all to hide the sword and the wallet. That's right. And now we must go to the Great Tower and talk."

When they had reached the top of the tower . . . Doctor Cornelius said,

"Dear Prince, you must leave this castle at once and go to seek your fortune in the wide world. Your life is in danger here."

"Why?" asked Caspian.

"Because you are the true King of Narnia: Caspian the Tenth, the true son and heir of Caspian the Ninth. Long life to your Majesty"—and suddenly, to Caspian's great surprise, the little man dropped down on one knee and kissed his hand.

—*Prince Caspian*

How might these events have changed if Caspian did not trust Doctor Cornelius so much? Who do you trust no matter what? Who trusts you in this way?

A Shocking Revelation

"WHAT DOES IT ALL MEAN? I don't understand," said Caspian.

"I wonder you have never asked me before," said the Doctor, "why, being the son of King Caspian, you are not King Caspian yourself. Everyone except your Majesty knows that Miraz is a usurper. When he first began to rule he did not even pretend to be the King: he called himself Lord Protector. But then your royal mother died, the good Queen and the only Telmarine who was ever kind to me. And then, one by one, all the great lords, who had known your father, died or disappeared. Not by accident, either. Miraz weeded them out. . . . And finally he persuaded the seven noble lords, who alone among all the Telmarines did not fear the sea, to sail away and look for new lands beyond the Eastern Ocean and, as he intended, they never came back. And when there was no one left who could speak a word for you, then his flatterers (as he had instructed them) begged him to become King. And of course he did."

"Do you mean he now wants to kill me too?" said Caspian.

"That is almost certain," said Doctor Cornelius.

"But why now?" said Caspian. "I mean, why didn't he do it long ago if he wanted to? And what harm have I done him?"

"He has changed his mind about you because of something that happened only two hours ago. The Queen has had a son."

"I don't see what that's got to do with it," said Caspian.

"Don't see!" exclaimed the Doctor. "Have all my lessons in History and Politics taught you no more than that? Listen. As long as he had no children of his own, he was willing enough that you should be King after he died. . . . Now that he has a son of his own he will want his own son to be the next King. You are in the way. . . ."

"Is he really as bad as that?" said Caspian. "Would he really murder me?"

"He murdered your Father," said Doctor Cornelius.

—*Prince Caspian*

How does Doctor Cornelius's information alter Caspian's picture of the world?
Have you ever received news that changed how you see the world?

FEBRUARY

Not Good Enough

W HY, IT'S ONLY A GIRL!" [Shasta] exclaimed.
"And what business is it of yours if I am *only* a girl?" snapped the stranger [Aravis]. "You're probably only a boy: a rude, common little boy—a slave probably, who's stolen his master's horse."

"That's all *you* know," said Shasta. . . .

"Look here," said the girl. "I don't mind going with *you*, Mr. War Horse, but what about this boy? How do I know he's not a spy?"

"Why don't you say at once that you think I'm not good enough for you?" said Shasta.

"Be quiet, Shasta," said Bree. "The Tarkheena's question is quite reasonable. I'll vouch for the boy, Tarkheena. He's been true to me and a good friend. And he's certainly either a Narnian or an Archenlander."

"All right, then. Let's go together." But she didn't say anything to Shasta and it was obvious that she wanted Bree, not him.

"Splendid!" said Bree. . . .

Both the children unsaddled their horses and the horses had a little grass and Aravis produced rather nice things to eat from her saddle-bag. But Shasta sulked and said, No thanks, and that he wasn't hungry. And he tried to put on what he thought very grand and stiff manners, but as a fisherman's hut is not usually a good place for learning grand manners, the result was dreadful. And he half knew that it wasn't a success and then became sulkier and more awkward than ever.

—The Horse and His Boy

What do Shasta and Aravis each do to make their first encounter less than ideal? Have you ever had to repair matters after a bad first encounter?

Good but Not Safe

YOU'LL UNDERSTAND when you see him."
"But shall we see him?" asked Susan.

"Why, Daughter of Eve, that's what I brought you here for. I'm to lead you where you shall meet him," said Mr. Beaver.

"Is—is he a man?" asked Lucy.

"Aslan a man!" said Mr. Beaver sternly. "Certainly not. I tell you he is the King of the wood and the son of the great Emperor-beyond-the-Sea. Don't you know who is the King of Beasts? Aslan is a lion—*the* Lion, the great Lion."

"Ooh!" said Susan, "I'd thought he was a man. Is he—quite safe? I shall feel rather nervous about meeting a lion."

"That you will, dearie, and no mistake," said Mrs. Beaver; "if there's anyone who can appear before Aslan without their knees knocking, they're either braver than most or else just silly."

"Then he isn't safe?" said Lucy.

"Safe?" said Mr. Beaver; "don't you hear what Mrs. Beaver tells you? Who said anything about safe? 'Course he isn't safe. But he's good. He's the King, I tell you."

—The Lion, the Witch, and the Wardrobe

What does it mean for someone to be good but not safe? Why do we value safety so much in our society? How can an overemphasis on safety cause us to miss what is good?

A Star at Rest

AND ARE WE NEAR the World's End now, Sir?" asked Caspian. "Have you any knowledge of the seas and lands further east than this?"

"I saw them long ago," said the Old Man, "but it was from a great height. I cannot tell you such things as sailors need to know."

"Do you mean you were flying in the air?" Eustace blurted out.

"I was a long way above the air, my son," replied the Old Man. "I am Ramandu. But I see that you stare at one another and have not heard this name. And no wonder, for the days when I was a star had ceased long before any of you knew this world, and all the constellations have changed."

"Golly," said Edmund under his breath. "He's a *retired* star."

"Aren't you a star any longer?" asked Lucy.

"I am a star at rest, my daughter," answered Ramandu. "When I set for the last time, decrepit and old beyond all that you can reckon, I was carried to this island. I am not so old now as I was then. Every morning a bird brings me a fire-berry from the valleys in the Sun, and each fire-berry takes away a little of my age. And when I have become as young as the child that was born yesterday, then I shall take my rising again (for we are at earth's eastern rim) and once more tread the great dance."

"In our world," said Eustace, "a star is a huge ball of flaming gas."

"Even in your world, my son, that is not what a star is but only what it is made of."

—*The Voyage of the* Dawn Treader

What is the distinction between what something is and what it is made of? In what ways do we often mix these two?

Puzzle and Shift

IN THE LAST DAYS OF NARNIA, far up to the west beyond
Lantern Waste and close beside the great waterfall, there lived an
Ape. He was so old that no one could remember when he had first come
to live in those parts, and he was the cleverest, ugliest, most wrinkled Ape
you can imagine. He had a little house, built of wood and thatched with
leaves, up in the fork of a great tree, and his name was Shift. There were
very few Talking Beasts or Men or Dwarfs, or people of any sort, in that
part of the wood, but Shift had one friend and neighbor who was a donkey
called Puzzle. At least they both said they were friends, but from the way
things went on you might have thought Puzzle was more like Shift's servant than his friend. He did all the work. When they went together to
the river, Shift filled the big skin bottles with water but it was Puzzle who
carried them back. When they wanted anything from the towns further
down the river it was Puzzle who went down with empty panniers on his
back and came back with the panniers full and heavy. And all the nicest
things that Puzzle brought back were eaten by Shift; for as Shift said, "You
see, Puzzle, I can't eat grass and thistles like you, so it's only fair I should
make it up in other ways." And Puzzle always said, "Of course, Shift, of
course. I see that." Puzzle never complained, because he knew that Shift
was far cleverer than himself and he thought it was very kind of Shift to be
friends with him at all. And if ever Puzzle did try to argue about anything,
Shift would always say, "Now, Puzzle, I understand what needs to be done
better than you. You know you're not clever, Puzzle." And Puzzle always
said, "No, Shift. It's quite true. I'm *not* clever." Then he would sigh and do
whatever Shift had said.

—*The Last Battle*

*How does Shift treat Puzzle and how does Puzzle respond? Have you ever
played Shift's or Puzzle's role in a relationship?*

Your Majesty's Tender Years

CASPIAN [SAID], "I want to know why you have permitted this abominable and unnatural traffic in slaves to grow up here, contrary to the ancient custom and usage of our dominions."

"Necessary, unavoidable," said his Sufficiency. "An essential part of the economic development of the islands, I assure you. Our present burst of prosperity depends on it."

"What need have you of slaves?"

"For export, your Majesty. Sell 'em to Calormen mostly; and we have other markets. We are a great center of the trade."

"In other words," said Caspian, "you don't need them. Tell me what purpose they serve except to put money into the pockets of such as Pug?"

"Your Majesty's tender years," said Gumpas, with what was meant to be a fatherly smile, "hardly make it possible that you should understand the economic problem involved. I have statistics, I have graphs, I have—"

"Tender as my years may be," said Caspian, "I believe I understand the slave trade from within quite as well as your Sufficiency. And I do not see that it brings into the islands meat or bread or beer or wine or timber or cabbages or books or instruments of music or horses or armor or anything else worth having. But whether it does or not, it must be stopped."

"But that would be putting the clock back," gasped the governor. "Have you no idea of progress, of development?"

"I have seen them both in an egg," said Caspian. "We call it 'Going Bad' in Narnia. This trade must stop."

—*The Voyage of the* **Dawn Treader**

What is Caspian's argument against the economic profit and prosperity of slavery? How do money and profit obscure morality in our world?

Narnia, Awake!

AND NOW, FOR THE FIRST TIME, the Lion was quite silent. He was going to and fro among the animals. And every now and then he would go up to two of them (always two at a time) and touch their noses with his. He would touch two beavers among all the beavers, two leopards among all the leopards, one stag and one deer among all the deer, and leave the rest. . . . [T]he creatures whom he had touched came and stood in a wide circle around him. . . .

The Lion, whose eyes never blinked, stared at the animals as hard as if he was going to burn them up with his mere stare. And gradually a change came over them. The smaller ones—the rabbits, moles, and such-like—grew a good deal larger. The very big ones—you noticed it most with the elephants—grew a little smaller. Many animals sat up on their hind legs. Most put their heads on one side as if they were trying very hard to understand. The Lion opened his mouth, but no sound came from it; he was breathing out, a long, warm breath; it seemed to sway all the beasts as the wind sways a line of trees. Far overhead from beyond the veil of blue sky which hid them the stars sang again; a pure, cold, difficult music. Then there came a swift flash like fire (but it burnt nobody) either from the sky or from the Lion itself, and every drop of blood tingled in the children's bodies, and the deepest, wildest voice they had ever heard was saying:

"Narnia, Narnia, Narnia, awake. Love. Think. Speak. Be walking trees. Be talking beasts. Be divine waters."

—*The Magician's Nephew*

As Aslan calls the animals to "awake," what three things does he command them to do? Why is this ordering significant? How would you measure yourself by these three commands?

Adam's Flesh and Adam's Bone

"When Adam's flesh and Adam's bone
Sits at Cair Paravel in throne,
The evil time will be over and done.

"So things must be drawing near their end now [Aslan's] come and you've come[, said Mr. Beaver]. We've heard of Aslan coming into these parts before—long ago, nobody can say when. But there's never been any of your race here before."

"That's what I don't understand, Mr. Beaver," said Peter, "I mean isn't the Witch herself human?"

"She'd like us to believe it," said Mr. Beaver, "and it's on that that she bases her claim to be Queen. But she's no Daughter of Eve. She comes of your father Adam's"—(here Mr. Beaver bowed) "your father Adam's first wife, her they called Lilith. And she was one of the Jinn. That's what she comes from on one side. And on the other she comes of the giants. No, no, there isn't a drop of real human blood in the Witch."

"That's why she's bad all through, Mr. Beaver," said Mrs. Beaver.

"True enough, Mrs. Beaver," replied he, "there may be two views about humans (meaning no offense to the present company). But there's no two views about things that look like humans and aren't."

"I've known good Dwarfs," said Mrs. Beaver.

"So've I, now you come to speak of it," said her husband, "but precious few, and they were the ones least like men. But in general, take my advice, when you meet anything that's going to be human and isn't yet, or used to be human once and isn't now, or ought to be human and isn't, you keep your eyes on it and feel for your hatchet."

—***The Lion, the Witch, and the Wardrobe***

How could Mr. Beaver's advice about watching out for anything that used to be human or ought to be human be applicable to our world?

Do Not Destroy Yourself

[ARAVIS SAID,] "Now it came to pass that my father's wife, my stepmother, hated me, and the sun appeared dark in her eyes as long as I lived in my father's house. And so she persuaded my father to promise me in marriage to Ahoshta Tarkaan. Now this Ahoshta is of base birth, though in these latter years he has won the favor of the Tisroc (may he live forever) by flattery and evil counsels, and is now made a Tarkaan and the lord of many cities and is likely to be chosen as the Grand Vizier when the present Grand Vizier dies. Moreover he is at least sixty years old and has a hump on his back and his face resembles that of an ape. Nevertheless my father, because of the wealth and power of this Ahoshta, and being persuaded by his wife, sent messengers offering me in marriage, and the offer was favorably accepted and Ahoshta sent word that he would marry me this very year at the time of high summer.

"When this news was brought to me the sun appeared dark in my eyes and I laid myself on my bed and wept for a day. But on the second day I rose up and washed my face and caused my mare Hwin to be saddled and took with me a sharp dagger which my brother had carried in the western wars and rode out alone. And when my father's house was out of sight and I was come to a green open place in a certain wood where there were no dwellings of men, I dismounted from Hwin my mare and took out the dagger. Then I parted my clothes where I thought the readiest way lay to my heart and I prayed to all the gods that as soon as I was dead I might find myself with my brother. After that I shut my eyes and my teeth and prepared to drive the dagger into my heart. But before I had done so, this mare spoke with the voice of one of the daughters of men and said, 'O my mistress, do not by any means destroy yourself, for if you live you may yet have good fortune but all the dead are dead alike.'"

—*The Horse and His Boy*

Would you find the mare's words persuasive? What keeps you going on the days when the sun appears dark in your eyes?

Preparation

Hullo! What's this?" said Edmund suddenly.

In the green valley to which they were descending, six or seven rough-looking men, all armed, were sitting by a tree.

"Don't tell them who we are," said Caspian.

"And pray, your Majesty, why not?" said Reepicheep, who had consented to ride on Lucy's shoulder.

"It just occurred to me," replied Caspian, "that no one here can have heard from Narnia for a long time. It's just possible they may not still acknowledge our over-lordship. In which case it might not be quite safe to be known as the King."

"We have our swords, Sire," said Reepicheep.

"Yes, Reep, I know we have," said Caspian. "But if it is a question of reconquering the three islands, I'd prefer to come back with a rather larger army."

—*The Voyage of the* **Dawn Treader**

How does one balance a call to be brave with the wisdom of caution?

The Worst Faun

[Mr. Tumnus the Faun] took out from its case on the dresser a strange little flute that looked as if it were made of straw and began to play. And the tune he played made Lucy want to cry and laugh and dance and go to sleep all at the same time. It must have been hours later when she shook herself and said:

"Oh, Mr. Tumnus—I'm so sorry to stop you, and I do love that tune— but really, I must go home. I only meant to stay for a few minutes."

"It's no good *now,* you know," said the Faun, laying down its flute and shaking its head at her very sorrowfully.

"No good?" said Lucy, jumping up and feeling rather frightened. "What do you mean? I've got to go home at once. The others will be wondering what has happened to me." But a moment later she asked, "Mr. Tumnus! Whatever is the matter?" for the Faun's brown eyes had filled with tears and then the tears began trickling down its cheeks, and soon they were running off the end of its nose; and at last it covered its face with its hands and began to howl.

"Mr. Tumnus! Mr. Tumnus!" said Lucy in great distress. "Don't! Don't! What is the matter? Aren't you well? Dear Mr. Tumnus, do tell me what is wrong." But the Faun continued sobbing as if its heart would break. And even when Lucy went over and put her arms round him and lent him her handkerchief, he did not stop. He merely took the handkerchief and kept on using it, wringing it out with both hands whenever it got too wet to be any more use, so that presently Lucy was standing in a damp patch.

"Mr. Tumnus!" bawled Lucy in his ear, shaking him. "Do stop. Stop it at once! You ought to be ashamed of yourself, a great big Faun like you. What on earth are you crying about?"

"Oh—oh—oh!" sobbed Mr. Tumnus. "I'm crying because I'm such a bad Faun."

"I don't think you're a bad Faun at all," said Lucy. "I think you are a very good Faun. You are the nicest Faun I've ever met."

"Oh—oh—you wouldn't say that if you knew," replied Mr. Tumnus between his sobs. "No, I'm a bad Faun. I don't suppose there ever was a worse Faun since the beginning of the world."

"But what have you done?" asked Lucy.

"My old father, now," said Mr. Tumnus; "that's his picture over the mantelpiece. He would never have done a thing like this."

"A thing like what?" said Lucy.

"Like what I've done," said the Faun. "Taken service under the White Witch. That's what I am. I'm in the pay of the White Witch."

"The White Witch? Who is she?"

"Why, it is she that has got all Narnia under her thumb. It's she that makes it always winter. Always winter and never Christmas; think of that!"

"How awful!" said Lucy. "But what does she pay *you* for?"

"That's the worst of it," said Mr. Tumnus with a deep groan. "I'm a kidnapper for her, that's what I am. Look at me, Daughter of Eve. Would you believe that I'm the sort of Faun to meet a poor innocent child in the wood, one that had never done me any harm, and pretend to be friendly with it, and invite it home to my cave, all for the sake of lulling it asleep and then handing it over to the White Witch?"

"No," said Lucy. "I'm sure you wouldn't do anything of the sort."

"But I have," said the Faun.

"Well," said Lucy rather slowly (for she wanted to be truthful and yet not be too hard on him), "well, that was pretty bad. But you're so sorry for it that I'm sure you will never do it again."

"Daughter of Eve, don't you understand?" said the Faun. "It isn't something I have done. I'm doing it now, this very moment."

—*The Lion, the Witch, and the Wardrobe*

Why do you think the Faun confesses to Lucy? When has your conscience prevented you from doing something you fully intended to do?

A Disagreeable Condition

Hwin said it looked to her as if the safest thing was to go right through the city itself from gate to gate because one was less likely to be noticed in the crowd. But she approved of the idea of disguise as well. She said, "Both the humans will have to dress in rags and look like peasants or slaves. And all Aravis's armor and our saddles and things must be made into bundles and put on our backs, and the children must pretend to drive us and people will think we're only pack-horses."

"My dear Hwin!" said Aravis rather scornfully. "As if anyone could mistake Bree for anything but a war horse however you disguised him!"

"I should think not, indeed," said Bree, snorting and letting his ears go ever so little back.

"I know it's not a *very* good plan," said Hwin. "But I think it's our only chance. And we haven't been groomed for ages and we're not looking quite ourselves (at least, I'm sure I'm not). I do think if we get well plastered with mud and go along with our heads down as if we're tired and lazy—and don't lift our hoofs hardly at all—we might not be noticed. And our tails ought to be cut shorter: not neatly, you know, but all ragged."

"My dear Madam," said Bree. "Have you pictured to yourself how very disagreeable it would be to arrive in Narnia in *that* condition?"

"Well," said Hwin humbly (she was a very sensible mare), "the main thing is to get there."

—*The Horse and His Boy*

What is at the heart of Bree's reluctance to accept Hwin's plan? How do such feelings block out common sense? How do you allow similar feelings to get in your way?

Always a Way Through

D O NOT FLY TOO HIGH," said Aslan. "Do not try to go over the tops of the great ice-mountains. Look out for the valleys, the green places, and fly through them. There will always be a way through. And now, begone with my blessing."

—*The Magician's Nephew*

Do you believe, as Aslan asserts, that there is always a way through? How have you seen this to be true in your own life?

The Solitary Journey

IF YOU GO BACK to the others now, and wake them up; and tell them you have seen me again; and that you must all get up at once and follow me—what will happen? There is only one way of finding out."

"Do you mean that is what you want me to do?" gasped Lucy.

"Yes, little one," said Aslan.

"Will the others see you too?" asked Lucy.

"Certainly not at first," said Aslan. "Later on, it depends."

"But they won't believe me!" said Lucy.

"It doesn't matter," said Aslan. . . .

Lucy buried her head in his mane to hide from his face. But there must have been magic in his mane. She could feel lion-strength going into her. Quite suddenly she sat up.

"I'm sorry, Aslan," she said. "I'm ready now."

"Now you are a lioness," said Aslan. "And now all Narnia will be renewed. But come. We have no time to lose."

He got up and walked with stately, noiseless paces back to the belt of dancing trees through which she had just come: and Lucy went with him, laying a rather tremulous hand on his mane. . . .

"Now, child," said Aslan, when they had left the trees behind them, "I will wait here. Go and wake the others and tell them to follow. If they will not, then you at least must follow me alone."

—*Prince Caspian*

Why doesn't Aslan care whether Lucy's siblings believe her? Have you ever felt like you had to move forward on your own, without the support of others?

The Slave Dealer and Reepicheep

THEN THE FOUR HUMAN PRISONERS were roped together, not cruelly but securely, and made to march down to the shore. Reepicheep was carried. He had stopped biting on a threat of having his mouth tied up, but he had a great deal to say, and Lucy really wondered how any man could bear to have the things said to him which were said to the slave dealer by the Mouse. But the slave dealer, far from objecting, only said "Go on" whenever Reepicheep paused for breath, occasionally adding, "It's as good as a play," or, "Blimey, you can't help almost thinking it knows what it's saying!" or, "Was it one of you what trained it?" This so infuriated Reepicheep that in the end the number of things he thought of saying all at once nearly suffocated him and he became silent.

—*The Voyage of the* **Dawn Treader**

Is Reepicheep brave or foolish to speak so boldly to the slave dealer? What is it about the dealer's response that infuriates Reepicheep so much? When have you been so angry that you were at a loss for words?

The Two Lords Plot

A N HOUR LATER two great lords in the army of Miraz, the Lord Glozelle and the Lord Sopespian, strolling along their lines and picking their teeth after breakfast, looked up and saw coming down to them from the wood the Centaur and Giant Wimbleweather, whom they had seen before in battle, and between them a figure they could not recognize. Nor indeed would the other boys at Edmund's school have recognized him if they could have seen him at that moment. For Aslan had breathed on him at their meeting and a kind of greatness hung about him.

"What's to do?" said the Lord Glozelle. "An attack?"

"A parley, rather," said Sopespian. "See, they carry green branches. They are coming to surrender most likely."

"He that is walking between the Centaur and the Giant has no look of surrender in his face," said Glozelle. "Who can he be? It is not the boy Caspian."

"No indeed," said Sopespian. "This is a fell warrior, I warrant you, wherever the rebels have got him from. He is (in your Lordship's private ear) a kinglier man than ever Miraz was. And what mail he wears! None of our smiths can make the like."

"I'll wager my dappled Pomely he brings a challenge, not a surrender," said Glozelle.

"How then?" said Sopespian. "We hold the enemy in our fist here. Miraz would never be so hair-brained as to throw away his advantage on a combat."

"He might be brought to it," said Glozelle in a much lower voice.

"Softly," said Sopespian. "Step a little aside here out of earshot of those sentries. Now. Have I taken your Lordship's meaning aright?"

"If the King undertook wager of battle," whispered Glozelle, "why, either he would kill or be killed."

"So," said Sopespian, nodding his head.

"And if he killed we should have won this war."

"Certainly. And if not?"

"Why, if not, we should be as able to win it without the King's grace as with him. For I need not tell your Lordship that Miraz is no very great captain. And after that, we should be both victorious and kingless."

"And it is your meaning, my Lord, that you and I could hold this land quite as conveniently without a King as with one?"

Glozelle's face grew ugly. "Not forgetting," said he, "that it was we who first put him on the throne. And in all the years that he has enjoyed it, what fruits have come our way? What gratitude has he shown us?"

"Say no more," answered Sopespian.

—*Prince Caspian*

Why do the two lords feel the way they do toward King Miraz? When is it appropriate to break loyalty with a King or ruler and when is it betrayal?

The Two Lords Goad Miraz

"As touching the challenge," [said Miraz,] "I suppose there is only one opinion between us?"

"I suppose so, indeed, Sire," said Glozelle.

"And what is that?" asked the King.

"Most infallibly to refuse it," said Glozelle. "For though I have never been called a coward, I must plainly say that to meet that young man in battle is more than my heart would serve me for. And if (as is likely) his brother, the High King, is more dangerous than he—why, on your life, my Lord King, have nothing to do with him."

"Plague on you!" cried Miraz. "It was not that sort of counsel I wanted. Do you think I am asking you if I should be afraid to meet this Peter (if there is such a man)? Do you think I fear him? I wanted your counsel of the policy of the matter; whether we, having the advantage, should hazard it on a wager of battle."

"To which I can only answer, your Majesty," said Glozelle, "that for all reasons the challenge should be refused. There is death in the strange knight's face."

"There you are again!" said Miraz, now thoroughly angry. "Are you trying to make it appear that I am as great a coward as your Lordship?"

"Your Majesty may say your pleasure," said Glozelle sulkily.

"You talk like an old woman, Glozelle," said the King. "What say you, my Lord Sopespian?"

"Do not touch it, Sire," was the reply. "And what your Majesty says of the policy of the thing comes in very happily. It gives your Majesty excellent grounds for a refusal without any cause for questioning your Majesty's honor or courage."

"Great Heaven!" exclaimed Miraz, jumping to his feet. "Are *you* also bewitched today? Do you think I am *looking* for grounds to refuse it? You might as well call me coward to my face."

The conversation was going exactly as the two lords wished, so they said nothing.

"I see what it is," said Miraz, after staring at them as if his eyes would start out of his head, "you are as lily-livered as hares yourselves and have the effrontery to imagine my heart after the likeness of yours! Grounds for a refusal, indeed! Excuses for not fighting! Are you soldiers? Are you Telmarines? Are you men? And if I do refuse it (as all good reasons of captaincy and martial policy urge me to do) you will think, and teach others to think, I was afraid. Is it not so?"

"No man of your Majesty's age," said Glozelle, "would be called coward by any wise soldier for refusing the combat with a great warrior in the flower of his youth."

"So I'm to be a dotard with one foot in the grave, as well as a dastard," roared Miraz. "I'll tell you what it is, my Lords. With your womanish counsels (ever shying from the true point, which is one of policy) you have done the very opposite of your intent. I had meant to refuse it. But I'll accept it. Do you hear, accept it! I'll not be shamed because some witchcraft or treason has frozen both your bloods."

—*Prince Caspian*

What tactics do the two lords use to convince Miraz to accept Peter's challenge of a single, person-to-person combat? When have you allowed yourself to be convinced by peer pressure to do something you might otherwise not have done?

Approaching Aslan

ASLAN STOOD IN THE CENTER of a crowd of creatures who had grouped themselves round him in the shape of a half-moon. There were Tree-Women there and Well-Women (Dryads and Naiads as they used to be called in our world) who had stringed instruments; it was they who had made the music. There were four great centaurs. The horse part of them was like huge English farm horses, and the man part was like stern but beautiful giants. There was also a unicorn, and a bull with the head of a man, and a pelican, and an eagle, and a great Dog. And next to Aslan stood two leopards of whom one carried his crown and the other his standard.

But as for Aslan himself, the Beavers and the children didn't know what to do or say when they saw him. People who have not been in Narnia sometimes think that a thing cannot be good and terrible at the same time. If the children had ever thought so, they were cured of it now. For when they tried to look at Aslan's face they just caught a glimpse of the golden mane and the great, royal, solemn, overwhelming eyes; and then they found they couldn't look at him and went all trembly.

"Go on," whispered Mr. Beaver.

"No," whispered Peter, "you first."

"No, Sons of Adam before animals," whispered Mr. Beaver back again.

"Susan," whispered Peter, "what about you? Ladies first."

"No, you're the eldest," whispered Susan. And of course the longer they went on doing this the more awkward they felt. Then at last Peter realized that it was up to him. He drew his sword and raised it to the salute and hastily saying to the others "Come on. Pull yourselves together," he advanced to the Lion and said:

"We have come—Aslan."

—*The Lion, the Witch, and the Wardrobe*

Why is it so hard for them to approach Aslan? Who or what in your life has required a great deal of courage for you to face?

Not Your Horse

ALL RIGHT THEN," said Aravis. "You've guessed it. Hwin and I are running away. We are trying to get to Narnia. And now, what about it?"

"Why, in that case, what is to prevent us all going together?" said Bree. "I trust, Madam Hwin, you will accept such assistance and protection as I may be able to give you on the journey?"

"Why do you keep talking to my horse instead of to me?" asked the girl.

"Excuse me, Tarkheena," said Bree (with just the slightest backward tilt of his ears), "but that's Calormene talk. We're free Narnians, Hwin and I, and I suppose, if you're running away to Narnia, you want to be one too. In that case Hwin isn't *your* horse any longer. One might just as well say you're *her* human."

The girl opened her mouth to speak and then stopped. Obviously she had not quite seen it in that light before.

—*The Horse and His Boy*

How do you think Aravis feels to hear the radical Narnian view of horse ownership? Have you ever felt possessive of another person as she felt about her horse, Hwin? If so, what can you do to view him or her more as a free person and less as yours?

We Simply Must Try

[M]R. TUMNUS'S] door had been wrenched off its hinges and broken to bits. Inside, the cave was dark and cold and had the damp feel and smell of a place that had not been lived in for several days. Snow had drifted in from the doorway and was heaped on the floor, mixed with something black, which turned out to be the charred sticks and ashes from the fire. Someone had apparently flung it about the room and then stamped it out. The crockery lay smashed on the floor and the picture of the Faun's father had been slashed into shreds with a knife.

"This is a pretty good washout," said Edmund; "not much good coming here."

"What is this?" said Peter, stooping down. He had just noticed a piece of paper which had been nailed through the carpet to the floor.

"Is there anything written on it?" asked Susan.

"Yes, I think there is," answered Peter, "but I can't read it in this light. Let's get out into the open air."

They all went out in the daylight and crowded round Peter as he read out the following words:

> *The former occupant of these premises, the Faun Tumnus, is under arrest and awaiting his trial on a charge of High Treason against her Imperial Majesty Jadis, Queen of Narnia, Chatelaine of Cair Paravel, Empress of the Lone Islands, etc., also of comforting her said Majesty's enemies, harboring spies and fraternizing with Humans.*
> *signed* MAUGRIM, *Captain of the Secret Police,*
> *LONG LIVE THE QUEEN!*

The children stared at each other.

"I don't know that I'm going to like this place after all," said Susan.

"Who is this Queen, Lu?" said Peter. "Do you know anything about her?"

"She isn't a real queen at all," answered Lucy; "she's a horrible witch, the White Witch. Everyone—all the wood people—hate her. She has made an enchantment over the whole country so that it is always winter here and never Christmas."

"I—I wonder if there's any point in going on," said Susan. "I mean, it doesn't seem particularly safe here and it looks as if it won't be much fun either. And it's getting colder every minute, and we've brought nothing to eat. What about just going home?"

"Oh, but we can't, we can't," said Lucy suddenly; "don't you see? We can't just go home, not after this. It is all on my account that the poor Faun has got into this trouble. He hid me from the Witch and showed me the way back. That's what it means by comforting the Queen's enemies and fraternizing with Humans. We simply must try to rescue him."

—*The Lion, the Witch, and the Wardrobe*

Why does Lucy feel that they must try to rescue Mr. Tumnus? What would you do in her situation? How should we balance loyalty with a concern for our own safety?

Eustace Clarence Scrubb

THERE WAS A BOY CALLED Eustace Clarence Scrubb, and he almost deserved it. His parents called him Eustace Clarence and masters called him Scrubb. I can't tell you how his friends spoke to him, for he had none. He didn't call his father and mother "Father" and "Mother," but Harold and Alberta. They were very up-to-date and advanced people. They were vegetarians, non-smokers and teetotalers and wore a special kind of underclothes. In their house there was very little furniture and very few clothes on beds and the windows were always open.

Eustace Clarence liked animals, especially beetles, if they were dead and pinned on a card. He liked books if they were books of information and had pictures of grain elevators or of fat foreign children doing exercises in model schools.

Eustace Clarence disliked his cousins, the four Pevensies, Peter, Susan, Edmund and Lucy. But he was quite glad when he heard that Edmund and Lucy were coming to stay. For deep down inside him he liked bossing and bullying; and, though he was a puny little person who couldn't have stood up even to Lucy, let alone Edmund, in a fight, he knew that there are dozens of ways to give people a bad time if you are in your own home and they are only visitors.

—*The Voyage of the* **Dawn Treader**

Why would Eustace Clarence Scrubb almost deserve his name? Why might someone like Eustace want to give Edmund and Lucy a bad time? Have you come across people in your life who fit Eustace's description?

Edmund Enters Narnia

[EDMUND] CAME INTO THE ROOM just in time to see Lucy vanishing into the wardrobe. He at once decided to get into it himself—not because he thought it a particularly good place to hide but because he wanted to go on teasing her about her imaginary country. He opened the door. There were the coats hanging up as usual, and a smell of moth-balls, and darkness and silence, and no sign of Lucy. "She thinks I'm Susan come to catch her," said Edmund to himself, "and so she's keeping very quiet in at the back." He jumped in and shut the door, forgetting what a very foolish thing this is to do. Then he began feeling about for Lucy in the dark. He had expected to find her in a few seconds and was very surprised when he did not. He decided to open the door again and let in some light. But he could not find the door either. He didn't like this at all and began groping wildly in every direction; he even shouted out, "Lucy! Lu! Where are you? I know you're here."

There was no answer and Edmund noticed that his own voice had a curious sound—not the sound you expect in a cupboard, but a kind of open-air sound. He also noticed that he was unexpectedly cold; and then he saw a light.

"Thank goodness," said Edmund, "the door must have swung open of its own accord." He forgot all about Lucy and went toward the light, which he thought was the open door of the wardrobe. But instead of finding himself stepping out into the spare room he found himself stepping out from the shadow of some thick dark fir trees into an open place in the middle of a wood.

There was crisp, dry snow under his feet and more snow lying on the branches of the trees. Overhead there was a pale blue sky, the sort of sky one sees on a fine winter day in the morning. Straight ahead of him he saw between the tree-trunks the sun, just rising, very red and clear. Everything was perfectly still, as if he were the only living creature in that country. There was not even a robin or a squirrel among the trees, and the wood stretched as far as he could see in every direction. He shivered.

He now remembered that he had been looking for Lucy; and also how unpleasant he had been to her about her "imaginary country" which now turned out not to have been imaginary at all. He thought that she must be somewhere quite close and so he shouted, "Lucy! Lucy! I'm here too— Edmund."

There was no answer.

"She's angry about all the things I've been saying lately," thought Edmund. And though he did not like to admit that he had been wrong, he also did not much like being alone in this strange, cold, quiet place; so he shouted again.

"I say, Lu! I'm sorry I didn't believe you. I see now you were right all along. Do come out. Make it Pax."

Still there was no answer.

—*The Lion, the Witch, and the Wardrobe*

Do you think Edmund's apology is sincere? When have you had trouble admitting you were wrong?

Talking Beasts

"CREATURES, I GIVE YOU YOURSELVES," said the strong, happy voice of Aslan. "I give to you forever this land of Narnia. I give you the woods, the fruits, the rivers. I give you the stars and I give you myself. The Dumb Beasts whom I have not chosen are yours also. Treat them gently and cherish them but do not go back to their ways lest you cease to be Talking Beasts. For out of them you were taken and into them you can return. Do not so."

—*The Magician's Nephew*

What would it mean for the Talking Beasts to go back to their former ways? How could they prevent that from happening?

How Can I Help It?

SHASTA HAD SO ENJOYED HIS DINNER and all the things Tumnus had been telling him that when he was left alone his thoughts took a different turn. He only hoped now that the real Prince Corin would not turn up until it was too late and that he would be taken away to Narnia by ship. I am afraid he did not think at all of what might happen to the real Corin when he was left behind in Tashbaan. He was a little worried about Aravis and Bree waiting for him at the Tombs. But then he said to himself, "Well, how can I help it?" and, "Anyway, that Aravis thinks she's too good to go about with me, so she can jolly well go alone," and at the same time he couldn't help feeling that it would be much nicer going to Narnia by sea than toiling across the desert.

—*The Horse and His Boy*

What are the excuses Shasta tells himself for not worrying about what may happen to the others? When have you left others at risk by putting your own interests first?

Happy Is the Horse

Aslan," said Bree in a shaken voice, "I'm afraid I must be rather a fool."

"Happy is the Horse who knows that while he is still young. Or the Human either."

—*The Horse and His Boy*

How could knowing we are fools make us happy?

Deathwater Island

"GET BACK!" [shouted Edmund.] "Back from the water. All of you. At once!!"

They all did and stared at him.

"Look," said Edmund, "look at the toes of my boots."

"They look a bit yellow," began Eustace.

"They're gold, solid gold," interrupted Edmund. "Look at them. Feel them. The leather's pulled away from it already. And they're as heavy as lead."

"By Aslan!" said Caspian. "You don't mean to say—?"

"Yes, I do," said Edmund. "That water turns things into gold. It turned the spear into gold, that's why it got so heavy. And it was just lapping against my feet (it's a good thing I wasn't barefoot) and it turned the toe-caps into gold. . . . And what a narrow shave *we've* had."

"Narrow indeed," said Reepicheep. "Anyone's finger, anyone's foot, anyone's whisker, or anyone's tail, might have slipped into the water at any moment."

"All the same," said Caspian, "we may as well test it." He stooped down and wrenched up a spray of heather. Then, very cautiously, he knelt beside the pool and dipped it in. It was heather that he dipped; what he drew out was a perfect model of heather made of the purest gold, heavy and soft as lead.

"The King who owned this island," said Caspian slowly, and his face flushed as he spoke, "would soon be the richest of all Kings of the world. I claim this land forever as a Narnian possession. It shall be called Gold-water Island. And I bind all of you to secrecy. No one must know of this. Not even Drinian—on pain of death, do you hear?"

"Who are you talking to?" said Edmund. "I'm no subject of yours. If anything it's the other way round. I am one of the four ancient sovereigns of Narnia and you are under allegiance to the High King my brother."

"So it has come to that, King Edmund, has it?" said Caspian, laying his hand on his sword-hilt.

"Oh, stop it, both of you," said Lucy. "That's the worst of doing anything with boys. You're all such swaggering, bullying idiots—oooh!—"

Her voice died away into a gasp. And everyone else saw what she had seen.

Across the grey hillside above them—grey, for the heather was not yet in bloom—without noise, and without looking at them, and shining as if he were in bright sunlight though the sun had in fact gone in, passed with slow pace the hugest lion that human eyes have ever seen. . . . They knew it was Aslan.

And nobody ever saw how or where he went. They looked at one another like people waking from sleep.

"What were we talking about?" said Caspian. "Have I been making rather an ass of myself?"

"Sire," said Reepicheep, "this is a place with a curse on it. Let us get back on board at once. And if I might have the honor of naming this island, I should call it Deathwater."

—*The Voyage of the* **Dawn Treader**

What is the effect of the gold transformation on Caspian, Edmund, and Lucy in turn? When have you been transfixed by the potential for wealth and riches?

Do You Feel Yourself Sufficient?

THEN PETER, LEADING CASPIAN, forced his way through the crowd of animals.

"This is Caspian, Sir," he said. And Caspian knelt and kissed the Lion's paw.

"Welcome, Prince," said Aslan. "Do you feel yourself sufficient to take up the Kingship of Narnia?"

"I—I don't think I do, Sir," said Caspian. "I'm only a kid."

"Good," said Aslan. "If you had felt yourself sufficient, it would have been a proof that you were not. Therefore, under us and under the High King, you shall be King of Narnia, Lord of Cair Paravel, and Emperor of the Lone Islands. You and your heirs while your race lasts."

—*Prince Caspian*

Why would feeling sufficient be proof that Caspian was not? When have you had to step up to a task for which you did not feel sufficient?

Into the Pool

L OOK! WHAT'S THAT?"
    "What's what?" said Puzzle.
"That yellow thing that's just come down the waterfall. Look! There it is again, it's floating. We must find out what it is."

"Must we?" said Puzzle.

"Of course we must," said Shift. "It may be something useful. Just hop into the Pool like a good fellow and fish it out. Then we can have a proper look at it."

"Hop into the Pool?" said Puzzle, twitching his long ears.

"Well how are we to get it if you don't?" said the Ape.

"But—but," said Puzzle, "wouldn't it be better if *you* went in? Because, you see, it's you who wants to know what it is, and I don't much. And you've got hands, you see. You're as good as a Man or a Dwarf when it comes to catching hold of things. I've only got hoofs."

"Really, Puzzle," said Shift, "I didn't think you'd ever say a thing like that. I didn't think it of you, really."

"Why, what have I said wrong?" said the Ass, speaking in rather a humble voice, for he saw that Shift was very deeply offended. "All I meant was—"

"Wanting *me* to go into the water," said the Ape. "As if you didn't know perfectly well what weak chests Apes always have and how easily they catch cold! Very well. I *will* go in. I'm feeling cold enough already in this cruel wind. But I'll go in. I shall probably die. Then you'll be sorry." And Shift's voice sounded as if he was just going to burst into tears.

"Please don't, please don't, please don't," said Puzzle, half braying, and half talking. "I never meant anything of the sort, Shift, really I didn't. You know how stupid I am and how I can't think of more than one thing at a time. I'd forgotten about your weak chest. Of course I'll go in. You mustn't think of doing it yourself. Promise me you won't, Shift."

—*The Last Battle*

Why does Puzzle give in? How do you attempt to get others to do something you know that you should do yourself?

We Can Only Ask Him

WHEN WE CAME BACK FROM That Place, Someone said that the two Pevensie kids (that's my two cousins) could never go there again. It was their third time, you see. I suppose they've had their share. But he never said I couldn't. Surely he would have said so, unless he meant that I was to get back? And I can't help wondering, can we—could we—?"

"Do you mean, do something to make it happen?" [Jill asked.]

Eustace nodded.

"You mean we might draw a circle on the ground—and write in queer letters in it—and stand inside it—and recite charms and spells?"

"Well," said Eustace after he had thought hard for a bit. "I believe that was the sort of thing I was thinking of, though I never did it. But now that it comes to the point, I've an idea that all those circles and things are rather rot. I don't think he'd like them. It would look as if we thought we could make him do things. But really, we can only ask him."

"Who is this person you keep on talking about?"

"They call him Aslan in That Place," said Eustace.

"What a curious name!"

"Not half so curious as himself," said Eustace solemnly. "But let's get on. It can't do any harm, just asking.

—*The Silver Chair*

Why wouldn't drawing circles and reciting spells help Eustace and his friend Jill get to Narnia? How would that be different from asking? Do you sometimes find yourself trying to make something happen rather than asking for it outright?

MARCH

The Ancient Treasure Chamber

FOR NOW ALL KNEW that it was indeed the ancient treasure chamber of Cair Paravel where they had once reigned as Kings and Queens of Narnia. There was a kind of path up the middle (as it might be in a greenhouse), and along each side at intervals stood rich suits of armor, like knights guarding the treasures. In between the suits of armor, and on each side of the path, were shelves covered with precious things—necklaces and arm rings and finger rings and golden bowls and dishes and long tusks of ivory, brooches and coronets and chains of gold, and heaps of unset stones lying piled anyhow as if they were marbles or potatoes—diamonds, rubies, carbuncles, emeralds, topazes, and amethysts. Under the shelves stood great chests of oak strengthened with iron bars and heavily padlocked. And it was bitterly cold, and so still that they could hear themselves breathing, and the treasures were so covered with dust that unless they had realized where they were and remembered most of the things, they would hardly have known they were treasures. There was something sad and a little frightening about the place, because it all seemed so forsaken and long ago. That was why nobody said anything for at least a minute.

Then, of course, they began walking about and picking things up to look at. It was like meeting very old friends. If you had been there you would have heard them saying things like, "Oh, look! Our coronation rings—do you remember first wearing this?—Why, this is the little brooch we all thought was lost—I say, isn't that the armor you wore in the great tournament in the Lone Islands?—do you remember the dwarf making that for me?—do you remember drinking out of that horn?—do you remember, do you remember?"

—*Prince Caspian*

Why do Edmund, Lucy, Peter, and Susan react as they do to the treasure chamber? What makes something a treasure?

He Has Betrayed Us All

I SAY—WHERE'S EDMUND?"
There was a dreadful pause, and then everyone began asking "Who saw him last? How long has he been missing? Is he outside?" and then all rushed to the door and looked out. The snow was falling thickly and steadily, the green ice of the pool had vanished under a thick white blanket, and from where the little house stood in the center of the dam you could hardly see either bank. Out they went, plunging well over their ankles into the soft new snow, and went round the house in every direction. "Edmund! Edmund!" they called till they were hoarse. But the silently falling snow seemed to muffle their voices and there was not even an echo in answer. . . .

"What on earth are we to do, Mr. Beaver?" said Peter.

"Do?" said Mr. Beaver, who was already putting on his snow-boots, "do? We must be off at once. We haven't a moment to spare!"

"We'd better divide into four search parties," said Peter, "and all go in different directions. . . ."

"Search parties, Son of Adam?" said Mr. Beaver; "what for?"

"Why, to look for Edmund, of course!"

"There's no point in looking for him," said Mr. Beaver.

"What do you mean?" said Susan. "He can't be far away yet. And we've got to find him. . . ."

"The reason there's no use looking," said Mr. Beaver, "is that we know already where he's gone!" Everyone stared in amazement. "Don't you understand?" said Mr. Beaver. "He's gone to *her,* to the White Witch. He has betrayed us all."

"Oh, surely—oh, really!" said Susan; "he can't have done that."

"Can't he?" said Mr. Beaver, looking very hard at the three children, and everything they wanted to say died on their lips, for each felt suddenly quite certain inside that this was exactly what Edmund had done.

—*The Lion, the Witch, and the Wardrobe*

How does Mr. Beaver know where Edmund has gone? Why does it sometimes take an outsider to point out the failings of those we love?

You Are Somebody?

Please, what task, Sir?" said Jill.

"The task for which I called you and him here out of your own world."

This puzzled Jill very much. "It's mistaking me for someone else," she thought. She didn't dare to tell the Lion this, though she felt things would get into a dreadful muddle unless she did.

"Speak your thought, Human Child," said the Lion.

"I was wondering—I mean—could there be some mistake? Because nobody called me and Scrubb, you know. It was we who asked to come here. Scrubb said we were to call to—to Somebody—it was a name I wouldn't know—and perhaps the Somebody would let us in. And we did, and then we found the door open."

"You would not have called to me unless I had been calling to you," said the Lion.

"Then you are Somebody, Sir?" said Jill.

"I am."

—*The Silver Chair*

Why is it hard for Jill to think that the Lion called her instead of the other way around? Do you tend to credit yourself with too much power or to accept too little responsibility for events in your life? What are some of the repercussions of each tendency?

The Old Days

"I WISH—I WISH—I WISH I could have lived in the Old Days," said Caspian. (He was only a very little boy at the time.)

Up till now King Miraz had been talking in the tiresome way that some grown-ups have, which makes it quite clear that they are not really interested in what you are saying, but now he suddenly gave Caspian a very sharp look.

"Eh? What's that?" he said. "What old days do you mean?"

"Oh, don't you know, Uncle?" said Caspian. "When everything was quite different. When all the animals could talk, and there were nice people who lived in the streams and the trees. Naiads and Dryads, they were called. And there were Dwarfs. And there were lovely little Fauns in all the woods. They had feet like goats. And—"

"That's all nonsense, for babies," said the King sternly. "Only fit for babies, do you hear? You're getting too old for that sort of stuff. At your age you ought to be thinking of battles and adventures, not fairy tales."

"Oh, but there *were* battles and adventures in those days," said Caspian. "Wonderful adventures. Once there was a White Witch and she made herself Queen of the whole country. And she made it so that it was always winter. And then two boys and two girls came from somewhere and so they killed the Witch and they were made Kings and Queens of Narnia, and their names were Peter and Susan and Edmund and Lucy. And so they reigned for ever so long and everyone had a lovely time, and it was all because of Aslan—"

"Who's he?" said Miraz. And if Caspian had been a very little older, the tone of his uncle's voice would have warned him that it would be wiser to shut up. But he babbled on,

"Oh, don't you know?" he said. "Aslan is the great Lion who comes from over the sea."

"Who has been telling you all this nonsense?" said the King in a voice of thunder. Caspian was frightened and said nothing.

"Your Royal Highness," said King Miraz, letting go of Caspian's hand, which he had been holding till now, "I insist upon being answered. Look me in the face. Who has been telling you this pack of lies?"

"N—Nurse," faltered Caspian, and burst into tears.

"Stop that noise," said his uncle, taking Caspian by the shoulders and giving him a shake. "Stop it. And never let me catch you talking—or *thinking* either—about all those silly stories again. There never were those Kings and Queens. How could there be two Kings at the same time? And there's no such person as Aslan. And there are no such things as lions. And there never was a time when animals could talk. Do you hear?"

—*Prince Caspian*

Why do the old stories hold such power for Caspian? At the same time, why does the King react to them the way he does? Have you ever felt the truth of something deeply only to have it denied by someone you trust?

I Apologize

O-O-OH!" SAID SUSAN SUDDENLY, and everyone asked her what was the matter.

"I'm sitting against a tree," said Susan, "and look! It's getting light—over there."

"By jove, you're right," said Peter, "and look there—and there. It's trees all round. And this wet stuff is snow. Why, I do believe we've got into Lucy's wood after all."

And now there was no mistaking it, and all four children stood blinking in the daylight of a winter day. Behind them were coats hanging on pegs, in front of them were snow-covered trees.

Peter turned at once to Lucy.

"I apologize for not believing you," he said, "I'm sorry. Will you shake hands?"

"Of course," said Lucy, and did.

—*The Lion, the Witch, and the Wardrobe*

Peter apologizes immediately when he realizes he was wrong not to believe Lucy. Do you think it is difficult for him to admit he was wrong? How quick are you to admit your errors or offenses? How does apologizing show strength?

A Wild Tune

THE LION WAS SINGING STILL. But now the song had once more changed. It was more like what we should call a tune, but it was also far wilder. It made you want to run and jump and climb. It made you want to shout. It made you want to rush at other people and either hug them or fight them. It made Digory hot and red in the face. It had some effect on Uncle Andrew, for Digory could hear him saying, "A spirited gel, sir. It's a pity about her temper, but a dem fine woman all the same, a dem fine woman." But what the song did to the two humans was nothing compared with what it was doing to the country.

Can you imagine a stretch of grassy land bubbling like water in a pot? For that is really the best description of what was happening. In all directions it was swelling into humps. There were of very different sizes, some no bigger than mole-hills, some as big as wheelbarrows, two the size of cottages. And the humps moved and swelled until they burst, and the crumbled earth poured out of them, and from each hump there came out an animal.

—*The Magician's Nephew*

Has anything in our world ever affected you as the song affects Digory?

The Fauns Arrive

CASPIAN HAD NEARLY DROPPED OFF to sleep when he thought he heard a faint musical sound from the depth of the woods at his back. Then he thought it was only a dream and turned over again; but as soon as his ear touched the ground he felt or heard (it was hard to tell which) a faint beating or drumming. He raised his head. The beating noise at once became fainter, but the music returned, clearer this time. It was like flutes. He saw that Trufflehunter was sitting up staring into the wood. The moon was bright; Caspian had been asleep longer than he thought. Nearer and nearer came the music, a tune wild and yet dreamy, and the noise of many light feet, till at last, out from the wood into the moonlight, came dancing shapes such as Caspian had been thinking of all his life. They were not much taller than dwarfs, but far slighter and more graceful. Their curly heads had little horns, the upper part of their bodies gleamed naked in the pale light, but their legs and feet were those of goats.

"Fauns!" cried Caspian, jumping up, and in a moment they were all round him. It took next to no time to explain the whole situation to them and they accepted Caspian at once. Before he knew what he was doing he found himself joining in the dance. Trumpkin, with heavier and jerkier movements, did likewise and even Trufflehunter hopped and lumbered about as best he could. Only Nikabrik stayed where he was, looking on in silence. The Fauns footed it all round Caspian to their reedy pipes. Their strange faces, which seemed mournful and merry all at once, looked into his; dozens of Fauns, Mentius and Obentinus and Dumnus, Voluns, Voltinus, Girbius, Nimienus, Nausus, and Oscuns. Pattertwig had sent them all.

When Caspian awoke next morning he could hardly believe that it had not all been a dream; but the grass was covered with little cloven hoofmarks.

—*Prince Caspian*

When have you had an experience so extraordinary that you could hardly believe it was not a dream?

Sleeping Under the Stars

THE PLACE WHERE THEY HAD MET the Fauns was, of course, Dancing Lawn itself, and here Caspian and his friends remained till the night of the great Council. To sleep under the stars, to drink nothing but well water and to live chiefly on nuts and wild fruit, was a strange experience for Caspian after his bed with silken sheets in a tapestried chamber at the castle, with meals laid out on gold and silver dishes in the anteroom, and attendants ready at his call. But he had never enjoyed himself more. Never had sleep been more refreshing nor food tasted more savory, and he began already to harden and his face wore a kinglier look.

—*Prince Caspian*

Why might just being away from the creature comforts of the castle give Caspian's face a more kingly look? When have you had an experience in which you were taken from your usual routine and found yourself changing? How did that change come about?

The Black Woods

THIS CASTLE IS A THING OF YESTERDAY. Your great-great-grand-father built it. But when the two sons of Adam and the two daughters of Eve were made Kings and Queens of Narnia by Aslan himself, they lived in the castle of Cair Paravel. No man alive has seen that blessed place and perhaps even the ruins of it have now vanished. But we believe it was far from here, down at the mouth of the Great River, on the very shore of the sea."

"Ugh!" said Caspian with a shudder. "Do you mean in the Black Woods? Where all the—the—you know, the ghosts live?"

"Your Highness speaks as you have been taught," said the Doctor. "But it is all lies. There are no ghosts there. That is a story invented by the Telmarines. Your Kings are in deadly fear of the sea because they can never quite forget that in all stories Aslan comes from over the sea. They don't want to go near it and they don't want anyone else to go near it. So they have let great woods grow up to cut their people off from the coast. But because they have quarreled with the trees they are afraid of the woods. And because they are afraid of the woods they imagine that they are full of ghosts. And the Kings and great men, hating both the sea and the wood, partly believe these stories, and partly encourage them. They feel safer if no one in Narnia dares to go down to the coast and look out to sea— toward Aslan's land and the morning and the eastern end of the world."

—*Prince Caspian*

Why don't the Kings want Narnians spending time at the coast? Do you think many modern ghost stories or superstitions have a similar basis? What does this story say about the power of fear?

Eustace's Diary

WHAT EUSTACE THOUGHT had best be told in his own words, for when they all got their clothes back, dried, next morning, he at once got out a little black notebook and a pencil and started to keep a diary. He always had this notebook with him and kept a record of his marks in it, for though he didn't care much about any subject for its own sake, he cared a great deal about marks and would even go to people and say, "I got so much. What did you get?" But as he didn't seem likely to get many marks on the *Dawn Treader* he now started a diary. This was the first entry.

August 7th. Have now been twenty-four hours on this ghastly boat if it isn't a dream. All the time a frightful storm has been raging (it's a good thing I'm not seasick). Huge waves keep coming in over the front and I have seen the boat nearly go under any number of times. All the others pretend to take no notice of this, either from swank or because Harold says one of the most cowardly things ordinary people do is to shut their eyes to Facts. It's madness to come out into the sea in a rotten little thing like this. Not much bigger than a lifeboat. And, of course, absolutely primitive indoors. No proper saloon, no radio, no bathrooms, no deck-chairs. I was dragged all over it yesterday evening and it would make anyone sick to hear Caspian showing off his funny little toy boat as if it was the Queen Mary. I tried to tell him what real ships are like, but he's too dense. E. and L., *of course,* didn't back me up. I suppose a kid like L. doesn't realize the danger and E. is buttering up C. as everyone does here. They call him a King. I said I was a Republican but he had to ask me what that meant! He doesn't seem to know anything at all. *Needless to say* I've been put in the worst cabin of the boat, a perfect dungeon, and Lucy has been given a whole room on deck to herself, almost a nice room compared with the rest of this place. C. says that's because she's a girl. I tried to make him see what Alberta says, that all that sort of thing is really lowering girls but he was too dense. Still, he might see that I shall be ill if I'm kept in that *hole* any longer. E. says we mustn't grumble because C. is sharing it with us himself to make room for L. As if that didn't make it more crowded and far worse. Nearly forgot to say that there is also a kind of Mouse thing that gives everyone the most frightful cheek. The others can put up with it if they like but I shall twist his tail pretty soon if he tries it on me. The food is frightful too.

—*The Voyage of the* **Dawn Treader**

How does Eustace, by assuming to know much more than those around him, distance himself and prevent himself from enjoying the adventure? Are there times in your life when you do the same thing?

Do Real Horses Roll?

WHEN SHASTA HAD finished his breakfast (which was by far the nicest he had ever eaten), Bree said, "I think I'll have a nice roll before we put on that saddle again." And he proceeded to do so. "That's good. That's very good," he said, rubbing his back on the turf and waving all four legs in the air. "You ought to have one too, Shasta," he snorted. "It's most refreshing."

But Shasta burst out laughing and said, "You do look funny when you're on your back!"

"I look nothing of the sort," said Bree. But then suddenly he rolled round on his side, raised his head and looked hard at Shasta, blowing a little.

"Does it really look funny?" he asked in an anxious voice.

"Yes, it does," replied Shasta. "But what does it matter?"

"You don't think, do you," said Bree, "that it might be a thing *talking* horses never do—a silly, clownish trick I've learned from the dumb ones? It would be dreadful to find, when I get back to Narnia, that I've picked up a lot of low, bad habits. What do you think, Shasta? Honestly, now. Don't spare my feelings. Should you think the real, free horses—the talking kind—do roll?"

"How should I know? Anyway, I don't think I should bother about it if I were you. We've got to get there first. Do you know the way?"

—*The Horse and His Boy*

Why is Bree so worried that he might have habits that the other talking horses wouldn't have? How would you respond to him if you were Shasta? When have you been worried about a habit of yours that might not be the same as everyone else's?

The Time of Greatest Need

IF YOUR MAJESTY is ever to use the Horn," said Trufflehunter, "I think the time has now come." Caspian had of course told them of his treasure several days ago.

"We are certainly in great need," answered Caspian. "But it is hard to be sure we are at our greatest. Supposing there came an even worse need and we had already used it?"

"By that argument," said Nikabrik, "your Majesty will never use it until it is too late."

"I agree with that," said Doctor Cornelius.

"And what do you think, Trumpkin?" asked Caspian.

"Oh, as for me," said the Red Dwarf, who had been listening with complete indifference, "your Majesty knows I think the Horn—and that bit of broken stone over there—and your great King Peter—and your Lion Aslan—are all eggs in moonshine. It's all one to me when your Majesty blows the Horn. All I insist on is that the army is told nothing about it. There's no good raising hopes of magical help which (as I think) are sure to be disappointed."

"Then in the name of Aslan we will wind Queen Susan's horn," said Caspian.

—*Prince Caspian*

Why is Caspian reluctant to use the horn? When have you waited, perhaps too long, to ask for help?

Slaves' and Fools' Talk

P**OOR LITTLE BEAST**," said the Horse in a gentler tone. "I forget you're only a foal. We'll make a fine rider of you in time. And now—we mustn't start until those two in the hut are asleep. Meantime we can make our plans. My Tarkaan is on his way North to the great city, to Tashbaan itself and the court of the Tisroc—"

"I say," put in Shasta in rather a shocked voice, "oughtn't you to say 'May he live forever'?"

"Why?" asked the Horse. "I'm a free Narnian. And why should I talk slaves' and fools' talk? I don't want him to live forever, and I know that he's not going to live forever whether I want him to or not. And I can see you're from the free North too. No more of this Southern jargon between you and me!"

—*The Horse and His Boy*

What power do you think is in Shasta and the Horse rejecting the "slaves' and fools' talk" of the South? How can the language we use affect our outlook?

A Better Man

THEN TWO WONDERS happened at the same moment. One was that the voice was suddenly joined by other voices; more voices than you could possibly count. They were in harmony with it, but far higher up the scale: cold, tingling, silvery voices. The second wonder was that the blackness overhead, all at once, was blazing with stars. They didn't come out gently one by one, as they do on a summer evening. One moment there had been nothing but darkness; next moment a thousand, thousand points of light leaped out—single stars, constellations, and planets, brighter and bigger than any in our world. There were no clouds. The new stars and the new voices began at exactly the same time. If you had seen and heard it, as Digory did, you would have felt quite certain that it was the stars themselves which were singing, and that it was the first voice, the deep one, which had made them appear and made them sing.

"Glory be!" said the Cabby. "I'd ha' been a better man all my life if I'd known there were things like this."

—*The Magician's Nephew*

What do you think the Cabby means by his remark? Have you ever experienced anything so awe-inspiring it made you want to be a better person?

The Knight and the Lady in Green

RIDING TOWARD [SCRUBB, Jill, and Puddleglum] on that ancient road were two people of normal grown-up human size. "Keep on. Move toward them," said Puddleglum. "Anyone you meet in a place like this is as likely as not to be an enemy, but we mustn't let them think we're afraid."

By the time they had stepped off the end of the bridge onto the grass, the two strangers were quite close. One was a knight in complete armor with his visor down. His armor and his horse were black; there was no device on his shield and no banneret on his spear. The other was a lady on a white horse, a horse so lovely that you wanted to kiss its nose and give it a lump of sugar at once. But the lady, who rode side-saddle and wore a long, fluttering dress of dazzling green, was lovelier still.

"Good day, t-r-r-avelers," she cried out in a voice as sweet as the sweetest bird's song, trilling her R's delightfully. "Some of you are young pilgrims to walk this rough waste."

"That's as may be, Ma'am," said Puddleglum very stiffly and on his guard.

"We're looking for the ruined city of the giants," said Jill.

"The r-r-ruined city?" said the Lady. "That is a strange place to be seeking. What will you do if you find it?"

"We've got to—" began Jill, but Puddleglum interrupted.

"Begging your pardon, ma'am. But we don't know you or your friend— a silent chap, isn't he?—and you don't know us. And we'd as soon not talk to strangers about our business, if you don't mind. Shall we have a little rain soon, do you think?"

The Lady laughed: the richest, most musical laugh you can imagine. "Well, children," she said, "you have a wise, solemn old guide with you. I think none the worse of him for keeping his own counsel, but I'll be free with mine. I have often heard the name of the giantish City Ruinous, but never met any who would tell me the way thither. This road leads to the burgh and castle of Harfang, where dwell the gentle giants. They are as mild, civil, prudent, and courteous as those of Ettinsmoor are foolish, fierce, savage, and given to all beastliness. And in Harfang you may or may not hear tidings of the City Ruinous, but certainly you shall find good lodgings and merry hosts. You would be wise to winter there, or, at the least, to tarry certain days for your ease and refreshment. There you shall have steaming baths, soft beds, and bright hearths; and the roast and the baked and the sweet and the strong will be on the table four times a day."

"I say!" exclaimed Scrubb. "That's something like! Think of sleeping in a bed again."

"Yes, and having a hot bath," said Jill. "Do you think they'll ask us to stay? We don't know them, you see."

"Only tell them," answered the Lady, "that She of the Green Kirtle salutes them by you, and has sent them two fair Southern children for the Autumn Feast."

—*The Silver Chair*

What about the Lady puts Puddleglum on his guard? Similarly, what about her leads Jill and Eustace to trust her?

Puddleglum and the Children Disagree

THE CHILDREN THANKED HER AGAIN, with shining eyes, and the Lady waved to them. The Marsh-wiggle took off his steeple-hat and bowed very stiffly. Then the silent Knight and the Lady started walking their horses up the slope of the bridge with a great clatter of hoofs.

"Well!" said Puddleglum. "I'd give a good deal to know where *she's* coming from and where she's going. Not the sort you expect to meet in the wilds of Giantland, is she? Up to no good, I'll be bound."

"Oh rot!" said Scrubb. "I thought she was simply super. And think of hot meals and warm rooms. I do hope Harfang isn't a long way off."

"Same here," said Jill. "And hadn't she a scrumptious dress? And the horse!"

"All the same," said Puddleglum, "I wish we knew a bit more about her."

"I *was* going to ask her all about herself," said Jill. "But how could I when you wouldn't tell her anything about us?"

"Yes," said Scrubb. "And why were you so stiff and unpleasant? Didn't you like them? . . ."

"I was wondering," remarked Puddleglum, "what you'd really see if you lifted up the visor of that helmet and looked inside. . . . How about a skeleton? . . . Or perhaps," he added as an afterthought, "nothing at all. I mean, nothing you could see. Someone invisible." . . .

"Oh, bother his ideas!" said Scrubb. "He's always expecting the worst, and he's always wrong. Let's think about those Gentle Giants and get on to Harfang as quickly as we can. I wish I knew how far it is."

—*The Silver Chair*

Why does Puddleglum urge caution? On what are Jill and Eustace basing their decision to travel to Harfang? How do our base needs get in the way of our judgment?

The Road Grows Long

AFTER THAT TALK WITH THE LADY things got worse in two different ways. In the first place the country was much harder. The road led through endless, narrow valleys down which a cruel north wind was always blowing in their faces. There was nothing that could be used for firewood, and there were no nice little hollows to camp in, as there had been on the moor. And the ground was all stony, and made your feet sore by day and every bit of you sore by night.

In the second place, whatever the Lady had intended by telling them about Harfang, the actual effect on the children was a bad one. They could think about nothing but beds and baths and hot meals and how lovely it would be to get indoors. They never talked about Aslan, or even about the lost prince, now. And Jill gave up her habit of repeating the signs over to herself every night and morning. She said to herself, at first, that she was too tired, but she soon forgot all about it. And though you might have expected that the idea of having a good time at Harfang would have made them more cheerful, it really made them more sorry for themselves and more grumpy and snappy with each other and with Puddleglum.

—*The Silver Chair*

Why would looking forward to comforts make the children so grumpy? Have you ever noticed this effect on yourself?

The Adventure Begins

[POLLY'S AND DIGORY'S] adventures began chiefly because it was one of the wettest and coldest summers there had been for years. That drove them to do indoor things: you might say, indoor exploration. It is wonderful how much exploring you can do with a stump of candle in a big house, or in a row of houses. Polly had discovered long ago that if you opened a certain little door in the box-room attic of her house you would find the cistern and a dark place behind it which you could get into by a little careful climbing. The dark place was like a long tunnel with brick wall on one side and sloping roof on the other. In the roof there were little chunks of light between the slates. There was no floor in this tunnel: you had to step from rafter to rafter, and between them there was only plaster. If you stepped on this you would find yourself falling through the ceiling of the room below. Polly had used the bit of the tunnel just beside the cistern as a smugglers' cave. She had brought up bits of old packing cases and the seats of broken kitchen chairs, and things of that sort, and spread them across from rafter to rafter so as to make a bit of floor. Here she kept a cash-box containing various treasures, and a story she was writing and usually a few apples. She had often drunk a quiet bottle of ginger-beer in there: the old bottles made it look more like a smugglers' cave.

—*The Magician's Nephew*

Like many children, Polly and Digory use their imaginations to create exciting places out of just about nothing. Do you still have this ability? What value do imagination and a sense of exploration have in today's world?

The Stone Lion

EDMUND CREPT UP to the arch and looked inside into the courtyard, and there he saw a sight that nearly made his heart stop beating. Just inside the gate, with the moonlight shining on it, stood an enormous lion crouched as if it was ready to spring. And Edmund stood in the shadow of the arch, afraid to go on and afraid to go back, with his knees knocking together. He stood there so long that his teeth would have been chattering with cold even if they had not been chattering with fear. How long this really lasted I don't know, but it seemed to Edmund to last for hours.

Then at last he began to wonder why the lion was standing so still—for it hadn't moved one inch since he first set eyes on it. Edmund now ventured a little nearer, still keeping in the shadow of the arch as much as he could. He now saw from the way the lion was standing that it couldn't have been looking at him at all. ("But supposing it turns its head?" thought Edmund.) In fact it was staring at something else—namely a little dwarf who stood with his back to it about four feet away. "Aha!" thought Edmund. "When it springs at the dwarf then will be my chance to escape." But still the lion never moved, nor did the dwarf. And now at last Edmund remembered what the others had said about the White Witch turning people into stone. Perhaps this was only a stone lion. And as soon as he had thought of that he noticed that the lion's back and the top of its head were covered with snow. Of course it must be only a statue! No living animal would have let itself get covered with snow. Then very slowly and with his heart beating as if it would burst, Edmund ventured to go up to the lion. Even now he hardly dared to touch it, but at last he put out his hand, very quickly, and did. It was cold stone. He had been frightened of a mere statue!

The relief which Edmund felt was so great that in spite of the cold he suddenly got warm all over right down to his toes, and at the same time there came into his head what seemed a perfectly lovely idea. "Probably," he thought, "this is the great Lion Aslan that they were all talking about. She's caught him already and turned him into stone. So *that's* the end of all their fine ideas about him! Pooh! Who's afraid of Aslan?"

And he stood there gloating over the stone lion, and presently he did something very silly and childish. He took a stump of lead pencil out of his pocket and scribbled a moustache on the lion's upper lip and then a pair of spectacles on its eyes. Then he said, "Yah! Silly old Aslan! How do you like being a stone? You thought yourself mighty fine, didn't you?" But in spite of the scribbles on it the face of the great stone beast still looked so terrible, and sad, and noble, staring up in the moonlight, that Edmund didn't really get any fun out of jeering at it. He turned away and began to cross the courtyard.

—*The Lion, the Witch, and the Wardrobe*

Why do you think Edmund is driven to draw on the stone lion? Why doesn't he get any enjoyment from his act? Have you ever jeered at someone or something? How did it make you feel?

Waiting All My Life

AT BEAVERSDAM they re-crossed the river and came east again along the southern bank. They came to a little cottage where a child stood in the doorway crying. "Why are you crying, my love?" asked Aslan. The child, who had never seen a picture of a lion, was not afraid of him. "Auntie's very ill," she said. "She's going to die." Then Aslan went to go in at the door of the cottage, but it was too small for him. So, when he had got his head through, he pushed with his shoulders (Lucy and Susan fell off when he did this) and lifted the whole house up and it fell backward and apart. And there, still in her bed, though the bed was now in the open air, lay a little old woman who looked as if she had Dwarf blood in her. She was at death's door, but when she opened her eyes and saw the bright, hairy head of the lion staring into her face, she did not scream or faint. She said, "Oh, Aslan! I knew it was true. I've been waiting for this all my life. Have you come to take me away?"

"Yes, dearest," said Aslan. "But not the long journey yet." And as he spoke, like the flush creeping along the underside of a cloud at sunrise, the color came back to her white face and her eyes grew bright and she sat up and said, "Why, I do declare I feel *that* better. I think I could take a little breakfast this morning."

—*Prince Caspian*

Why might just seeing Aslan make the woman feel so much better? How does seeing something you've longed for give you life?

The Most Unfortunate
Boy That Ever Lived

I DO THINK," said Shasta, "that I must be the most unfortunate boy that ever lived in the whole world. Everything goes right for everyone except me. Those Narnian lords and ladies got safe away from Tashbaan; I was left behind. Aravis and Bree and Hwin are all as snug as anything with that old Hermit: of course I was the one who was sent on. King Lune and his people must have got safely into the castle and shut the gates long before Rabadash arrived, but I get left out."

And being very tired and having nothing inside him, he felt so sorry for himself that the tears rolled down his cheeks.

—*The Horse and His Boy*

When have you reached a low point such as this one? What contributed to your despair? What helped to bring you out of it?

Gay and Frolicsome Puddleglum

"OUR ONLY CHANCE," said Scrubb, "is to try to sneak away by daylight. Mightn't there be an hour in the afternoon when most of the giants are asleep?—and if we could steal down into the kitchen, mightn't there be a back door open? . . . We must put them off their guard, though. . . . We must pretend we love being here and are longing for this Autumn Feast."

"That's tomorrow night," said Puddleglum. "I heard one of them say so."

"I see," said Jill. "We must pretend to be awfully excited about it, and keep on asking questions. They think we're absolute infants anyway, which will make it easier."

"Gay," said Puddleglum with a deep sigh. "That's what we've got to be. Gay. As if we hadn't a care in the world. Frolicsome. You two youngsters haven't always got very high spirits, I've noticed. You must watch me, and do as I do. I'll be gay. Like this"—and he assumed a ghastly grin. "And frolicsome"—here he cut a most mournful caper. "You'll soon get into it, if you keep your eyes on me. They think I'm a funny fellow already, you see. I dare say you two thought I was a trifle tipsy last night, but I do assure you it was—well, most of it was—put on. I had an idea it would come in useful, somehow."

The children, when they talked over their adventures afterward, could never feel sure whether this last statement was quite strictly true; but they were sure that Puddleglum thought it was true when he made it.

—*The Silver Chair*

Is Puddleglum trying to convince himself, or the children, that he wasn't really tipsy the night before? When have you convinced yourself of an alternate story that was more palatable than reality?

Edmund Lets Lucy Down

L UCY BURST OUT:
"Peter! Susan! It's all true. Edmund has seen it too. There *is* a country you can get to through the wardrobe. Edmund and I both got in. We met one another in there, in the wood. Go on, Edmund; tell them all about it."

"What's all this about, Ed?" said Peter.

And now we come to one of the nastiest things in this story. Up to that moment Edmund had been feeling sick, and sulky, and annoyed with Lucy for being right, but he hadn't made up his mind what to do. When Peter suddenly asked him the question he decided all at once to do the meanest and most spiteful thing he could think of. He decided to let Lucy down.

"Tell us, Ed," said Susan.

And Edmund gave a very superior look as if he were far older than Lucy (there was really only a year's difference) and then a little snigger and said, "Oh, yes, Lucy and I have been playing—pretending that all her story about a country in the wardrobe is true. Just for fun, of course. There's nothing there really."

Poor Lucy gave Edmund one look and rushed out of the room.

Edmund, who was becoming a nastier person every minute, thought that he had scored a great success, and went on at once to say, "There she goes again. What's the matter with her? That's the worst of young kids, they always—"

"Look here," said Peter, turning on him savagely, "shut up! You've been perfectly beastly to Lu ever since she started this nonsense about the wardrobe, and now you go playing games with her about it and setting her off again. I believe you did it simply out of spite."

—*The Lion, the Witch, and the Wardrobe*

Why does Edmund lie about their experiences in Narnia? When have you lied to someone to avoid a truth that didn't make you look good?

One Good Deed

[SHASTA] TURNED AND RACED for the gate in the green wall which, now for the first time, he remembered seeing. Hwin, stumbling and nearly fainting, was just entering the gate: Aravis still kept her seat but her back was covered with blood.

"Come in, my daughter, come in," the robed and bearded man was saying, and then, "Come in, my son," as Shasta panted up to him. . . .

They were in a wide and perfectly circular enclosure, protected by a high wall of green turf. A pool of perfectly still water, so full that the water was almost exactly level with the ground, lay before him. At one end of the pool, completely overshadowing it with its branches, there grew the hugest and most beautiful tree that Shasta had ever seen. Beyond the pool was a little low house of stone roofed with deep and ancient thatch. . . .

"Are—are—are you," panted Shasta, "are you King Lune of Archenland?"

The old man shook his head. "No," he replied in a quiet voice, "I am the Hermit of the Southern March. And now, my son, waste no time on questions, but obey. This damsel is wounded. Your horses are spent. Rabadash is at this moment finding a ford over the Winding Arrow. If you run now, without a moment's rest, you will still be in time to warn King Lune."

Shasta's heart fainted at these words for he felt he had no strength left. And he writhed inside at what seemed the cruelty and unfairness of the demand. He had not yet learned that if you do one good deed your reward usually is to be set to do another and harder and better one. But all he said out loud was:

"Where is the King?"

—*The Horse and His Boy*

Despite his internal reaction, why do you think Shasta obeys immediately? How could completing one good deed and then having another one waiting be a reward?

The Knight's Enchantment

THE KNIGHT WAS SEATED in a curious silver chair, to which he was bound by his ankles, his knees, his elbows, his wrists, and his waist. There was sweat on his forehead, and his face was filled with anguish.

"Come in, friends," he said, glancing quickly up. "The fit is not yet upon me. Make no noise, for I told that prying chamberlain that you were in bed. Now . . . I can feel it coming. Quick! Listen while I am master of myself. When the fit is upon me, it well may be that I shall beg and implore you, with entreaties and threatenings, to loosen my bonds. They say I do. I shall call upon you by all that is most dear and most dreadful. But do not listen to me. Harden your hearts and stop your ears. For while I am bound you are safe. But if once I were up and out of this chair, then first would come my fury, and after that"—he shuddered—"the change into a loathsome serpent."

"There's no fear of our loosing you," said Puddleglum. "We've no wish to meet wild men; or serpents either."

"I should think not," said Scrubb and Jill together.

"All the same," added Puddleglum in a whisper. "Don't let's be too sure. Let's be on our guard. We've muffed everything else, you know. He'll be cunning, I shouldn't wonder, once he gets started. Can we trust one another? Do we all promise that whatever he says we don't touch those cords? *Whatever* he says, mind you?"

"Rather!" said Scrubb.

"There's nothing in the world he can say or do that'll make me change my mind," said Jill.

"Hush! Something's happening," said Puddleglum.

The Knight was moaning. His face was as pale as putty, and he writhed in his bonds. And whether because she was sorry for him, or for some other reason, Jill thought that he looked a nicer sort of man than he had looked before.

"Ah," he groaned. "Enchantments, enchantments . . . the heavy, tangled, cold, clammy web of evil magic. Buried alive. Dragged down under the earth, down into the sooty blackness . . . how many years is it? . . .

Have I lived ten years, or a thousand years, in the pit? Maggotmen all around me. Oh, have mercy. Let me out, let me go back. Let me feel the wind and see the sky. . . . There used to be a little pool. When you looked down into it you could see all the trees growing upside-down in the water, all green, and below them, deep, very deep, the blue sky."

He had been speaking in a low voice; now he looked up, fixed his eyes upon them, and said loud and clear:

"Quick! I am sane now. Every night I am sane. If only I could get out of this enchanted chair, it would last. I should be a man again. But every night they bind me, and so every night my chance is gone. But you are not enemies. I am not *your* prisoner. Quick! Cut these cords."

"Stand fast! Steady," said Puddleglum to the two children.

—*The Silver Chair*

When in your life have you had to band together with others to keep a commitment?

The Knight's Enchantment

I BESEECH YOU TO HEAR ME," said the Knight, forcing himself to speak calmly. "Have they told you that if I am released from this chair I shall kill you and become a serpent? I see by your faces that they have. It is a lie. It is at this hour that I am in my right mind: it is all the rest of the day that I am enchanted. You are not Earthmen nor witches. Why should you be on their side? Of your courtesy, cut my bonds.". . .

"This is dreadful. I do wish we'd stayed away till it was over," said Jill.

"Steady!" said Puddleglum.

The prisoner's voice was now rising into a shriek. "Let me go, I say. Give me my sword. My sword! Once I am free, I shall take such revenge on Earthmen that Underland will talk of it for a thousand years!"

"Now the frenzy is beginning," said Scrubb. "I hope those knots are all right."

"Yes," said Puddleglum. "He'd have twice his natural strength if he got free now. And I'm not clever with my sword. He'd get us both, I shouldn't wonder; and then Pole on her own would be left to tackle the snake.". . .

"Once and for all," said the prisoner, "I adjure you to set me free. By all fears and all loves, by the bright skies of Overland, by the great Lion, by Aslan himself, I charge you—"

"Oh!" cried the three travelers as though they had been hurt. "It's the sign," said Puddleglum. "It was the *words* of the sign," said Scrubb more cautiously. "Oh, what *are* we to do?" said Jill.

It was a dreadful question. What had been the use of promising one another that they would not on any account set the Knight free, if they were now to do so the first time he happened to call upon a name they really cared about? On the other hand, what had been the use of learning the signs if they weren't going to obey them? Yet could Aslan have really meant them to unbind anyone—even a lunatic—who asked it in his name? Could it be a mere accident? Or how if the Queen of the Underworld knew all about the signs and had made the Knight learn this name simply in order to entrap them? But then, supposing this was the real sign? . . . They had muffed three [signs] already; they daren't muff the fourth.

"Oh, if only we knew!" said Jill.

"I think we do know," said Puddleglum.

"Do you mean you think everything will come right if we do untie him?" said Scrubb.

"I don't know about that," said Puddleglum. "You see, Aslan didn't tell Pole what would happen. He only told her what to do. That fellow will be the death of us once he's up, I shouldn't wonder. But that doesn't let us off following the sign."

They all stood looking at one another with bright eyes. It was a sickening moment. "All right!" said Jill suddenly. "Let's get it over. Good-bye, everyone . . . !" They all shook hands.

—*The Silver Chair*

Why is it so hard to decide to loose the Knight? Why did Aslan tell Jill what to do and not what would happen?

Beasts Don't Change

[PETER SAID,] "And you, I suppose, are King Caspian?"

"Yes," said the other boy. "But I've no idea who you are."

"It's the High King, King Peter," said Trumpkin.

"Your Majesty is very welcome," said Caspian.

"And so is *your* Majesty," said Peter. "I haven't come to take your place, you know, but to put you into it."

"Your Majesty," said another voice at Peter's elbow. He turned and found himself face to face with the Badger. Peter leaned forward, put his arms round the beast and kissed the furry head: it wasn't a girlish thing for him to do, because he was the High King.

"Best of badgers," he said. "You never doubted us all through."

"No credit to me, your Majesty," said Trufflehunter. "I'm a beast and we don't change. I'm a badger, what's more, and we hold on."

—*Prince Caspian*

What does Trufflehunter mean by saying that beasts don't change? In what ways can such constancy be good? In what ways can it be limiting?

The Queen Rises

THE CHILDREN WERE FACING one another across the pillar where the bell hung, still trembling, though it no longer gave out any note. Suddenly they heard a soft noise from the end of the room which was still undamaged. They turned as quick as lightning to see what it was. One of the robed figures, the furthest-off one of all, the woman whom Digory thought so beautiful, was rising from its chair. When she stood up they realized that she was even taller than they had thought. And you could see at once, not only from her crown and robes, but from the flash of her eyes and the curve of her lips, that she was a great queen. She looked round the room and saw the damage and saw the children, but you could not guess from her face what she thought of either or whether she was surprised. She came forward with long, swift strides.

"Who has awaked me? Who has broken the spell?" she asked.

"I think it must have been me," said Digory.

"You!" said the Queen, laying her hand on his shoulder—a white, beautiful hand, but Digory could feel that it was strong as steel pincers. "You? But you are only a child, a common child. Anyone can see at a glance that you have no drop of royal or noble blood in your veins. How did such as you dare to enter this house?"

—*The Magician's Nephew*

The children can see from her eyes and lips that she is a "great queen." Great in what sense? How do we measure greatness these days?

Eustace Wakes as a Dragon

[JUST AS EUSTACE] reached the edge of the pool two things happened. First of all, it came over him like a thunder-clap that he had been running on all fours—and why on earth had he been doing that? And secondly, as he bent toward the water, he thought for a second that yet another dragon was staring up at him out of the pool. But in an instant he realized the truth. The dragon face in the pool was his own reflection. There was no doubt of it. It moved as he moved: it opened and shut its mouth as he opened and shut his.

He had turned into a dragon while he was asleep. Sleeping on a dragon's hoard with greedy, dragonish thoughts in his heart, he had become a dragon himself.

—*The Voyage of the* **Dawn Treader**

How do the thoughts we allow into our heart affect who we become?

No Fear

[H]IS FIRST FEELING was one of relief. There was nothing to be afraid of any more. He was a terror himself and nothing in the world but a knight (and not all of those) would dare to attack him. He could get even with Caspian and Edmund now—

But the moment he thought this he realized that he didn't want to. He wanted to be friends. He wanted to get back among humans and talk and laugh and share things. He realized that he was a monster cut off from the whole human race. An appalling loneliness came over him. He began to see that the others had not really been fiends at all. He began to wonder if he himself had been such a nice person as he had always supposed. He longed for their voices. He would have been grateful for a kind word even from Reepicheep.

When he thought of this the poor dragon that had been Eustace lifted up its voice and wept. A powerful dragon crying its eyes out under the moon in a deserted valley is a sight and a sound hardly to be imagined.

At last he decided he would try to find his way back to the shore. He realized now that Caspian would never have sailed away and left him. And he felt sure that somehow or other he would be able to make people understand who he was.

—*The Voyage of the* **Dawn Treader**

Why does Eustace at first feel that there is nothing to be afraid of anymore? What about being a dragon makes Eustace finally appreciate his companions? When in your life has a dramatic change helped you to appreciate those around you?

May You Live Forever

"OH-MY-FATHER-and-oh-the-delight-of-my-eyes," began the young man, muttering the words very quickly and sulkily and not at all as if the Tisroc *were* the delight of his eyes. "May you live forever, but you have utterly destroyed me. If you had given me the swiftest of the galleys at sunrise when I first saw that the ship of the accursed barbarians was gone from her place I would perhaps have overtaken them. But you persuaded me to send first and see if they had not merely moved round the point into better anchorage. And now the whole day has been wasted. And they are gone—gone—out of my reach! The false jade, the—" and here he added a great many descriptions of Queen Susan which would not look at all nice in print. For of course this young man was Prince Rabadash and of course the false jade was Susan of Narnia. . . .

"I desire and propose, O my father," said Rabadash, "that you immediately call out your invincible armies and invade the thrice-accursed land of Narnia and waste it with fire and sword and add it to your illimitable empire, killing their High King and all of his blood except the queen Susan. For I must have her as my wife, though she shall learn a sharp lesson first."

"Understand, O my son," said the Tisroc, "that no words you can speak will move me to open war against Narnia."

"If you were not my father, O ever-living Tisroc," said the Prince, grinding his teeth, "I should say that was the word of a coward."

"And if you were not my son, O most inflammable Rabadash," replied his father, "your life would be short and your death slow when you had said it." (The cool, placid voice in which he spoke these words made Aravis's blood run cold.)

—*The Horse and His Boy*

What is the contrast between the terms the Prince and the Tisroc use to address each other and the actual meaning of their words? Do you think addressing his father with such overblown terms of respect—"Oh the delight of my eyes" and "May you live forever"—has any impact on the way the Prince feels about his father?

APRIL

Plan of the
Dawn Treader

FORECASTLE

POOP

lookout man

galley

quarters

starboard

port

hen coop

boat

hatch

poop deck

tiller

Lucy's cabin

Drinian's cabin

stern cabin

Caspian's cabin

Susan's Bow

W E MUST TAKE THE GIFTS," said Peter. For long ago at a Christmas in Narnia he and Susan and Lucy had been given certain presents which they valued more than their whole kingdom. . . .

They all agreed with Peter and walked up the path to the wall at the far end of the treasure chamber, and there, sure enough, the gifts were still hanging. Lucy's was the smallest for it was only a little bottle. But the bottle was made of diamond instead of glass, and it was still more than half full of the magical cordial which would heal almost every wound and every illness. Lucy said nothing and looked very solemn as she took her gift down from its place and slung the belt over her shoulder and once more felt the bottle at her side where it used to hang in the old days. Susan's gift had been a bow and arrows and a horn. The bow was still there, and the ivory quiver, full of well-feathered arrows, but—"Oh, Susan," said Lucy. "Where's the horn?"

"Oh, bother, bother, bother," said Susan after she had thought for a moment. "I remember now. I took it with me the last day of all, the day we went hunting the White Stag. It must have got lost when we blundered back into that other place—England, I mean. . . .

"Never mind," said Susan, "I've still got the bow." And she took it.

"Won't the string be perished, Su?" said Peter.

But whether by some magic in the air of the treasure chamber or not, the bow was still in working order. . . . In a moment she had bent the bow and then she gave one little pluck to the string. It twanged: a chirruping twang that vibrated through the whole room. And that one small noise brought back the old days to the children's minds more than anything that had happened yet. All the battles and hunts and feasts came rushing into their heads together.

—*Prince Caspian*

Why do you think the sound of Susan's bow has the power to bring back all those old memories, more so even than walking through their old castle? When has a sound or smell brought back a series of memories for you?

He Has Shown Another Face

NOW, MADAM," the King was saying to Queen Susan (the lady who had kissed Shasta). "What think you? We have been in this city fully three weeks. Have you yet settled in your mind whether you will marry this dark-faced lover of yours, this Prince Rabadash, or no?"

The lady shook her head. "No, brother," she said, "not for all the jewels in Tashbaan." ("Hullo!" thought Shasta. "Although they're king and queen, they're brother and sister, not married to one another.")

"Truly, sister," said the King, "I should have loved you the less if you had taken him. And I tell you that at the first coming of the Tisroc's ambassadors into Narnia to treat of this marriage, and later when the Prince was our guest at Cair Paravel, it was a wonder to me that ever you could find it in your heart to show him so much favor."

"That was my folly, Edmund," said Queen Susan, "of which I cry you mercy. Yet when he was with us in Narnia, truly this Prince bore himself in another fashion than he does now in Tashbaan. For I take you all to witness what marvelous feats he did in that great tournament and hastilude which our brother the High King made for him, and how meekly and courteously he consorted with us the space of seven days. But here, in his own city, he has shown another face."

"Ah!" croaked the Raven. "It is an old saying: See the bear in his own den before you judge of his conditions."

"That's very true, Sallowpad," said one of the Dwarfs. "And another is, Come, live with me and you'll know me."

"Yes," said the King. "We have now seen him for what he is: that is, a most proud, bloody, luxurious, cruel, and self-pleasing tyrant."

—The Horse and His Boy

Do you relate to the Raven's and the Dwarf's statements? When have you known someone who acted one way in one place and a different way in another? Are you ever guilty of this?

Royal Responsibilities

W ELL," SAID ASLAN, "can you use a spade and a plough and raise food out of the earth?"

"Yes, sir, I could do a bit of that sort of work: being brought up to it, like."

"Can you rule these creatures kindly and fairly, remembering that they are not slaves like the dumb beasts of the world you were born in, but Talking Beasts and free subjects?"

"I see that, sir," replied the Cabby. "I'd try to do the square thing by them all."

"And would you bring up your children and grandchildren to do the same?"

"It'd be up to me to try, sir. I'd do my best: wouldn't we, Nellie?"

"And you wouldn't have favorites either among your own children or among the other creatures, or let any hold another under or use it hardly?"

"I never could abide such goings on, sir, and that's the truth. I'd give 'em what for if I caught 'em at it," said the Cabby. (All through this conversation his voice was growing slower and richer. More like the country voice he must have had as a boy and less like the sharp, quick voice of a cockney.)

"And if enemies came against the land (for enemies will arise) and there was war, would you be the first in the charge and the last in the retreat?"

"Well, sir," said the Cabby very slowly, "a chap don't exactly know till he's been tried. I dare say I might turn out ever such a soft 'un. Never did no fighting except with my fists. I'd try—that is, I 'ope I'd try—to do my bit."

"Then," said Aslan, "you will have done all that a King should do."
                                          —*The Magician's Nephew*

What are the main tasks that Aslan outlines for the new king and queen? What virtues do these tasks represent? How are these virtues represented in your life?

The Story of Prince Rilian

THEN IN GOOD TIME on the next day they saddled their horses and rode a great gallop into the northern woods and alighted at the same fountain where the Queen got her death. Drinian thought it strange that the Prince should choose that place of all places, to linger in. And there they rested till it came to high noon: and at noon Drinian looked up and saw the most beautiful lady he had ever seen; and she stood at the north side of the fountain and said no word but beckoned to the Prince with her hand as if she bade him come to her. And she was tall and great, shining, and wrapped in a thin garment as green as poison. And the Prince stared at her like a man out of his wits. But suddenly the lady was gone, Drinian knew not where; and they two returned to Cair Paravel. It stuck in Drinian's mind that this shining green woman was evil.

Drinian doubted very much whether he ought not to tell this adventure to the King, but he had little wish to be a blab and a tale-bearer and so he held his tongue. But afterward he wished he had spoken. For next day Prince Rilian rode out alone. That night he came not back, and from that hour no trace of him was ever found in Narnia nor any neighboring land, and neither his horse nor his hat nor his cloak nor anything else was ever found. Then Drinian in the bitterness of his heart went to Caspian and said, "Lord King, slay me speedily as a great traitor: for by my silence I have destroyed your son." And he told him the story. Then Caspian caught up a battle-axe and rushed upon the Lord Drinian to kill him, and Drinian stood still as a stock for the death blow. But when the axe was raised, Caspian suddenly threw it away and cried out, "I have lost my queen and my son: shall I lose my friend also?" And he fell upon the Lord Drinian's neck and embraced him and both wept, and their friendship was not broken.

Such was the story of Rilian.

—*The Silver Chair*

When have you kept something to yourself only to regret it? How do we balance respecting others' privacy with watching out for them?

Rabadash Made Ridiculous

"LET ME DOWN, EDMUND," howled Rabadash. "Let me down and fight me like a king and a man; or if you are too great a coward to do that, kill me at once."

"Certainly," began King Edmund, but King Lune interrupted.

"By your Majesty's good leave," said King Lune to Edmund. "Not so." Then turning to Rabadash he said, "Your royal Highness, if you had given that challenge a week ago, I'll answer for it there was no one in King Edmund's dominion, from the High King down to the smallest Talking Mouse, who would have refused it. But by attacking our castle of Anvard in time of peace without defiance sent, you have proved yourself no knight, but a traitor, and one rather to be whipped by the hangman than to be suffered to cross swords with any person of honor. Take him down, bind him, and carry him within till our pleasure is further known."

Strong hands wrenched Rabadash's sword from him and he was carried away into the castle, shouting, threatening, cursing, and even crying. For though he could have faced torture he couldn't bear being made ridiculous. In Tashbaan everyone had always taken him seriously.

—The Horse and His Boy

Why does King Lune no longer consider Rabadash worthy of a duel? How does that wound Rabadash more than a blow?

APRIL 6

Excuses

JUST AS MR. BEAVER had been repeating the rhyme about *Adam's flesh and Adam's bone* Edmund had been very quietly turning the door-handle; and just before Mr. Beaver had begun telling them that the White Witch wasn't really human at all but half a Jinn and half a giantess, Edmund had got outside into the snow and cautiously closed the door behind him.

You mustn't think that even now Edmund was quite so bad that he actually wanted his brother and sisters to be turned into stone. He did want Turkish Delight and to be a Prince (and later a King) and to pay Peter out for calling him a beast. As for what the Witch would do with the others, he didn't want her to be particularly nice to them—certainly not to put them on the same level as himself; but he managed to believe, or to pretend he believed, that she wouldn't do anything very bad to them. "Because," he said to himself, "all these people who say nasty things about her are her enemies and probably half of it isn't true. She was jolly nice to me, anyway, much nicer than they are. I expect she is the rightful Queen really. Anyway, she'll be better than that awful Aslan!" At least, that was the excuse he made in his own mind for what he was doing. It wasn't a very good excuse, however, for deep down inside him he really knew that the White Witch was bad and cruel.

—*The Lion, the Witch, and the Wardrobe*

How do you make excuses for yourself? Do you think that deep down you really know the truth?

Reepicheep Joins Caspian

THE NEXT PLACE they were to visit was quite near at hand, but they had to go a long way round in order to avoid a region in which Men lived. It was well into the afternoon before they found themselves in level fields, warm between hedgerows. There Trufflehunter called at the mouth of a little hole in a green bank and out popped the last thing Caspian expected—a Talking Mouse. He was of course bigger than a common mouse, well over a foot high when he stood on his hind legs, and with ears nearly as long as (though broader than) a rabbit's. His name was Reepicheep and he was a gay and martial mouse. He wore a tiny little rapier at his side and twirled his long whiskers as if they were a moustache. "There are twelve of us, Sire," he said with a dashing and graceful bow, "and I place all the resources of my people unreservedly at your Majesty's disposal." Caspian tried hard (and successfully) not to laugh, but he couldn't help thinking that Reepicheep and all his people could very easily be put in a washing basket and carried home on one's back.

—Prince Caspian

Why does Caspian have a hard time seeing the worth Reepicheep and his people can bring to their cause? When have you underestimated someone's worth?

The Spell

[Lucy] TURNED ON and found to her surprise a page with no pictures at all; but the first words were *A Spell to make hidden things visible.* She read it through to make sure of all the hard words and then said it out loud. And she knew at once that it was working because as she spoke the colors came into the capital letters at the top of the page and the pictures began appearing in the margins. It was like when you hold to the fire something written in Invisible Ink and the writing gradually shows up; only instead of the dingy color of lemon juice (which is the easiest Invisible Ink) this was all gold and blue and scarlet. . . . And then she thought, "I suppose I've made everything visible, and not only the Thumpers. There might be lots of other invisible things hanging about a place like this. I'm not sure that I want to see them all."

At that moment she heard soft, heavy footfalls coming along the corridor behind her; and of course she remembered what she had been told about the Magician walking in his bare feet and making no more noise than a cat. It is always better to turn round than to have anything creeping up behind your back. Lucy did so.

Then her face lit up till, for a moment (but of course she didn't know it), she looked almost as beautiful as that other Lucy in the picture, and she ran forward with a little cry of delight and with her arms stretched out. For what stood in the doorway was Aslan himself, the Lion, the highest of all High Kings. And he was solid and real and warm and he let her kiss him and bury herself in his shining mane. And from the low, earthquake-like sound that came from inside him, Lucy even dared to think that he was purring.

"Oh, Aslan," said she, "it was kind of you to come."

"I have been here all the time," said he, "but you have just made me visible."

"Aslan!" said Lucy almost a little reproachfully. "Don't make fun of me. As if anything *I* could do would make *you* visible!"

"It did," said Aslan. "Do you think I wouldn't obey my own rules?"

—*The Voyage of the* **Dawn Treader**

What exactly do you think Aslan means by saying he was there all the time?

He Wouldn't Send Them
If It Weren't

[ASLAN SAID,] "Tell your mistress, Son of Earth, that I grant her safe conduct on condition that she leaves her wand behind her at that great oak."

This was agreed to and two leopards went back with the dwarf to see that the conditions were properly carried out. "But supposing she turns the two leopards into stone?" whispered Lucy to Peter. I think the same idea had occurred to the leopards themselves; at any rate, as they walked off their fur was all standing up on their backs and their tails were bristling—like a cat's when it sees a strange dog.

"It'll be all right," whispered Peter in reply. "He wouldn't send them if it weren't."

—*The Lion, the Witch, and the Wardrobe*

Peter has just met Aslan, yet he expresses complete faith in his judgment. Have you ever felt such trust in someone shortly after meeting him or her?

Thou Art My Heir

A<small>ND TOMORROW</small>, C<small>OR</small>," [King Lune] added, "shalt come over all the castle with me and see the estate, and mark all its strength and weakness, for it will be thine to guard when I'm gone."

"But Corin will be the King then, Father," said Cor.

"Nay, lad," said King Lune, "thou art my heir. The crown comes to thee."

"But I don't want it," said Cor. "I'd far rather—"

"'Tis no question what thou wantest, Cor, nor I either. 'Tis in the course of law."

"But if we're twins we must be the same age."

"Nay," said the King with a laugh. "One must come first. Art Corin's elder by full twenty minutes. And his better too, let's hope, though that's no great mastery." And he looked at Corin with a twinkle in his eyes.

"But, Father, couldn't you make whichever you like to be the next King?"

"No. The king's under the law, for it's the law makes him a king. Hast no more power to start away from thy crown than any sentry from his post."

"Oh dear," said Cor. "I don't want to at all. And Corin—I am most dreadfully sorry. I never dreamed my turning up was going to chisel you out of your kingdom."

"Hurrah! Hurrah!" said Corin. "I shan't have to be King. I shan't have to be King. I'll always be a prince. It's princes have all the fun."

"And that's truer than thy brother knows, Cor," said King Lune. "For this is what it means to be a king: to be first in every desperate attack and last in every desperate retreat, and when there's hunger in the land (as must be now and then in bad years) to wear finer clothes and laugh louder over a scantier meal than any man in your land."

—*The Horse and His Boy*

Why does no one—neither Cor nor Corin nor even the present King—seem at all anxious to be king? How do you interpret King Lune's last comments about being a king? How are they true for those in power today?

Enjoying the Journey

[THE SECOND JOURNEY] was even better than yesterday, partly because everyone was feeling so fresh, and partly because the newly risen sun was at their backs and, of course, everything looks nicer when the light is behind you. It was a wonderful ride. The big snowy mountains rose above them in every direction. The valleys, far beneath them, were so green, and all the streams which tumbled down from the glaciers into the main river were so blue, that it was like flying over gigantic pieces of jewelry. They would have liked this part of the adventure to go on longer than it did. But quite soon they were all sniffing the air and saying "What is it?" and "Did you smell something?" and "Where's it coming from?" For a heavenly smell, warm and golden, as if from all the most delicious fruits and flowers of the world, was coming up to them from somewhere ahead.

"It's coming from that valley with the lake in it," said Fledge.

"So it is," said Digory. "And look! There's a green hill at the far end of the lake. And look how blue the water is."

"It must be the place," said all three.

—The Magician's Nephew

What about the journey described here appeals to you? When have you experienced the feeling that the journey was even better than the destination? What could it mean to live your entire life this way?

The Great Bridge Builder

B UT BETWEEN THEM and the foot of the sky there was something so white on the green grass that even with their eagles' eyes they could hardly look at it. They came on and saw that it was a Lamb.

"Come and have breakfast," said the Lamb in its sweet milky voice.

Then they noticed for the first time that there was a fire lit on the grass and fish roasting on it. They sat down and ate the fish, hungry now for the first time for many days. And it was the most delicious food they had ever tasted.

"Please, Lamb," said Lucy, "is this the way to Aslan's country?"

"Not for you," said the Lamb. "For you the door into Aslan's country is from your own world."

"What!" said Edmund. "Is there a way into Aslan's country from our world too?"

"There is a way into my country from all the worlds," said the Lamb; but as he spoke, his snowy white flushed into tawny gold and his size changed and he was Aslan himself, towering above them and scattering light from his mane.

"Oh, Aslan," said Lucy. "Will you tell us how to get into your country from our world?"

"I shall be telling you all the time," said Aslan. "But I will not tell you how long or short the way will be; only that it lies across a river. But do not fear that, for I am the great Bridge Builder. And now come; I will open the door in the sky and send you to your own land."

—*The Voyage of the* **Dawn Treader**

What does Aslan mean when he says he is the great Bridge Builder? What does Aslan's country represent for you?

What a Horse Can Stand

"WELL, I CAN'T GO ON without a snack," said Bree. "Take my bridle off, Shasta."

"P-please," said Hwin, very shyly, "I feel just like Bree that I *can't* go on. But when Horses have humans (with spurs and things) on their backs, aren't they often made to go on when they're feeling like this? And then they find they can. I m-mean—oughtn't we to be able to do even more, now that we're free? It's all for Narnia."

"I think, Ma'am," said Bree very crushingly, "that I know a little more about campaigns and forced marches and what a horse can stand than you do."

To this Hwin made no answer, being, like most highly bred mares, a very nervous and gentle person who was easily put down. In reality she was quite right, and if Bree had had a Tarkaan on his back at that moment to make him go on, he would have found that he was good for several hours' hard going. But one of the worst results of being a slave and being forced to do things is that when there is no one to force you any more you find you have almost lost the power of forcing yourself.

—*The Horse and His Boy*

What makes you push yourself to go on during those times when you're no longer sure you can? How do you put limits on yourself?

Bargaining

SON OF ADAM," said Aslan. "Are you ready to undo the wrong that you have done to my sweet country of Narnia on the very first day of its birth?"

"Well, I don't see what I can do," said Digory. "You see, the Queen ran away and—"

"I asked, are you ready?" said the Lion.

"Yes," said Digory. He had had for a second some wild idea of saying, "I'll try to help you if you'll promise to help my Mother," but he realized in time that the Lion was not at all the sort of person one could try to make bargains with.

—*The Magician's Nephew*

How does Digory initially avoid Aslan's question? Why would Aslan not be someone to bargain with? What would have been a better way for Digory to approach Aslan for help for his mother?

What Ever Am I to Say to Him?

WITH A JINGLING OF MAIL the others climbed up behind [Lucy]. Aslan glided on before them and they walked after him.

"Lucy," said Susan in a very small voice.

"Yes?" said Lucy.

"I see him now. I'm sorry."

"That's all right."

"But I've been far worse than you know. I really believed it was him—he, I mean—yesterday. When he warned us not to go down to the fir wood. And I really believed it was him tonight, when you woke us up. I mean, deep down inside. Or I could have, if I'd let myself. But I just wanted to get out of the woods and—and—oh, I don't know. And what ever am I to say to him?"

"Perhaps you won't need to say much," suggested Lucy.

—*Prince Caspian*

Why might not saying much be the best option for Susan after denying Aslan's presence with them? What do you think the best strategy is when we realize we have made bad choices?

You Have Listened to Fears

Hush!" SAID THE OTHER FOUR, for now Aslan had stopped and turned and stood facing them, looking so majestic that they felt as glad as anyone can who feels afraid, and as afraid as anyone can who feels glad. The boys strode forward: Lucy made way for them: Susan and the Dwarf shrank back.

"Oh, Aslan," said King Peter, dropping on one knee and raising the Lion's heavy paw to his face, "I'm so glad. And I'm so sorry. I've been leading them wrong ever since we started and especially yesterday morning."

"My dear son," said Aslan.

Then he turned and welcomed Edmund. "Well done," were his words.

Then, after an awful pause, the deep voice said, "Susan." Susan made no answer but the others thought she was crying. "You have listened to fears, child," said Aslan. "Come, let me breathe on you. Forget them. Are you brave again?"

"A little, Aslan," said Susan.

—*Prince Caspian*

Peter and Susan don't initially believe Lucy when she says she can see Aslan and asks them to follow her. Why might listening to fears prevent Susan from seeing Aslan? When have your fears prevented you from doing the right thing?

Spring

EVERY MOMENT the patches of green grew bigger and the patches of snow grew smaller. Every moment more and more of the trees shook off their robes of snow. Soon, wherever you looked, instead of white shapes you saw the dark green of firs or the black prickly branches of bare oaks and beeches and elms. Then the mist turned from white to gold and presently cleared away altogether. Shafts of delicious sunlight struck down onto the forest floor and overhead you could see a blue sky between the tree tops.

Soon there were more wonderful things happening. Coming suddenly round a corner into a glade of silver birch trees Edmund saw the ground covered in all directions with little yellow flowers—celandines.

The noise of water grew louder. Presently they actually crossed a stream. Beyond it they found snowdrops growing.

"Mind your own business!" said the dwarf when he saw that Edmund had turned his head to look at them; and he gave the rope a vicious jerk.

But of course this didn't prevent Edmund from seeing. Only five minutes later he noticed a dozen crocuses growing round the foot of an old tree—gold and purple and white. Then came a sound even more delicious than the sound of the water. Close beside the path they were following a bird suddenly chirped from the branch of a tree. It was answered by the chuckle of another bird a little further off. And then, as if that had been a signal, there was chattering and chirruping in every direction, and then a moment of full song, and within five minutes the whole wood was ringing with birds' music, and wherever Edmund's eyes turned he saw birds alighting on branches, or sailing overhead or chasing one another or having their little quarrels or tidying up their feathers with their beaks.

—*The Lion, the Witch, and the Wardrobe*

What does the spring symbolize? Can you imagine perpetual winter with no relief? How can the turning of seasons be helpful to us as humans?

The Albatross

"DRINIAN," [CASPIAN] said in a very low voice. "How long did we take rowing in?—I mean rowing to where we picked up the stranger?"

"Five minutes, perhaps," whispered Drinian. "Why?"

"Because we've been more than that already trying to get out."

Drinian's hand shook on the tiller and a line of cold sweat ran down his face. The same idea was occurring to everyone on board. "We shall never get out, never get out," moaned the rowers. "He's steering us wrong. We're going round and round in circles. We shall never get out.". . .

Lucy leant her head on the edge of the fighting-top and whispered, "Aslan, Aslan, if ever you loved us at all, send us help now." The darkness did not grow any less, but she began to feel a little—a very, very little— better. "After all, nothing has really happened to us yet," she thought.

"Look!" cried Rynelf's voice hoarsely from the bows. There was a tiny speck of light ahead, and while they watched, a broad beam of light fell from it upon the ship. It did not alter the surrounding darkness, but the whole ship was lit up as if by searchlight. Caspian blinked, stared round, saw the faces of his companions all with wild, fixed expressions. Everyone was staring in the same direction: behind everyone lay his black, sharply edged shadow.

Lucy looked along the beam and presently saw something in it. At first it looked like a cross, then it looked like an aeroplane, then it looked like a kite, and at last with a whirring of wings it was right overhead and was an albatross. It circled three times round the mast and then perched for an instant on the crest of the gilded dragon at the prow. It called out in a strong sweet voice what seemed to be words though no one understood them. After that it spread its wings, rose, and began to fly slowly ahead, bearing a little to starboard. Drinian steered after it not doubting that it offered good guidance. But no one except Lucy knew that as it circled the mast it had whispered to her, "Courage, dear heart," and the voice, she felt sure, was Aslan's, and with the voice a delicious smell breathed in her face.

In a few moments the darkness turned into a greyness ahead, and then, almost before they dared to begin hoping, they had shot out into the sunlight and were in the warm, blue world again. And all at once every-body realized that there was nothing to be afraid of and never had been. They blinked their eyes and looked about them. The brightness of the ship herself astonished them: they had half expected to find that the darkness would cling to the white and the green and the gold in the form of some grime or scum. And then first one, and then another, began laughing.

"I reckon we've made pretty good fools of ourselves," said Rynelf.

—*The Voyage of the* **Dawn Treader**

Why does Rynelf feel they've made fools of themselves? When have you been terrified and later realized there was nothing to be afraid of? How do we allow ourselves to be fooled?

The Forgotten Story

O**N THE NEXT PAGE** she came to a spell "for the refreshment of the spirit." The pictures were fewer here but very beautiful. And what Lucy found herself reading was more like a story than a spell. It went on for three pages and before she had read to the bottom of the page she had forgotten that she was reading at all. She was living in the story as if it were real, and all the pictures were real too. When she had got to the third page and come to the end, she said, "That is the loveliest story I've ever read or ever shall read in my whole life. Oh, I wish I could have gone on reading it for ten years. At least I'll read it over again."

But here part of the magic of the Book came into play. You couldn't turn back. The right-hand pages, the ones ahead, could be turned; the left-hand pages could not.

"Oh, what a shame!" said Lucy. "I did so want to read it again. Well, at least I must remember it. Let's see . . . it was about . . . about . . . oh dear, it's all fading away again. And even this last page is going blank. This is a very queer book. How can I have forgotten? It was about a cup and a sword and a tree and a green hill, I know that much. But I can't remember and what *shall* I do?"

And she never could remember; and ever since that day what Lucy means by a good story is a story which reminds her of the forgotten story in the Magician's Book.

—*The Voyage of the* **Dawn Treader**

Why do you think the book does not allow its reader to go back? What is the best story you've ever read? Upon rereading, did you love it as much?

Many Sink Down, and Few Return

A ND OUT OF THAT CAVE they passed into another, and then into another and another, and so on till Jill lost count, but always they were going downhill and each cave was lower than the last, till the very thought of the weight and depth of the earth above you was suffocating. . . .

"One thing I'd like to know," said Puddleglum, "is whether anyone from our world—from up-a-top, I mean—has ever done this trip before?"

"Many have taken ship at the pale beaches," replied the Warden, "and—"

"Yes, I know," interrupted Puddleglum. *"And few return to the sunlit lands.* You needn't say it again. You *are* a chap of one idea, aren't you?"

The children huddled close together on each side of Puddleglum. They had thought him a wet blanket while they were still above ground, but down here he seemed the only comforting thing they had. Then the pale lantern was hung up amidships, the Earthmen sat to the oars, and the ship began to move. The lantern cast its light only a very short way. Looking ahead, they could see nothing but smooth, dark water, fading into absolute blackness.

"Oh, whatever will become of us?" said Jill despairingly.

"Now, don't you let your spirits down, Pole," said the Marsh-wiggle. "There's one thing you've got to remember. We're back on the right lines. We were to go under the Ruined City, and we *are* under it. We're following the instructions again."

—*The Silver Chair*

Confronted with the pessimistic Warden, who keeps repeating that many come down to the underground realm but few return, the normally negative Puddleglum the Marsh-wiggle starts sounding downright optimistic. What might be the reason for this change?

Narnian Air

THEN [TIRIAN] had tried to teach Eustace how to use his sword and shield. Eustace had learned quite a lot about sword fighting on his earlier adventures but that had been all with a straight Narnian sword. He had never handled a curved Calormene scimitar and that made it hard, for many of the strokes are quite different and some of the habits he had learned with the long sword had now to be unlearned again. But Tirian found that he had a good eye and was very quick on his feet. He was surprised at the strength of both children: in fact they both seemed to be already much stronger and bigger and more grown-up than they had been when he first met them a few hours ago. It is one of the effects which Narnian air often has on visitors from our world.

—*The Last Battle*

What about Narnia makes Jill and Eustace appear stronger and bigger and more grown-up? Has any place or circumstance had a similar effect on you?

Eustace's Sufferings

If we could, of course, the sensible thing would be to turn west at once and make for the Lone Islands. But it took us eighteen days to get where we are, running like mad with a gale behind us. Even if we got an east wind it might take us far longer to get back. And at present there's no sign of an east wind—in fact there's no wind at all. As for rowing back, it would take far too long and Caspian says the men couldn't row on half a pint of water a day. I'm pretty sure this is wrong. I tried to explain that perspiration really cools people down, so the men would need less water if they were working. He didn't take any notice of this, which is always his way when he can't think of an answer. The others all voted for going *on* in the hope of finding land. I felt it my duty to point out that we didn't know there *was* any land ahead and tried to get them to see the dangers of *wishful thinking*. Instead of producing a better plan they had the cheek to ask me what I proposed. So I just explained coolly and quietly that I had been kidnapped and brought away on this *idiotic* voyage without my consent, and it was hardly *my* business to get them out of their scrape.

September 4. Still becalmed. Very short rations for dinner and I got less than anyone. Caspian is very clever at helping and thinks I don't see! Lucy for some reason tried to make up to me by offering me some of hers but that *interfering prig* Edmund wouldn't let her. Pretty hot sun. Terribly thirsty all evening.

—*The Voyage of the* Dawn Treader

What is your reaction to Eustace's description of the situation? What do you think Caspian's, Edmund's, or Lucy's account of the same events might be? What is your tendency in times of crisis: to offer comment or criticism or to offer help and solutions? Which is easier?

The Water Thief

September 6. A horrible day. Woke up in the night *knowing* I was feverish and *must* have a drink of water. Any doctor would have said so. Heaven knows I'm the last person to try to get any unfair advantage but I never *dreamed* that this water-rationing would be meant to apply to a sick man. In fact I would have woken the others up and asked for some only I thought it would be selfish to wake them. . . . I got out all right into the big room, if you can call it a room, where the rowing benches and the luggage are. The thing of water is at this end. All was going beautifully, but before I'd drawn a cupful who should catch me but that *little spy* Reep. I tried to explain that I was going on deck for a breath of air (the business about the water had nothing to do with him) and he asked me why I had a cup. He made such a noise that the whole ship was roused. They treated me scandalously. I asked, as I think anyone would have, why Reepicheep was sneaking about the water cask in the middle of the night. He said that as he was too small to be any use on deck, he did sentry over the water every night so that one more man could go to sleep. Now comes their rotten unfairness: they all believed *him*. Can you beat it?

—*The Voyage of the* **Dawn Treader**

Have you ever known someone who was so self-centered that he or she did not seem capable of thinking of others? Under what circumstances does such a tendency become especially plain?

Lucy and the Trees

INSTEAD OF GETTING DROWSIER [Lucy] was getting more awake—with an odd, night-time, dreamish kind of wakefulness. The Creek was growing brighter. She knew now that the moon was on it, though she couldn't see the moon. And now she began to feel that the whole forest was coming awake like herself. Hardly knowing why she did it, she got up quickly and walked a little distance away from their bivouac.

"This is lovely," said Lucy to herself. It was cool and fresh; delicious smells were floating everywhere. . . .

Lucy's eyes began to grow accustomed to the light, and she saw the trees that were nearest her more distinctly. A great longing for the old days when the trees could talk in Narnia came over her. She knew exactly how each of these trees would talk if only she could wake them, and what sort of human form it would put on. She looked at a silver birch: it would have a soft, showery voice and would look like a slender girl, with hair blown all about her face, and fond of dancing. She looked at the oak: he would be a wizened, but hearty old man with a frizzled beard and warts on his face and hands, and hair growing out of the warts. She looked at the beech under which she was standing. Ah!—she would be the best of all. She would be a gracious goddess, smooth and stately, the lady of the wood.

"Oh, Trees, Trees, Trees," said Lucy (though she had not been intending to speak at all). "Oh, Trees, wake, wake, wake. Don't you remember it? Don't you remember *me*? Dryads and Hamadryads, come out, come to me."

Though there was not a breath of wind they all stirred about her. The rustling noise of the leaves was almost like words. The nightingale stopped singing as if to listen to it. Lucy felt that at any moment she would begin to understand what the trees were trying to say. But the moment did not come. The rustling died away. The nightingale resumed its song. Even in the moonlight the wood looked more ordinary again.

—*Prince Caspian*

What do you think causes the trees around Lucy to stir? Have you ever wished that desperately for something to happen?

Them

"OH, GO AWAY and mind your own business," she said. "Nobody asked you to come barging in, did they? And you're a nice person to start telling us what we all ought to do, aren't you? I suppose you mean we ought to spend all our time sucking up to Them, and currying favor, and dancing attendance on Them like you do."

"Oh, Lor!" said the boy, sitting down on the grassy bank at the edge of the shrubbery and very quickly getting up again because the grass was soaking wet. His name unfortunately was Eustace Scrubb, but he wasn't a bad sort.

"Pole!" he said. "Is that fair? Have I been doing anything of the sort this term? Didn't I stand up to Carter about the rabbit? And didn't I keep the secret about Spivvins—under torture too? And didn't I—"

"I d-don't know and I don't care," sobbed Jill.

Scrubb saw that she wasn't quite herself yet and very sensibly offered her a peppermint. He had one too. Presently Jill began to see things in a clearer light.

"I'm sorry, Scrubb," she said presently. "I wasn't fair. You have done all that—this term."

"Then wash out last term if you can," said Eustace. "I was a different chap then. I was—gosh! what a little tick I was."

"Well, honestly, you were," said Jill.

"You think there has been a change, then?" said Eustace.

"It's not only me," said Jill. "Everyone's been saying so. *They*'ve noticed it. Eleanor Blakiston heard Adela Pennyfather talking about it in our changing room yesterday. She said, 'Someone's got hold of that Scrubb kid. He's quite unmanageable this term. We shall have to attend to *him* next.'"

Eustace gave a shudder. Everyone at Experiment House knew what it was like being "attended to" by *Them*.

—*The Silver Chair*

Who in your childhood represented "Them"? Did you ever undergo a change as Eustace does when you were a child? Or stand up to Them?

The Lion-Skin Coat

I WONDER WHO KILLED the poor lion," said Puzzle presently. "It ought to be buried. We must have a funeral."

"Oh, it wasn't a Talking Lion," said Shift. "You needn't bother about *that*. There are no Talking Beasts up beyond the Falls, up in the Western Wild. This skin must have belonged to a dumb, wild lion.". . .

"All the same, Shift," said Puzzle, "even if the skin only belonged to a dumb, wild lion, oughtn't we to give it a decent burial? I mean, aren't all lions rather—well, rather solemn? Because of you know Who. Don't you see?"

"Don't you start getting ideas into your head, Puzzle," said Shift. "Because, you know, thinking isn't your strong point. We'll make this skin into a fine warm winter coat for you."

"Oh, I don't think I'd like that," said the Donkey. "It would look—I mean, the other Beasts might think—that is to say, I shouldn't feel—"

"What are you talking about?" said Shift, scratching himself the wrong way up as Apes do.

"I don't think it would be respectful to the Great Lion, to Aslan himself, if an ass like me went about dressed up in a lion-skin," said Puzzle.

"Now don't stand arguing, please," said Shift. "What does an ass like you know about things of that sort? You know you're no good at thinking, Puzzle, so why don't you let me do your thinking for you? Why don't you treat me as I treat you? I don't think I can do everything. I know you're better at some things than I am. That's why I let you go into the Pool; I knew you'd do it better than me. But why can't I have my turn when it comes to something I *can* do and you can't? Am I never to be allowed to do anything? Do be fair. Turn and turn about."

—*The Last Battle*

How does Shift talk Puzzle into the lion-skin coat? What would happen if Puzzle really did as Shift asked, and treated Shift as Shift treats him?

The Plan to Impersonate Aslan

"COME AND TRY ON your beautiful new lion-skin coat," said Shift.

"Oh bother that old skin," said Puzzle. "I'll try it on in the morning. I'm too tired tonight."

"You *are* unkind, Puzzle," said Shift. "If *you're* tired what do you think I am? All day long, while you've been having a lovely refreshing walk down the valley, I've been working hard to make you a coat. My paws are so tired I can hardly hold these scissors. And now you won't say thank you—and you won't even look at the coat—and you don't care—and—and—"

"My dear Shift," said Puzzle, getting up at once, "I am so sorry. I've been horrid. Of course I'd love to try it on. And it looks simply splendid. Do try it on me at once. Please do."

"Well, stand still then," said the Ape. The skin was very heavy for him to lift, but in the end, with a lot of pulling and pushing and puffing and blowing, he got it onto the donkey. He tied it underneath Puzzle's body and he tied the legs to Puzzle's legs and the tail to Puzzle's tail. A good deal of Puzzle's grey nose and face could be seen through the open mouth of the lion's head. No one who had ever seen a real lion would have been taken in for a moment. But if someone who had never seen a lion looked at Puzzle in his lion-skin he just might mistake him for a lion, if he didn't come too close, and if the light was not too good, and if Puzzle didn't let out a bray and didn't make any noise with his hoofs.

"You look wonderful, wonderful," said the Ape. "If anyone saw you now, they'd think you were Aslan, the Great Lion, himself."

"That would be dreadful," said Puzzle.

"No it wouldn't," said Shift. "Everyone would do whatever you told them."

"But I don't want to tell them anything."

—*The Last Battle*

Why do Puzzle and Shift want such opposite things? How could two such different creatures be friends?

A Sign

BUT YOU THINK OF THE GOOD we could do!" said Shift. "You'd have me to advise you, you know. I'd think of sensible orders for you to give. And everyone would have to obey us, even the King himself. We would set everything right in Narnia."

"But isn't everything right already?" said Puzzle.

"What!" cried Shift. "Everything right?—when there are no oranges or bananas?"

"Well, you know," said Puzzle, "there aren't many people—in fact, I don't think there's anyone but yourself—who wants those sort of things."

"There's sugar too," said Shift.

"H'm, yes," said the Ass. "It would be nice if there was more sugar."

"Well then, that's settled," said the Ape. "You will pretend to be Aslan, and I'll tell you what to say."

"No, no, no," said Puzzle. "Don't say such dreadful things. It would be wrong, Shift. I may be not very clever but I know that much. What would become of us if the real Aslan turned up?"

"I expect he'd be very pleased," said Shift. "Probably he sent us the lion-skin on purpose, so that we could set things to right. Anyway, he never *does* turn up, you know. Not nowadays."

At that moment there came a great thunderclap right overhead and the ground trembled with a small earthquake. Both the animals lost their balance and were flung on their faces.

"There!" gasped Puzzle, as soon as he had breath to speak. "It's a sign, a warning. I knew we were doing something dreadfully wicked. . . ."

"No, no," said the Ape (whose mind worked very quickly). "It's a sign the other way. I was just going to say that if the real Aslan, as you call him, meant us to go on with this, he would send us a thunderclap and an earth-tremor. It was just on the tip of my tongue, only the sign itself came before I could get the words out. . . ."

—*The Last Battle*

How could Puzzle know if the earthquake and thunder were a warning or a positive sign? Have you ever experienced something you took as a sign?

Can You Ever Forgive Me?

THEY BOTH GOT UP and left the tea things on the table, and Mr. Tumnus once more put up his umbrella and gave Lucy his arm, and they went out into the snow. The journey back was not at all like the journey to the Faun's cave; they stole along as quickly as they could, without speaking a word, and Mr. Tumnus kept to the darkest places. Lucy was relieved when they reached the lamp-post again.

"Do you know your way from here, Daughter of Eve?" said Tumnus.

Lucy looked very hard between the trees and could just see in the distance a patch of light that looked like daylight. "Yes," she said, "I can see the wardrobe door."

"Then be off home as quick as you can," said the Faun, "and—c-can you ever forgive me for what I meant to do?"

"Why, of course I can," said Lucy, shaking him heartily by the hand. "And I do hope you won't get into dreadful trouble on my account."

"Farewell, Daughter of Eve," said he. "Perhaps I may keep the handkerchief?"

"Rather!" said Lucy, and then ran toward the far-off patch of daylight as quickly as her legs would carry her.

—*The Lion, the Witch, and the Wardrobe*

Why do you think Lucy is so quick to forgive Mr. Tumnus? Do you find it's easier to forgive someone who asks for forgiveness? What conditions make it more difficult for you to offer forgiveness?

Into the Picture

THE THINGS IN THE PICTURE were moving. . . . Down went the prow of the ship into the wave and up went a great shock of spray. And then up went the wave behind her, and her stern and her deck became visible for the first time. . . . Lucy felt all her hair whipping round her face as it does on a windy day. And this was a windy day; but the wind was blowing out of the picture toward them. And suddenly with the wind came the noises—the swishing of waves and the slap of water against the ship's sides and the creaking and the over-all high steady roar of air and water. But it was the smell, the wild, briny smell, which really convinced Lucy that she was not dreaming.

"Stop it," came Eustace's voice, squeaky with fright and bad temper. "It's some silly trick you two are playing. Stop it. I'll tell Alberta—Ow!"

The other two were much more accustomed to adventures but, just exactly as Eustace Clarence said "Ow," they both said "Ow" too. The reason was that a great cold, salt splash had broken right out of the frame and they were breathless from the smack of it, besides being wet through.

"I'll smash the rotten thing," cried Eustace; and then several things happened at the same time. Eustace rushed toward the picture. Edmund, who knew something about magic, sprang after him, warning him to look out and not to be a fool. Lucy grabbed at him from the other side and was dragged forward. And by this time either they had grown much smaller or the picture had grown bigger. Eustace jumped to try to pull it off the wall and found himself standing on the frame; in front of him was not glass but real sea, and wind and waves rushing up to the frame as they might to a rock. He lost his head and clutched at the other two who had jumped up beside him. There was a second of struggling and shouting, and just as they thought they had got their balance a great blue roller surged up round them, swept them off their feet, and drew them down into the sea.

—*The Voyage of the* **Dawn Treader**

Why do you think Eustace's first reactions are to think the others are tricking him and then to smash the picture? Why is it impossible to get back into Narnia the same way twice?

MAY

The Battle Goes Badly

THAT MORNING Caspian had arranged what was his biggest battle yet, and all had hung their hopes on it. He, with most of the Dwarfs, was to have fallen on the King's right wing at daybreak, and then, when they were heavily engaged, Giant Wimbleweather, with the Centaurs and some of the fiercest beasts, was to have broken out from another place and endeavored to cut the King's right off from the rest of the army. But it had all failed. No one had warned Caspian (because no one in these later days of Narnia remembered) that Giants are not at all clever. Poor Wimbleweather, though as brave as a lion, was a true Giant in that respect. He had broken out at the wrong time and from the wrong place, and both his party and Caspian's had suffered badly and done the enemy little harm. The best of the Bears had been hurt, a Centaur terribly wounded, and there were few in Caspian's party who had not lost blood. It was a gloomy company that huddled under the dripping trees to eat their scanty supper.

The gloomiest of all was Giant Wimbleweather. He knew it was all his fault. He sat in silence shedding big tears which collected on the end of his nose and then fell off with a huge splash on the whole bivouac of the Mice, who had just been beginning to get warm and drowsy. They all jumped up, shaking the water out of their ears and wringing their little blankets, and asked the Giant in shrill but forcible voices whether he thought they weren't wet enough without this sort of thing. And then other people woke up and told the Mice they had been enrolled as scouts and not as a concert party, and asked why they couldn't keep quiet. And Wimbleweather tiptoed away to find some place where he could be miserable in peace, and stepped on somebody's tail and somebody (they said afterward it was a fox) bit him. And so everyone was out of temper.

—*Prince Caspian*

What might you say to Wimbleweather if you were there? Have you ever had a day when everything seemed to go as badly as possible? How did you react?

A Very Bad Donkey

"WHERE HAS PUZZLE GOT TO?" said Eustace.

They all shouted out Puzzle's name and Jill went round to the other side of the Tower to see if he had gone there.

They were quite tired of looking for him when at last his large grey head peered cautiously out of the doorway and he said, "Has it gone away?" And when at last they got him to come out, he was shivering the way a dog shivers before a thunderstorm.

"I see now," said Puzzle, "that I really have been a very bad donkey. I ought never to have listened to Shift. I never thought things like this would begin to happen."

"If you'd spent less time saying you weren't clever and more time trying to be as clever as you could—" began Eustace but Jill interrupted him.

"Oh leave poor old Puzzle alone," she said. "It was all a mistake; wasn't it, Puzzle dear?" And she kissed him on the nose.

—*The Last Battle*

As Eustace suggests, "I'm not clever" is a kind of refrain for Puzzle. Is this a good enough excuse for Puzzle having allowed the Ape to talk him into impersonating Aslan? Do you have a similar refrain that you use as an excuse to keep from taking full responsibility?

The Beautiful Terror

HE TURNED AND SAW, pacing beside him, taller than the horse, a Lion. The horse did not seem to be afraid of it or else could not see it. It was from the Lion that the light came. No one ever saw anything more terrible or beautiful.

—The Horse and His Boy

How can something be both terrible and beautiful? Can you think of anything in our world that might warrant such a description?

Falling at the Lion's Feet

LUCKILY SHASTA HAD LIVED all his life too far south in Calormen to have heard the tales that were whispered in Tashbaan about a dreadful Narnian demon that appeared in the form of a lion. And of course he knew none of the true stories about Aslan, the great Lion, the son of the Emperor over-the-Sea, the King above all High Kings in Narnia. But after one glance at the Lion's face he slipped out of the saddle and fell at its feet. He couldn't say anything but then he didn't want to say anything, and he knew he needn't say anything.

The High King above all kings stooped toward him. Its mane, and some strange and solemn perfume that hung about the mane, was all round him. It touched his forehead with its tongue. He lifted his face and their eyes met. Then instantly the pale brightness of the mist and the fiery brightness of the Lion rolled themselves together into a swirling glory and gathered themselves up and disappeared. He was alone with the horse on a grassy hillside under a blue sky. And there were birds singing.

—*The Horse and His Boy*

What do you think makes Shasta fall at the Lion's feet? Have you ever sensed another's greatness in the way Shasta senses Aslan's?

Queen of Narnia, Indeed

"SIRE, THERE IS A MESSENGER from the enemy who craves audience."

"Let him approach," said Aslan.

The leopard went away and soon returned leading the Witch's dwarf.

"What is your message, Son of Earth?" asked Aslan.

"The Queen of Narnia and Empress of the Lone Islands desires a safe conduct to come and speak with you," said the dwarf, "on a matter which is as much to your advantage as to hers."

"Queen of Narnia, indeed!" said Mr. Beaver. "Of all the cheek—"

"Peace, Beaver," said Aslan. "All names will soon be restored to their proper owners. In the meantime we will not dispute about them. Tell your mistress, Son of Earth, that I grant her safe conduct on condition that she leaves her wand behind her at that great oak."

—*The Lion, the Witch, and the Wardrobe*

Why is Mr. Beaver so angered by the title the dwarf uses? What does Aslan mean when he says all names will soon be restored to their proper owners? What significance do names and titles hold in Narnia? How do you see this reflected in our world?

Sibling Tensions

IT WAS A COLD AND CHEERLESS waking for them all next morning, with a grey twilight in the wood (for the sun had not yet risen) and everything damp and dirty.

"Apples, heigh-ho," said Trumpkin with a rueful grin. "I must say you ancient kings and queens don't overfeed your courtiers!"

They stood up and shook themselves and looked about. The trees were thick and they could see no more than a few yards in any direction.

"I suppose your Majesties know the way all right?" said the Dwarf.

"I don't," said Susan. "I've never seen these woods in my life before. In fact I thought all along that we ought to have gone by the river."

"Then I think you might have said so at the time," answered Peter, with pardonable sharpness.

"Oh, don't take any notice of her," said Edmund. "She always is a wet blanket. You've got that pocket compass of yours, Peter, haven't you? Well, then, we're as right as rain. We've only got to keep on going northwest—cross that little river, the what-do-you-call-it?—the Rush—"

"I know," said Peter. "The one that joins the big river at the Fords of Beruna, or Beruna's Bridge, as the D.L.F. calls it."

"That's right. Cross it and strike uphill, and we'll be at the Stone Table (Aslan's How, I mean) by eight or nine o'clock. I hope King Caspian will give us a good breakfast!"

—*Prince Caspian*

Days of eating nothing but apples and now being lost in the woods have taken their toll on the siblings. Why is Peter's sharpness pardonable? What causes you to lose your temper or act sharp with those you love?

The Lion's Task

[ASLAN SAID TO DIGORY,] "Now the land of Narnia ends where the waterfall comes down, and once you have reached the top of the cliffs you will be out of Narnia and into the Western Wild. You must journey through those mountains till you find a green valley with a blue lake in it, walled round by mountains of ice. At the end of the lake there is a steep, green hill. On the top of that hill there is a garden. In the center of that garden is a tree. Pluck an apple from that tree and bring it back to me."

—*The Magician's Nephew*

Why do you think Aslan charges Digory with this task when it seems the Lion himself could do it, and much more quickly and efficiently? Do you feel charged with certain tasks in the world? If so, what are they?

Forget Your Pride and Your Anger

R ABADASH," SAID ASLAN. "Take heed. Your doom is very near, but you may still avoid it. Forget your pride (what have you to be proud of?) and your anger (who has done you wrong?) and accept the mercy of these good kings."

Then Rabadash rolled his eyes and spread out his mouth into a horrible, long mirthless grin like a shark, and wagged his ears up and down (anyone can learn how to do this if they take the trouble). He had always found this very effective in Calormen. The bravest had trembled when he made these faces, and ordinary people had fallen to the floor, and sensitive people had often fainted. But what Rabadash hadn't realized is that it is very easy to frighten people who know you can have them boiled alive the moment you give the word. The grimaces didn't look at all alarming in Archenland; indeed Lucy only thought Rabadash was going to be sick.

"Demon! Demon! Demon!" shrieked the Prince. "I know you. You are the foul fiend of Narnia. You are the enemy of the gods. Learn who *I* am, horrible phantasm. I am descended from Tash, the inexorable, the irresistible. The curse of Tash is upon you. Lightning in the shape of scorpions shall be rained on you. The mountains of Narnia shall be ground into dust. The—"

"Have a care, Rabadash," said Aslan quietly. "The doom is nearer now: it is at the door; it has lifted the latch."

"Let the skies fall," shrieked Rabadash. "Let the earth gape! Let blood and fire obliterate the world! But be sure I will never desist till I have dragged to my palace by her hair the barbarian queen, the daughter of dogs, the—"

"The hour has struck," said Aslan: and Rabadash saw, to his supreme horror, that everyone had begun to laugh.

They couldn't help it. Rabadash had been wagging his ears all the time and as soon as Aslan said, "The hour has struck!" the ears began to change. They grew longer and more pointed and soon were covered with grey hair. And while everyone was wondering where they had seen ears like that before, Rabadash's face began to change too. It grew longer, and thicker at the top and larger eyed, and the nose sank back into the face (or else the face swelled out and became all nose) and there was hair all over it. And his arms grew longer and came down in front of him till his hands were resting on the ground: only they weren't hands, now, they were hoofs. And he was standing on all fours, and his clothes disappeared, and everyone laughed louder and louder (because they couldn't help it) for now what had been Rabadash was, simply and unmistakably, a donkey.

The terrible thing was that his human speech lasted just a moment longer than his human shape, so that when he realized the change that was coming over him, he screamed out:

"Oh, not a Donkey! Mercy! If it were even a horse—e'en—a hor—eeh—auh, eeh-auh." And so the words died away into a donkey's bray.

—*The Horse and His Boy*

How would becoming a donkey be the ultimate doom for Rabadash?

Evil Comes to Narnia

"THIS IS THE BOY," said Aslan, looking, not at Digory, but at his councillors. "This is the Boy who did it."

"Oh dear," thought Digory, "what have I done now?"

"Son of Adam," said the Lion. "There is an evil Witch abroad in my new land of Narnia. Tell these good Beasts how she came here."

A dozen different things that he might say flashed through Digory's mind, but he had the sense to say nothing except the exact truth.

"I brought her, Aslan," he answered in a low voice.

"For what purpose?"

"I wanted to get her out of my own world back into her own. I thought I was taking her back to her own place."

"How came she to be in your world, son of Adam?"

"By—by Magic."

The Lion said nothing and Digory knew that he had not told enough.

"It was my Uncle, Aslan," he said. "He sent us out of our own world by magic rings, at least I had to go because he sent Polly first, and then we met the Witch in a place called Charn and she just held on to us when—"

"You *met* the Witch?" said Aslan in a low voice which had the threat of a growl in it.

"She woke up," said Digory wretchedly. And then, turning very white, "I mean, I woke her. Because I wanted to know what would happen if I struck a bell. Polly didn't want to. It wasn't her fault. I—I fought her. I know I shouldn't have. I think I was a bit enchanted by the writing under the bell."

"Do you?" asked Aslan; still speaking very low and deep.

"No," said Digory. "I see now I wasn't. I was only pretending."

There was a long pause. And Digory was thinking all the time, "I've spoiled everything. There's no chance of getting anything for Mother now."

When the Lion spoke again it was not to Digory.

"You see, friends," he said, "that before the new, clean world I gave you is seven hours old, a force of evil has already entered it; waked and brought hither by this son of Adam." The Beasts, even Strawberry, all turned their eyes on Digory till he felt that he wished the ground would swallow him up. "But do not be cast down," said Aslan, still speaking to the Beasts. "Evil will come of that evil, but it is still a long way off, and I will see to it that the worst falls upon myself. In the meantime, let us take such order that for many hundred years yet this shall be a merry land in a merry world. And as Adam's race has done the harm, Adam's race shall help to heal it."

—*The Magician's Nephew*

How does Digory try to avoid accepting responsibility for his role in bringing the Witch to Narnia? Does the fact that Digory didn't know the extent of what he'd done provide any excuse for his actions? Why or why not? When have you had to make amends for something you unwittingly set into motion?

No Offense . . .

"MEANWHILE," said the Dwarf, "what are we to do? I suppose I'd better go back to King Caspian and tell him no help has come."

"No help?" said Susan. "But it *has* worked. And here we are."

"Um—um—yes, to be sure. I see that," said the Dwarf, whose pipe seemed to be blocked (at any rate he made himself very busy cleaning it). "But—well—I mean—"

"But don't you yet see who we are?" shouted Lucy. "You *are* stupid."

"I suppose you are the four children out of the old stories," said Trumpkin. "And I'm very glad to meet you of course. And it's very interesting, no doubt. But—no offense?"—and he hesitated again.

"Do get on and say whatever you're going to say," said Edmund.

"Well, then—no offense," said Trumpkin. "But, you know, the King and Trufflehunter and Doctor Cornelius were expecting—well, if you see what I mean, help. To put it in another way, I think they'd been imagining you as great warriors. As it is—we're awfully fond of children and all that, but just at the moment, in the middle of a war—but I'm sure you understand."

"You mean you think we're no good," said Edmund, getting red in the face.

"Now pray don't be offended," interrupted the Dwarf. "I assure you, my dear little friends—"

"*Little* from you is really a bit too much," said Edmund, jumping up. "I suppose you don't believe we won the Battle of Beruna? Well, you can say what you like about me because I know—"

"There's no good losing our tempers," said Peter. "Let's fit him out with fresh armor and fit ourselves out from the treasure chamber, and have a talk after that."

—*Prince Caspian*

Why does the Dwarf write off Peter, Susan, Edmund, and Lucy? When have you been underestimated or dismissed in this way? How did you react?

The Archery Contest

"Not hurt, I hope, my dear little friend?" said Edmund, panting a little and returning his own sword to its sheath.

"I see the point," said Trumpkin drily. "You know a trick I never learned."

"That's quite true," put in Peter. "The best swordsman in the world may be disarmed by a trick that's new to him. I think it's only fair to give Trumpkin a chance at something else. Will you have a shooting match with my sister? There are no tricks in archery, you know."

"Ah, you're jokers, you are," said the Dwarf. "I begin to see. As if I didn't know how she can shoot, after what happened this morning. All the same, I'll have a try." He spoke gruffly, but his eyes brightened, for he was a famous bowman among his own people.

All five of them came out into the courtyard.

"What's to be the target?" asked Peter.

"I think that apple hanging over the wall on the branch there would do," said Susan.

"That'll do nicely, lass," said Trumpkin. "You mean the yellow one near the middle of the arch?"

"No, not that," said Susan. "The red one up above—over the battlement."

The Dwarf's face fell. "Looks more like a cherry than an apple," he muttered, but he said nothing out loud.

They tossed up for first shot (greatly to the interest of Trumpkin, who had never seen a coin tossed before) and Susan lost. They were to shoot from the top of the steps that led from the hall into the courtyard. Everyone could see from the way the Dwarf took his position and handled his bow that he knew what he was about.

Twang went the string. It was an excellent shot. The tiny apple shook as the arrow passed, and a leaf came fluttering down. Then Susan went to the top of the steps and strung her bow. She was not enjoying her match half so much as Edmund had enjoyed his; not because she had any doubt about hitting the apple but because Susan was so tender-hearted that she almost hated to beat someone who had been beaten already. The Dwarf watched her keenly as she drew the shaft to her ear. A moment later, with a little soft thump which they could all hear in that quiet place, the apple fell to the grass with Susan's arrow in it.

"Oh, well done, Su," shouted the other children.

"It wasn't really any better than yours," said Susan to the Dwarf. "I think there was a tiny breath of wind as you shot."

—*Prince Caspian*

Why does Susan not enjoy arching against the Dwarf as much as Edmund enjoyed their earlier fencing match? Is one attitude preferable to the other? Why or why not?

My Humble Duty to Your Majesties

O H, ARE YOU WOUNDED?" asked Lucy. "Do let me look."
"It's not a sight for little girls," began Trumpkin, but then he
suddenly checked himself. "There I go talking like a fool again," he said. "I
suppose you're as likely to be a great surgeon as your brother was to be a great
swordsman or your sister to be a great archer." He sat down on the steps and
took off his hauberk and slipped down his little shirt, showing an arm hairy
and muscular (in proportion) as a sailor's though not much bigger than a
child's. There was a clumsy bandage on the shoulder which Lucy proceeded
to unroll. Underneath, the cut looked very nasty and there was a good deal of
swelling. "Oh, poor Trumpkin," said Lucy. "How horrid." Then she carefully
dripped onto it one single drop of the cordial from her flask.

"Hullo. Eh? What have you done?" said Trumpkin. But however
he turned his head and squinted and whisked his beard to and fro, he
couldn't quite see his own shoulder. Then he felt it as well as he could,
getting his arms and fingers into very difficult positions as you do when
you're trying to scratch a place that is just out of reach. Then he swung
his arm and raised it and tried the muscles, and finally jumped to his feet
crying, "Giants and junipers! It's cured! It's as good as new." After that he
burst into a great laugh and said, "Well, I've made as big a fool of myself as
ever a Dwarf did. No offense, I hope? My humble duty to your Majesties
all—humble duty. And thanks for my life, my cure, my breakfast—and
my lesson."

The children all said it was quite all right and not to mention it.

"And now," said Peter, "if you've really decided to believe in us—"

"I have," said the Dwarf.

"It's quite clear what we have to do. We must join King Caspian at once."

"The sooner the better," said Trumpkin. "My being such a fool has
already wasted about an hour."

—*Prince Caspian*

What does Peter mean when he asks the Dwarf if he now believes in them?
What does it say about the Dwarf that he can admit he was wrong?

Invisible Enemies

"INVISIBLE ENEMIES," muttered Caspian. "And cutting us off from the boat. This is an ugly furrow to plow."

"You've no idea what *sort* of creatures they are, Lu?" asked Edmund.

"How can I, Ed, when I couldn't see them?"

"Did they sound like humans from their footsteps?"

"I didn't hear any noise of feet—only voices and this frightful thudding and thumping—like a mallet."

"I wonder," said Reepicheep, "do they become visible when you drive a sword into them?"

"It looks as if we shall find out," said Caspian. "But let's get out of this gateway. There's one of these gentry at that pump listening to all we say."

They came out and went back on to the path where the trees might possibly make them less conspicuous. "Not that it's any good *really*," said Eustace, "trying to hide from people you can't see. They may be all round us."

"Now, Drinian," said Caspian. "How would it be if we gave up the boat for lost, went down to another part of the bay, and signaled to the *Dawn Treader* to stand in and take us aboard?"

"Not depth for her, Sire," said Drinian.

"We could swim," said Lucy.

"Your Majesties all," said Reepicheep, "hear me. It is folly to think of avoiding an invisible enemy by any amount of creeping and skulking. If these creatures mean to bring us to battle, be sure they will succeed. And whatever comes of it I'd sooner meet them face to face than be caught by the tail."

"I really think Reep is in the right this time," said Edmund.

"Surely," said Lucy, "if Rhince and the others on the *Dawn Treader* see us fighting on the shore they'll be able to do *something*."

"But they won't see us fighting if they can't see any enemy," said Eustace miserably. "They'll think we're just swinging our swords in the air for fun."

There was an uncomfortable pause.

"Well," said Caspian at last, "let's get on with it. We must go and face them. Shake hands all round—arrow on the string, Lucy—swords out, everyone else—and now for it. Perhaps they'll parley."

—*The Voyage of the* **Dawn Treader**

Why do they ultimately decide to face their enemies, even though they are invisible? What is the purpose of shaking hands before going into a battle situation? What kind of feeling might that build among the companions?

The Whole Truth

A ND SO, before they were half-way through Tashbaan, all their plans were ruined, and without even a chance to say good-bye to the others Shasta found himself being marched off among strangers and quite unable to guess what might be going to happen next. The Narnian King—for Shasta began to see by the way the rest spoke to him that he must be a king—kept on asking him questions; where he had been, how he had got out, what he had done with his clothes, and didn't he know that he had been very naughty. Only the king called it "naught" instead of naughty.

And Shasta said nothing in answer, because he couldn't think of anything to say that would not be dangerous.

"What! All mum?" asked the king. "I must plainly tell you, prince, that this hangdog silence becomes one of your blood even less than the scape itself. To run away might pass for a boy's frolic with some spirit in it. But the king's son of Archenland should avouch his deed; not hang his head like a Calormene slave.". . .

"This is perfectly dreadful," thought Shasta. It never came into his head to tell these Narnians the whole truth and ask for their help. Having been brought up by a hard, closefisted man like Arsheesh, he had a fixed habit of never telling grown-ups anything if he could help it; he thought they would always spoil or stop whatever you were trying to do. . . . "I simply daren't tell them I'm not Prince Corin *now*," thought Shasta. "I've heard all their plans. If they knew I wasn't one of themselves, they'd never let me out of this house alive. They'd be afraid I'd betray them to the Tisroc. They'd kill me. And if the real Corin turns up, it'll all come out, and they *will*!" He had, you see, no idea of how noble and free-born people behave.

—The Horse and His Boy

Mistaking Shasta for the lost prince, the king tells him that not explaining why he ran away "becomes one of your blood even less than the scape itself." What is the difference between his perspective on truth and Shasta's? What changes could more honesty, with ourselves and with others around us, bring about in our world?

Jill and Eustace's Task

AND NOW HEAR YOUR TASK. Far from here in the land of Narnia there lives an aged king who is sad because he has no prince of his blood to be king after him. He has no heir because his only son was stolen from him many years ago, and no one in Narnia knows where that prince went or whether he is still alive. But he is. I lay on you this command, that you seek this lost prince until either you have found him and brought him to his father's house, or else died in the attempt, or else gone back to your own world."

"How, please?" said Jill.

"I will tell you, Child," said the Lion. "These are the signs by which I will guide you in your quest. First; as soon as the Boy Eustace sets foot in Narnia, he will meet an old and dear friend. He must greet that friend at once; if he does, you will both have good help. Second; you must journey out of Narnia to the north till you come to the ruined city of the ancient giants. Third; you shall find a writing on a stone in that ruined city, and you must do what the writing tells you. Fourth; you will know the lost prince (if you find him) by this, that he will be the first person you have met in your travels who will ask you to do something in my name, in the name of Aslan."

As the Lion seemed to have finished, Jill thought she should say something. So she said, "Thank you very much. I see."

"Child," said Aslan, in a gentler voice than he had yet used, "perhaps you do not see quite as well as you think. But the first step is to remember."

—*The Silver Chair*

Jill reacts quite calmly to the task and the signs Aslan gives her, at least outwardly. What does this tell us about Jill? How would you react to the Lion's words? What might he mean by saying that perhaps she does not see as well as she thinks?

Making It All Up

"STILL PLAYING YOUR OLD GAME?" said Eustace Clarence, who had been listening outside the door and now came grinning into the room. Last year, when he had been staying with the Pevensies, he had managed to hear them all talking of Narnia and he loved teasing them about it. He thought of course that they were making it all up; and as he was far too stupid to make anything up himself, he did not approve of that.

"You're not wanted here," said Edmund curtly.

"I'm trying to think of a limerick," said Eustace. "Something like this:

"Some kids who played games about Narnia
Got gradually balmier and balmier—"

"Well, *Narnia* and *balmier* don't rhyme, to begin with," said Lucy.

"It's an assonance," said Eustace.

"Don't ask him what an assy-thingummy is," said Edmund. "He's only longing to be asked. Say nothing and perhaps he'll go away."

—*The Voyage of the* **Dawn Treader**

Why do Edmund's and Lucy's stories about Narnia make Eustace not like them very much? Do you normally think of someone with a great imagination as intelligent? Why or why not?

A Dark and Doubtful Enterprise

"Bᴜᴛ ᴡʜʏ, ᴏ ᴍʏ ꜰᴀᴛʜᴇʀ," said the Prince—this time in a much more respectful voice, "why should we think twice about punishing Narnia any more than about hanging an idle slave or sending a worn-out horse to be made into dog's-meat? It is not the fourth size of one of your least provinces. A thousand spears could conquer it in five weeks. It is an unseemly blot on the skirts of your empire."

"Most undoubtedly," said the Tisroc. "These little barbarian countries that call themselves *free* (which is as much as to say, idle, disordered, and unprofitable) are hateful to the gods and to all persons of discernment."

"Then why have we suffered such a land as Narnia to remain thus long unsubdued?"

"Know, O enlightened Prince," said the Grand Vizier, "that until the year in which your exalted father began his salutary and unending reign, the land of Narnia was covered with ice and snow and was moreover ruled by a most powerful enchantress."

"This I know very well, O loquacious Vizier," answered the Prince. "But I know also that the enchantress is dead. And the ice and snow have vanished, so that Narnia is now wholesome, fruitful, and delicious."

"And this change, O most learned Prince, has doubtless been brought to pass by the powerful incantations of those wicked persons who now call themselves kings and queens of Narnia."

"I am rather of the opinion," said Rabadash, "that it has come about by the alteration of the stars and the operation of natural causes."

"All this," said the Tisroc, "is a question for the disputations of learned men. I will never believe that so great an alteration, and the killing of the old enchantress, were effected without the aid of strong magic. And such things are to be expected in that land, which is chiefly inhabited by demons in the shape of beasts that talk like men, and monsters that are half man and half beast. It is commonly reported that the High King of Narnia (whom may the gods utterly reject) is supported by a demon of hideous aspect and irresistible maleficence who appears in the shape of a Lion. Therefore the attacking of Narnia is a dark and doubtful enterprise, and I am determined not to put my hand out farther than I can draw it back."

—*The Horse and His Boy*

The Tisroc believes the change in Narnia was wrought by sorcery, and the Prince believes it has come about by the stars and natural causes. What does each man's idea show about him? What explanations would appeal to you to describe a change as dramatic as this one?

The True Sign of Maturity

ASLAN, ASLAN. DEAR ASLAN," sobbed Lucy. "At last."
The great beast rolled over on his side so that Lucy fell, half sitting and half lying between his front paws. He bent forward and just touched her nose with his tongue. His warm breath came all round her. She gazed up into the large wise face.

"Welcome, child," he said.

"Aslan," said Lucy, "you're bigger."

"That is because you are older, little one," answered he.

"Not because you are?"

"I am not. But every year you grow, you will find me bigger."

—*Prince Caspian*

What could it mean that Aslan appears bigger to Lucy? Over the years, how has your perception of certain things changed?

The Cabby Strikes Up a Hymn

"THIS IS NOT CHARN," came the Witch's voice. "This is an empty world. This is nothing."

And really it was uncommonly like Nothing. There were no stars. It was so dark that they couldn't see one another at all and it made no difference whether you kept your eyes shut or opened. Under their feet there was a cool, flat something which might have been earth, and was certainly not grass or wood. The air was cold and dry and there was no wind.

"My doom has come upon me," said the Witch in a voice of horrible calmness.

"Oh don't say that," babbled Uncle Andrew. "My dear young lady, pray don't say such things. It can't be as bad as that. Ah—Cabman—my good man—you don't happen to have a flask about you? A drop of spirits is just what I need."

"Now then, now then," came the Cabby's voice, a good firm, hardy voice. "Keep cool, everyone, that's what I say. No bones broken, anyone? Good. Well there's something to be thankful for straight away, and more than anyone could expect after falling all that way. Now, if we've fallen down some diggings—as it might be for a new station on the Underground—someone will come and get us out presently, see! And if we're dead—which I don't deny it might be—well, you got to remember that worse things 'appen at sea and a chap's got to die sometime. And there ain't nothing to be afraid of if a chap's led a decent life. And if you ask me, I think the best thing we could do to pass the time would be sing a 'ymn."

And he did. He struck up at once a harvest thanksgiving hymn, all about crops being "safely gathered in." It was not very suitable to a place which felt as if nothing had ever grown there since the beginning of time, but it was the one he could remember best. He had a fine voice and the children joined in; it was very cheering. Uncle Andrew and the Witch did not join in.

—*The Magician's Nephew*

What does the way each adult responds to the new world reveal about him or her? Whose response do you think your own would most closely imitate?

What Your Friends Really Think

A LITTLE LATER she came to a spell which would let you know what your friends thought about you. . . . And all in a hurry, for fear her mind would change, she said the words (nothing will induce me to tell you what they were). Then she waited for something to happen.

. . . And all at once she saw the very last thing she expected—a picture of a third-class carriage in a train, with two schoolgirls sitting in it. . . . Only now it was much more than a picture. It was alive. . . . Then gradually (like when the radio is "coming on") she could hear what they were saying.

"Shall I see anything of you this term?" said Anne, "or are you still going to be all taken up with Lucy Pevensie?"

"Don't know what you mean by *taken up*," said Marjorie.

"Oh yes, you do," said Anne. "You were crazy about her last term."

"No, I wasn't," said Marjorie. "I've got more sense than that. Not a bad little kid in her way. But I was getting pretty tired of her before the end of term."

"Well, you jolly well won't have the chance any other term!" shouted Lucy. "Two-faced little beast." But the sound of her own voice at once reminded her that she was talking to a picture and that the real Marjorie was far away in another world.

"Well," said Lucy to herself, "I did think better of her than that. And I did all sorts of things for her last term, and I stuck to her when not many other girls would. And she knows it too. And to Anne Featherstone of all people! I wonder are all my friends the same? There are lots of other pictures. No. I won't look at any more. I won't, I won't"—and with a great effort she turned over the page, but not before a large, angry tear had splashed on it.

—*The Voyage of the* **Dawn Treader**

Would you have been able to resist the spell, or resist looking at the other pictures on the page? How are we sometimes better off not knowing everything? Why do we have such a desire to know all things?

You Have Been Eavesdropping

"CHILD," [ASLAN] SAID, "I think you have been eavesdropping."

"Eavesdropping?"

"You listened to what your two schoolfellows were saying about you."

"Oh that? I never thought that was eavesdropping, Aslan. Wasn't it magic?"

"Spying on people by magic is the same as spying on them in any other way. And you have misjudged your friend. She is weak, but she loves you. She was afraid of the older girl and said what she does not mean."

"I don't think I'd ever be able to forget what I heard her say."

"No, you won't."

"Oh dear," said Lucy. "Have I spoiled everything? Do you mean we would have gone on being friends if it hadn't been for this—and been really great friends—all our lives perhaps—and now we never shall?"

"Child," said Aslan, "did I not explain to you once before that no one is ever told what *would have happened*?"

"Yes, Aslan, you did," said Lucy. "I'm sorry. But please—"

"Speak on, dear heart."

"Shall I ever be able to read that story again; the one I couldn't remember? Will you tell it to me, Aslan? Oh do, do, do."

"Indeed, yes, I will tell it to you for years and years. But now, come. We must meet the master of this house."

—*The Voyage of the* Dawn Treader

What strikes you about the tone Aslan takes with Lucy as he corrects her? Do you spend a lot of time thinking about what would have happened? If so, what might Aslan say to that?

Shasta Turns Back to Help

A HUGE TAWNY CREATURE, its body low to the ground, like a cat streaking across the lawn to a tree when a strange dog has got into the garden, was behind them. And it was nearer every second and half second.

He looked forward again and saw something which he did not take in, or even think about. Their way was barred by a smooth green wall about ten feet high. In the middle of that wall there was a gate, open. In the middle of the gateway stood a tall man dressed, down to his bare feet, in a robe colored like autumn leaves, leaning on a straight staff. His beard fell almost to his knees.

Shasta saw all this in a glance and looked back again. The lion had almost got Hwin now. It was making snaps at her hind legs, and there was no hope now in her foam-flecked, wide-eyed face.

"Stop," bellowed Shasta in Bree's ear. "Must go back. Must help!"

Bree always said afterward that he never heard, or never understood this; and as he was in general a very truthful horse we must accept his word.

Shasta slipped his feet out of the stirrups, slid both his legs over on the left side, hesitated for one hideous hundredth of a second, and jumped. It hurt horribly and nearly winded him; but before he knew how it hurt him he was staggering back to help Aravis. He had never done anything like this in his life before and hardly knew why he was doing it now.

One of the most terrible noises in the world, a horse's scream, broke from Hwin's lips. Aravis was stooping low over Hwin's neck and seemed to be trying to draw her sword. And now all three—Aravis, Hwin, and the lion—were almost on top of Shasta. Before they reached him the lion rose on its hind legs, larger than you would have believed a lion could be, and jabbed at Aravis with its right paw. Shasta could see all the terrible claws extended. Aravis screamed and reeled in the saddle. The lion was tearing her shoulders. Shasta, half mad with horror, managed to lurch toward the brute. He had no weapon, not even a stick or a stone. He shouted out, idiotically, at the lion as one would at a dog. "Go home! Go home!" For a fraction of a second he was staring right into its wide-opened, raging mouth. Then, to his utter astonishment, the lion, still on its hind legs, checked itself suddenly, turned head over heels, picked itself up, and rushed away.

—*The Horse and His Boy*

Why do you think Shasta turns back to try to help Aravis and Hwin? Do you think he would react the same way if he had more time to think about it? How have you reacted in a split-second moment of great need?

A Most Horrible Feeling

FOR THE LAST PART of the journey it was Susan and Lucy who saw most of [Aslan]. He did not talk very much and seemed to them to be sad. It was still afternoon when they came down to a place where the river valley had widened out and the river was broad and shallow. This was the Fords of Beruna and Aslan gave orders to halt on this side of the water. But Peter said,

"Wouldn't it be better to camp on the far side—for fear she should try a night attack or anything?"

Aslan, who seemed to have been thinking about something else, roused himself with a shake of his magnificent mane and said, "Eh? What's that?" Peter said it all over again.

"No," said Aslan in a dull voice, as if it didn't matter. "No. She will not make an attack tonight." And then he sighed deeply. But presently he added, "All the same it was well thought of. That is how a soldier ought to think. But it doesn't really matter." So they proceeded to pitch their camp.

Aslan's mood affected everyone that evening. Peter was feeling uncomfortable too at the idea of fighting the battle on his own; the news that Aslan might not be there had come as a great shock to him. Supper that evening was a quiet meal. Everyone felt how different it had been last night or even that morning. It was as if the good times, having just begun, were already drawing to their end.

This feeling affected Susan so much that she couldn't get to sleep when she went to bed. And after she had lain counting sheep and turning over and over she heard Lucy give a long sigh and turn over just beside her in the darkness.

"Can't you get to sleep either?" said Susan.

"No," said Lucy. "I thought you were asleep. I say, Susan!"

"What?"

"I've a most horrible feeling—as if something were hanging over us."

"Have you? Because, as a matter of fact, so have I."

"Something about Aslan," said Lucy. "Either some dreadful thing is going to happen to him, or something dreadful that he's going to do."

"There's been something wrong with him all afternoon," said Susan. "Lucy! What was that he said about not being with us at the battle? You don't think he could be stealing away and leaving us tonight, do you?"

"Where is he now?" said Lucy. "Is he here in the pavilion?"

"I don't think so."

"Susan! Let's go outside and have a look round. We might see him."

"All right. Let's," said Susan; "we might just as well be doing that as lying awake here."

Very quietly the two girls groped their way among the other sleepers and crept out of the tent. The moonlight was bright and everything was quite still except for the noise of the river chattering over the stones. Then Susan suddenly caught Lucy's arm and said, "Look!" On the far side of the camping ground, just where the trees began, they saw the Lion slowly walking away from them into the wood. Without a word they both followed him.

—*The Lion, the Witch, and the Wardrobe*

Why do you think Susan and Lucy choose to follow Aslan rather than ask him about their sense of foreboding? Have you ever had a similar feeling of foreboding? What faith do you place in such feelings?

I Should Be Glad of Company

HE LOOKED SOMEHOW DIFFERENT from the Aslan they knew. His tail and his head hung low and he walked slowly as if he were very, very tired. Then, when they were crossing a wide open place where there were no shadows for them to hide in, he stopped and looked round. It was no good trying to run away so they came toward him. When they were closer he said,

"Oh, children, children, why are you following me?"

"We couldn't sleep," said Lucy—and then felt sure that she need say no more and that Aslan knew all they had been thinking.

"Please, may we come with you—wherever you're going?" asked Susan.

"Well—" said Aslan, and seemed to be thinking. Then he said, "I should be glad of company tonight. Yes, you may come, if you will promise to stop when I tell you, and after that leave me to go on alone."

"Oh, thank you, thank you. And we will," said the two girls.

Forward they went again and one of the girls walked on each side of the Lion. But how slowly he walked! And his great, royal head drooped so that his nose nearly touched the grass. Presently he stumbled and gave a low moan.

"Aslan! Dear Aslan!" said Lucy, "what is wrong? Can't you tell us?"

"Are you ill, dear Aslan?" asked Susan.

"No," said Aslan. "I am sad and lonely. Lay your hands on my mane so that I can feel you are there and let us walk like that."

And so the girls did what they would never have dared to do without his permission, but what they had longed to do ever since they first saw him—buried their cold hands in the beautiful sea of fur and stroked it and, so doing, walked with him.

—*The Lion, the Witch, and the Wardrobe*

What must Lucy and Susan be feeling to see Aslan so sad? Why is touch such a comfort when we feel sad and lonely?

Only a Great Cat

A HOWL AND A GIBBER of dismay went up from the creatures when they first saw the great Lion pacing toward them, and for a moment even the Witch herself seemed to be struck with fear. Then she recovered herself and gave a wild fierce laugh.

"The fool!" she cried. "The fool has come. Bind him fast."

Lucy and Susan held their breaths waiting for Aslan's roar and his spring upon his enemies. But it never came. Four Hags, grinning and leering, yet also (at first) hanging back and half afraid of what they had to do, had approached him. "Bind him, I say!" repeated the White Witch. The Hags made a dart at him and shrieked with triumph when they found that he made no resistance at all. Then others—evil dwarfs and apes—rushed in to help them, and between them they rolled the huge Lion over on his back and tied all his four paws together, shouting and cheering as if they had done something brave, though, had the Lion chosen, one of those paws could have been the death of them all. But he made no noise, even when the enemies, straining and tugging, pulled the cords so tight that they cut into his flesh. Then they began to drag him toward the Stone Table.

"Stop!" said the Witch. "Let him first be shaved."

Another roar of mean laughter went up from her followers as an ogre with a pair of shears came forward and squatted down by Aslan's head. Snip-snip-snip went the shears and masses of curling gold began to fall to the ground. Then the ogre stood back and the children, watching from their hiding-place, could see the face of Aslan looking all small and different without its mane. The enemies also saw the difference.

"Why, he's only a great cat after all!" cried one.

"Is *that* what we were afraid of?" said another.

And they surged round Aslan, jeering at him, saying things like "Puss, Puss! Poor Pussy," and "How many mice have you caught today, Cat?" and "Would you like a saucer of milk, Pussums?"

"Oh, how *can* they?" said Lucy, tears streaming down her cheeks. "The brutes, the brutes!" for now that the first shock was over the shorn face of Aslan looked to her braver, and more beautiful, and more patient than ever.

"Muzzle him!" said the Witch. And even now, as they worked about his face putting on the muzzle, one bite from his jaws would have cost two or three of them their hands. But he never moved. And this seemed to enrage all that rabble. Everyone was at him now. Those who had been afraid to come near him even after he was bound began to find their courage, and for a few minutes the two girls could not even see him—so thickly was he surrounded by the whole crowd of creatures kicking him, hitting him, spitting on him, jeering at him.

—*The Lion, the Witch, and the Wardrobe*

What purpose does humiliating Aslan serve? Why does Aslan's lack of resistance seem to enrage his enemies all the more?

Despair and Die

THEY BEGAN TO DRAG the bound and muzzled Lion to the Stone Table, some pulling and some pushing. He was so huge that even when they got him there it took all their efforts to hoist him onto the surface of it. Then there was more tying and tightening of cords.

"The cowards! The cowards!" sobbed Susan. "Are they *still* afraid of him, even now?"

When once Aslan had been tied (and tied so that he was really a mass of cords) on the flat stone, a hush fell on the crowd. Four Hags, holding four torches, stood at the corners of the Table. The Witch bared her arms as she had bared them the previous night when it had been Edmund instead of Aslan. Then she began to whet her knife. It looked to the children, when the gleam of the torchlight fell on it, as if the knife were made of stone, not of steel, and it was of a strange and evil shape.

At last she drew near. She stood by Aslan's head. Her face was working and twitching with passion, but his looked up at the sky, still quiet, neither angry nor afraid, but a little sad. Then, just before she gave the blow, she stooped down and said in a quivering voice,

"And now, who has won? Fool, did you think that by all this you would save the human traitor? Now I will kill you instead of him as our pact was and so the Deep Magic will be appeased. But when you are dead what will prevent me from killing him as well? And who will take him out of my hand *then*? Understand that you have given me Narnia forever, you have lost your own life and you have not saved his. In that knowledge, despair and die."

—*The Lion, the Witch, and the Wardrobe*

Why is it so important to the Witch that Aslan die in despair?

The Storm at Sea

THERE CAME AN EVENING when Lucy, gazing idly astern at the long furrow or wake they were leaving behind them, saw a great rack of clouds building itself up in the west with amazing speed. Then a gap was torn in it and a yellow sunset poured through the gap. All the waves behind them seemed to take on unusual shapes and the sea was a drab or yellowish color like dirty canvas. The air grew cold. The ship seemed to move uneasily as if she felt danger behind her. The sail would be flat and limp one minute and wildly full the next. While she was noting these things and wondering at a sinister change which had come over the very noise of the wind, Drinian cried, "All hands on deck." In a moment everyone became frantically busy. The hatches were battened down, the galley fire was put out, men went aloft to reef the sail. Before they had finished, the storm struck them. It seemed to Lucy that a great valley in the sea opened just before their bows, and they rushed down into it, deeper down than she would have believed possible. A great grey hill of water, far higher than the mast, rushed to meet them; it looked like certain death but they were tossed to the top of it. Then the ship seemed to spin round. A cataract of water poured over the deck; the poop and forecastle were like two islands with a fierce sea between them. Up aloft the sailors were lying out along the yard desperately trying to get control of the sail. A broken rope stood out sideways in the wind as straight and stiff as if it were a poker. . . .

And all the next day and all the next it went on. It went on till one could hardly even remember a time before it had begun. And there always had to be three men at the tiller and it was as much as three could do to keep any kind of a course. And there always had to be men at the pump. And there was hardly any rest for anyone, and nothing could be cooked and nothing could be dried, and one man was lost overboard, and they never saw the sun.

—*The Voyage of the* Dawn Treader

What would the most difficult part of the storm be for you? When in your life has time seemed to stand still like this?

Owning Up

Dஂ OWN BELOW THEM, spread out like a map, lay the flat hill-
top which they had struggled over yesterday afternoon; seen
from the castle, it could not be mistaken for anything but the ruins of a
gigantic city. . . . To crown all, in large, dark lettering across the center of
the pavement, ran the words UNDER ME.

The three travelers looked at each other in dismay, and, after a short
whistle, Scrubb said what they were all thinking, "The second and third
signs muffed." And at that moment Jill's dream rushed back into her
mind.

"It's my fault," she said in despairing tones. "I—I'd given up repeating
the signs every night. If I'd been thinking about them I could have seen it
was the city, even *in* all that snow."

"I'm worse," said Puddleglum. "I *did* see, or nearly. I thought it looked
uncommonly like a ruined city."

"You're the only one who isn't to blame," said Scrubb. "You *did* try to
make us stop."

"Didn't try hard enough, though," said the Marsh-wiggle. "And I'd no
call to be trying. I ought to have done it. As if I couldn't have stopped you
two with one hand each!"

"The truth is," said Scrubb, "we were so jolly keen on getting to this
place that we weren't bothering about anything else. At least I know I was.
Ever since we met the woman with the knight who didn't talk, we've been
thinking of nothing else. We'd nearly forgotten about Prince Rilian."

"I shouldn't wonder," said Puddleglum, "if that wasn't exactly what she
intended."

"What I don't quite understand," said Jill, "is how we didn't see the lettering? Or could it have come there since last night. Could he—Aslan—
have put it there in the night? I had such a queer dream." And she told
them all about it.

"Why, you chump!" said Scrubb. "We did see it. We got into the lettering. Don't you see? We got into the letter *E* in ME. That was your sunk
lane. We walked along the bottom stroke of the *E*, due north—turned to
our right along the upright—came to another turn to the right—that's the

middle stroke—and then went on to the top left-hand corner, or (if you like) the northeastern corner of the letter, and came back. Like the bally idiots that we are." He kicked the window seat savagely, and went on, "So it's no good, Pole. I know what you were thinking because I was thinking the same. You were thinking how nice it would have been if Aslan hadn't put the instructions on the stones of the ruined city till after we'd passed it. And then it would have been his fault, not ours. So likely, isn't it? No. We must just own up. We've only four signs to go by, and we've muffed the first three."

—*The Silver Chair*

Jill, Scrubb, and Puddleglum have just realized the place they struggled over yesterday was the very place Aslan told them to seek. Why is it so important for each of them to own up to their mistakes? How might this scene have played out if, instead of each blaming themselves, they pointed fingers at one another?

Facing the Dragon

BUT LATER IN THE NIGHT Lucy was wakened, very softly, and found the whole company gathered close together and talking in whispers.

"What is it?" said Lucy.

"We must all show great constancy," Caspian was saying. "A dragon has just flown over the tree-tops and lighted on the beach. Yes, I am afraid it is between us and the ship. And arrows are no use against dragons. And they're not at all afraid of fire."

"With your Majesty's leave—" began Reepicheep.

"No, Reepicheep," said the King very firmly, "you are *not* to attempt a single combat with it. And unless you promise to obey me in this matter I'll have you tied up. We must just keep close watch and, as soon as it is light, go down to the beach and give it battle. . . ."

"Perhaps it will go away," said Lucy.

"It'll be worse if it does," said Edmund, "because then we shan't know where it is. If there's a wasp in the room I like to be able to see it."

The rest of the night was dreadful, and when the meal came, though they knew they ought to eat, many found that they had very poor appetites. And endless hours seemed to pass before the darkness thinned and birds began chirping here and there and the world got colder and wetter than it had been all night and Caspian said, "Now for it, friends."

They got up, all with swords drawn, and formed themselves into a solid mass with Lucy in the middle and Reepicheep on her shoulder. It was nicer than the waiting about and everyone felt fonder of everyone else than at ordinary times.

—*The Voyage of the* **Dawn Treader**

Why would facing the dragon together make the company feel fonder of each other than usual? Have you ever experienced a similar sense of camaraderie in a time of danger?

Who Believes Nowadays?

DON'T YOU GO TALKING about things you don't understand, Nikabrik," said Trufflehunter. "You Dwarfs are as forgetful and changeable as the Humans themselves. I'm a beast, I am, and a Badger what's more. We don't change. We hold on. I say great good will come of it. This is the true King of Narnia we've got here: a true King, coming back to true Narnia. And we beasts remember, even if Dwarfs forget, that Narnia was never right except when a Son of Adam was King."

"Whistles and whirligigs, Trufflehunter!" said Trumpkin. "You don't mean you want to give the country to the Humans?"

"I said nothing about that," answered the Badger. "It's not Men's country (who should know that better than me?) but it's a country for a man to be King of. We badgers have long enough memories to know that. Why, bless us all, wasn't the High King Peter a Man?"

"Do you believe all those old stories?" asked Trumpkin.

"I tell you, we don't change, we beasts," said Trufflehunter. "We don't forget. I believe in the High King Peter and the rest that reigned at Cair Paravel, as firmly as I believe in Aslan himself."

"As firmly as *that,* I dare say," said Trumpkin. "But who believes in Aslan nowadays?"

"I do," said Caspian. "And if I hadn't believed in him before, I would now. Back there among the Humans the people who laughed at Aslan would have laughed at stories about Talking Beasts and Dwarfs. Sometimes I did wonder if there really was such a person as Aslan: but then sometimes I wondered if there were really people like you. Yet there you are."

—*Prince Caspian*

What are Trufflehunter and Caspian's reasons for believing Aslan is real? Why is it hard for Trumpkin to believe in Aslan? Are there certain things that you have trouble believing in because of others' scorn?

The Witch-Queen's Green Powder

[THE WITCH-QUEEN] stood dead still in the doorway, and they could see her eyes moving as she took in the whole situation—the three strangers, the silver chair destroyed, and the Prince free, with his sword in his hand. . . .

"How now, my lord Prince," she said. "Has your nightly fit not yet come upon you, or is it over so soon? Why stand you here unbound? Who are these aliens? And is it they who have destroyed the chair which was your only safety?"

Prince Rilian shivered as she spoke to him. And no wonder: it is not easy to throw off in half an hour an enchantment which has made one a slave for ten years. Then, speaking with a great effort, he said:

"Madam, there will be no more need of that chair. And you, who have told me a hundred times how deeply you pitied me for the sorceries by which I was bound, will doubtless hear with joy that they are now ended forever. There was, it seems, some small error in your Ladyship's way of treating them. These, my true friends, have delivered me. I am now in my right mind, and there are two things I will say to you. First—as for your Ladyship's design of putting me at the head of an army of Earthmen so that I may break out into the Overworld and there, by main force, make myself king over some nation that never did me wrong—murdering their natural lords and holding their throne as a bloody and foreign tyrant—now that I know myself, I do utterly abhor and renounce it as plain villainy. And second: I am the King's son of Narnia, Rilian, the only child of Caspian, Tenth of that name, whom some call Caspian the Seafarer. Therefore, Madam, it is my purpose, as it is also my duty, to depart suddenly from your Highness's court into my own country. Please it you to grant me and my friends safe conduct and a guide through your dark realm."

Now the Witch said nothing at all, but moved gently across the room, always keeping her face and eyes very steadily toward the Prince. When she had come to a little ark set in the wall not far from the fireplace, she opened it, and took out first a handful of a green powder. This she threw on the fire. It did not blaze much, but a very sweet and drowsy smell came from it. And all through the conversation which followed, that smell grew stronger, and filled the room, and made it harder to think. Secondly, she took out a musical instrument rather like a mandolin. She began to play it with her fingers—a steady, monotonous thrumming that you didn't notice after a few minutes. But the less you noticed it, the more it got into your brain and your blood. This also made it hard to think. After she had thrummed for a time (and the sweet smell was now strong) she began speaking in a sweet, quiet voice.

"Narnia?" she said. "Narnia? I have often heard your Lordship utter that name in your ravings. Dear Prince, you are very sick. There is no land called Narnia."

—The Silver Chair

How might the Witch-queen's speaking so gently and playing soothing music be more effective in convincing them than if she yelled and became angry? Would this technique work on you? Has anyone ever argued an untruth to you so convincingly that you began to believe it?

JUNE

The Blind Dwarfs

LUCY LED THE WAY and soon they could all see the Dwarfs. They had a very odd look. They weren't strolling about or enjoying themselves (although the cords with which they had been tied seemed to have vanished) nor were they lying down and having a rest. They were sitting very close together in a little circle facing one another. They never looked round or took any notice of the humans till Lucy and Tirian were almost near enough to touch them. Then the Dwarfs all cocked their heads as if they couldn't see anyone but were listening hard and trying to guess by the sound what was happening.

"Look out!" said one of them in a surly voice. "Mind where you're going. Don't walk into our faces!"

"All right!" said Eustace indignantly. "We're not blind. We've got eyes in our heads."

"They must be darn good ones if you can see in here," said the same Dwarf whose name was Diggle.

"In where?" asked Edmund.

"Why you bone-head, in *here* of course," said Diggle. "In this pitch-black, poky, smelly little hole of a stable."

"Are you blind?" said Tirian.

"Ain't we all blind in the dark!" said Diggle.

"But it isn't dark, you poor stupid Dwarfs," said Lucy. "Can't you see? Look up! Look round! Can't you see the sky and the trees and the flowers? Can't you see *me*?"

"How in the name of all Humbug can I see what ain't there? And how can I see you any more than you can see me in this pitch darkness?"

"But I *can* see you," said Lucy. "I'll prove I can see you. You've got a pipe in your mouth."

"Anyone that knows the smell of baccy could tell that," said Diggle.

"Oh the poor things! This is dreadful," said Lucy. Then she had an idea. She stooped and picked some wild violets. "Listen, Dwarf," she said. "Even if your eyes are wrong, perhaps your nose is all right: can you smell *that*?" She leaned across and held the fresh, damp flowers to Diggle's ugly nose. But she had to jump back quickly in order to avoid a blow from his hard little fist.

"None of that!" he shouted. "How dare you! What do you mean by shoving a lot of filthy stable-litter in my face? There was a thistle in it too. It's like your sauce! And who are you anyway?"

—*The Last Battle*

Why couldn't the Dwarfs see what the others could? How do we close off our own minds to what's right in front of us?

Aslan Tries to Help

"Aslan," said Lucy through her tears, "could you—will you—do something for these poor Dwarfs?"

"Dearest," said Aslan, "I will show you both what I can, and what I cannot, do." He came close to the Dwarfs and gave a low growl: low, but it set all the air shaking. But the Dwarfs said to one another, "Hear that? That's the gang at the other end of the stable. Trying to frighten us. They do it with a machine of some kind. Don't take any notice. They won't take *us* in again!"

Aslan raised his head and shook his mane. Instantly a glorious feast appeared on the Dwarfs' knees: pies and tongues and pigeons and trifles and ices, and each Dwarf had a goblet of good wine in his right hand. But it wasn't much use. They began eating and drinking greedily enough, but it was clear that they couldn't taste it properly. They thought they were eating and drinking only the sort of things you might find in a stable. One said he was trying to eat hay and another said he had got a bit of an old turnip and a third said he'd found a raw cabbage leaf. . . . But very soon every Dwarf began suspecting that every other Dwarf had found something nicer than he had, and they started grabbing and snatching, and went on to quarreling, till in a few minutes there was a free fight and all the good food was smeared on their faces and clothes or trodden under foot. But when at last they sat down to nurse their black eyes and their bleeding noses, they all said:

"Well, at any rate there's no Humbug here. We haven't let anyone take us in. The Dwarfs are for the Dwarfs."

"You see," said Aslan. "They will not let us help them. They have chosen cunning instead of belief. Their prison is only in their own minds, yet they are in that prison; and so afraid of being taken in that they cannot be taken out."

—*The Last Battle*

What does it mean to choose cunning over belief? Why is believing so hard for the Dwarfs? Have you ever felt imprisoned in your own mind? How?

The Giant King and Queen

GO ON, POLE, do your stuff," whispered Scrubb.

Jill found that her mouth was so dry that she couldn't speak a word. She nodded savagely at Scrubb.

Thinking to himself that he would never forgive her (or Puddleglum either), Scrubb licked his lips and shouted up to the King giant.

"If you please, Sire, the Lady of the Green Kirtle salutes you by us and said you'd like to have us for your Autumn Feast."

The giant King and Queen looked at each other, nodded to each other, and smiled in a way that Jill didn't exactly like. She liked the King better than the Queen. He had a fine, curled beard and a straight eagle-like nose, and was really rather good-looking as giants go. The Queen was dreadfully fat and had a double chin and a fat, powdered face—which isn't a very nice thing at the best of times, and of course looks much worse when it is ten times too big. Then the King put out his tongue and licked his lips. Anyone might do that: but his tongue was so very large and red, and came out so unexpectedly, that it gave Jill quite a shock.

"Oh, what *good* children!" said the Queen. ("Perhaps she's the nice one after all," thought Jill.)

"Yes indeed," said the King. "Quite excellent children. We welcome you to our court. Give me your hands."

He stretched down his great right hand—very clean and with any number of rings on the fingers, but also with terrible pointed nails. He was much too big to shake the hands which the children, in turn, held up to him; but he shook the arms. . . .

I hope you won't lose all interest in Jill for the rest of the book if I tell you that at this moment she began to cry. There was a good deal of excuse for her. Her feet and hands and ears and nose were still only just beginning to thaw; melted snow was trickling off her clothes; she had had hardly anything to eat or drink that day; and her legs were aching so that she felt she could not go on standing much longer. Anyway, it did more good at the moment than anything else would have done, for the Queen said:

"Ah, the poor child! My lord, we do wrong to keep our guests standing. Quick, some of you! Take them away. Give them food and wine and baths. Comfort the little girl. Give her lollipops, give her dolls, give her physics, give her all you can think of—possets and comfits and caraways and lullabies and toys. Don't cry, little girl, or you won't be good for anything when the feast comes."

—The Silver Chair

Are there moments when crying is exactly what should happen? Do you try to avoid emotion in front of others? Why or why not?

Wild Inside

THEY HAD PLODDED ON for about half an hour (three of them very stiff from yesterday's rowing) when Trumpkin suddenly whispered, "Stop." They all stopped. "There's something following us," he said in a low voice. "Or rather, something keeping up with us: over there on the left." They all stood still, listening and staring till their ears and eyes ached. "You and I'd better each have an arrow on the string," said Susan to Trumpkin. The Dwarf nodded, and when both bows were ready for action the party went on again.

They went a few dozen yards through fairly open woodland, keeping a sharp look-out. Then they came to a place where the undergrowth thickened and they had to pass nearer to it. Just as they were passing the place, there came a sudden something that snarled and flashed, rising out from the breaking twigs like a thunderbolt. Lucy was knocked down and winded, hearing the twang of a bowstring as she fell. When she was able to take notice of things again, she saw a great grim-looking grey bear lying dead with Trumpkin's arrow in its side.

"The D.L.F. beat you in *that* shooting match, Su," said Peter, with a slightly forced smile. Even he had been shaken by this adventure.

"I—I left it too late," said Susan, in an embarrassed voice. "I was so afraid it might be, you know—one of our kind of bears, a *talking* bear." She hated killing things.

"That's the trouble of it," said Trumpkin, "when most of the beasts have gone enemy and gone dumb, but there are still some of the other kind left. You never know, and you daren't wait to see."

"Poor old Bruin," said Susan. "You don't think he *was*?"

"Not he," said the Dwarf. "I saw the face and I heard the snarl. He only wanted Little Girl for his breakfast. And talking of breakfast, I didn't want to discourage your Majesties when you said you hoped King Caspian would give you a good one: but meat's precious scarce in camp. And there's good eating on a bear. It would be a shame to leave the carcass without taking a bit, and it won't delay us more than half an hour. I dare say you two youngsters—Kings, I should say—know how to skin a bear?"

"Let's go and sit down a fair way off," said Susan to Lucy. "I know what a horrid messy business *that* will be." Lucy shuddered and nodded. When they had sat down she said: "Such a horrible idea has come into my head, Su."

"What's that?"

"Wouldn't it be dreadful if some day in our own world, at home, men started going wild inside, like the animals here, and still looked like men, so that you'd never know which were which?"

"We've got enough to bother about here and now in Narnia," said the practical Susan, "without imagining things like that."

—*Prince Caspian*

Does Susan err by waiting to see if the bear might be one of their kind? What do you think Lucy means by men going wild inside? How might that manifest itself?

The Deplorable Word

"LOOK WELL ON THAT WHICH no eyes will ever see again," said the Queen. "Such was Charn, that great city, the city of the King of Kings, the wonder of the world, perhaps of all worlds. Does your uncle rule any city as great as this, boy?"

"No," said Digory. He was going to explain that Uncle Andrew didn't rule any cities, but the Queen went on: ·

"It is silent now. But I have stood here when the whole air was full of the noises of Charn; the trampling of feet, the creaking of wheels, the cracking of the whips and the groaning of slaves, the thunder of chariots, and the sacrificial drums beating in the temples. I have stood here (but that was near the end) when the roar of battle went up from every street and the river of Charn ran red." She paused and added, "All in one moment one woman blotted it out forever."

"Who?" said Digory in a faint voice; but he had already guessed the answer.

"I," said the Queen. "I, Jadis, the last Queen, but the Queen of the World."

The two children stood silent, shivering in the cold wind.

"It was my sister's fault," said the Queen. "She drove me to it. May the curse of all the Powers rest upon her forever! At any moment I was ready to make peace—yes and to spare her life too, if only she would yield me the throne. But she would not. Her pride has destroyed the whole world. Even after the war had begun, there was a solemn promise that neither side would use Magic. But when she broke her promise, what could I do? Fool! As if she did not know that I had more Magic than she! She even knew that I had the secret of the Deplorable Word. Did she think—she was always a weakling—that I would not use it?"

"What was it?" said Digory.

"That was the secret of secrets," said the Queen Jadis. "It had long been known to the great kings of our race that there was a word which, if spoken with the proper ceremonies, would destroy all living things except the one who spoke it. But the ancient kings were weak and soft-hearted and bound themselves and all who should come after them with great oaths never even to seek after the knowledge of that word. But I learned it in a secret place and paid a terrible price to learn it. I did not use it until she forced me to it. I fought to overcome her by every other means. I poured out the blood of my armies like water—"

"Beast!" muttered Polly.

"The last great battle," said the Queen, "raged for three days here in Charn itself. For three days I looked down upon it from this very spot. I did not use my power till the last of my soldiers had fallen, and the accursed woman, my sister, at the head of her rebels was halfway up those great stairs that lead up from the city to the terrace. Then I waited till we were so close that we could see one another's faces. She flashed her horrible, wicked eyes upon me and said, 'Victory.' 'Yes,' said I, 'Victory, but not yours.' Then I spoke the Deplorable Word. A moment later I was the only living thing beneath the sun."

—*The Magician's Nephew*

What excuse does Jadis give for ending the world with a word? How have you witnessed the destructive power of pride?

I Was the Lion

ONCE MORE HE FELT the warm breath of the Thing on his hand and face. "There," it said, "that is not the breath of a ghost. Tell me your sorrows."

Shasta was a little reassured by the breath: so he told how he had never known his real father or mother and had been brought up sternly by the fisherman. And then he told the story of his escape and how they were chased by lions and forced to swim for their lives; and of all their dangers in Tashbaan and about his night among the tombs and how the beasts howled at him out of the desert. And he told about the heat and thirst of their desert journey and how they were almost at their goal when another lion chased them and wounded Aravis. . . .

"I do not call you unfortunate," said the Large Voice.

"Don't you think it was bad luck to meet so many lions?" said Shasta.

"There was only one lion," said the Voice.

"What on earth do you mean? I've just told you there were at least two the first night, and—"

"There was only one: but he was swift of foot."

"How do you know?"

"I was the lion." And as Shasta gaped with open mouth and said nothing, the voice continued. "I was the lion who forced you to join with Aravis. I was the cat who comforted you among the houses of the dead. I was the lion who drove the jackals from you while you slept. I was the lion who gave the Horses the new strength of fear for the last mile so that you should reach King Lune in time. And I was the lion you do not remember who pushed the boat in which you lay, a child near death, so that it came to shore where a man sat, wakeful at midnight, to receive you."

—*The Horse and His Boy*

Why did Aslan not reveal himself earlier? How would it feel to know that someone was watching over you in that way?

The In-Between Place

[D]IGORY] WAS STANDING by the edge of a small pool—not more than ten feet from side to side—in a wood. The trees grew close together and were so leafy that he could get no glimpse of the sky. All the light was green light that came through the leaves: but there must have been a very strong sun overhead, for this green daylight was bright and warm. It was the quietest wood you could possibly imagine. There were no birds, no insects, no animals, and no wind. You could almost feel the trees growing. The pool he had just got out of was not the only pool. There were dozens of others—a pool every few yards as far as his eyes could reach. You could almost feel the trees drinking the water up with their roots. This wood was very much alive. When he tried to describe it afterward Digory always said, "It was a *rich* place: as rich as plumcake."

The strangest thing was that, almost before he had looked about him, Digory had half forgotten how he had come there. . . . He was not in the least frightened, or excited, or curious. If anyone had asked him "Where did you come from?" he would probably have said, "I've always been here." That was what it felt like—as if one had always been in that place and never been bored although nothing had ever happened. . . .

"What do we do now?" said Polly. "Take the guinea-pig and go home?"

"There's no hurry," said Digory with a huge yawn.

"I think there is," said Polly. "This place is too quiet. It's so—so dreamy. You're almost asleep. If we once give in to it we shall just lie down and drowse forever and ever."

"It's very nice here," said Digory.

"Yes, it is," said Polly. "But we've got to get back."

—*The Magician's Nephew*

What kind of feeling does the in-between place evoke in Polly and Digory? How could such a state be dangerous? Have you ever felt paralyzed or overcome by lethargy while in an in-between place or stage in your life? How did you move past it?

Father Christmas Arrives

"COME ON!" cried Mr. Beaver, who was almost dancing with delight. "Come and see! This is a nasty knock for the Witch! It looks as if her power is already crumbling."

"What *do* you mean, Mr. Beaver?" panted Peter as they all scrambled up the steep bank of the valley together.

"Didn't I tell you," answered Mr. Beaver, "that she'd made it always winter and never Christmas? Didn't I tell you? Well, just come and see!"

And then they were all at the top and did see.

It *was* a sledge, and it *was* reindeer with bells on their harness. But they were far bigger than the Witch's reindeer, and they were not white but brown. And on the sledge sat a person whom everyone knew the moment they set eyes on him. He was a huge man in a bright red robe (bright as hollyberries) with a hood that had fur inside it and a great white beard that fell like a foamy waterfall over his chest. Everyone knew him because, though you see people of his sort only in Narnia, you see pictures of them and hear them talked about even in our world—the world on this side of the wardrobe door. But when you really see them in Narnia it is rather different. Some of the pictures of Father Christmas in our world make him look only funny and jolly. But now that the children actually stood looking at him they didn't find it quite like that. He was so big, and so glad, and so real, that they all became quite still. They felt very glad, but also solemn.

"I've come at last," said he. "She has kept me out for a long time, but I have got in at last. Aslan is on the move. The Witch's magic is weakening."

And Lucy felt running through her that deep shiver of gladness which you only get if you are being solemn and still.

—The Lion, the Witch, and the Wardrobe

What is the connection between gladness and solemnness? Why must Lucy be solemn to experience that kind of gladness?

Eustace's Escape

[Eustace] ROSE QUIETLY from his place and walked away among the trees, taking care to go slowly and in an aimless manner so that anyone who saw him would think he was merely stretching his legs. He was surprised to find how quickly the noise of conversation died away behind him and how very silent and warm and dark green the wood became. . . .

The ground began sloping steeply up in front of him. The grass was dry and slippery but manageable if he used his hands as well as his feet, and though he panted and mopped his forehead a good deal, he plugged away steadily. This showed, by the way, that his new life, little as he suspected it, had already done him some good; the old Eustace, Harold and Alberta's Eustace, would have given up the climb after about ten minutes.

Slowly, and with several rests, he reached the ridge. Here he had expected to have a view into the heart of the island, but the clouds had now come lower and nearer and a sea of fog was rolling to meet him. He sat down and looked back. He was now so high that the bay looked small beneath him and miles of sea were visible. Then the fog from the mountains closed in all round him, thick but not cold, and he lay down and turned this way and that to find the most comfortable position to enjoy himself.

But he didn't enjoy himself, or not for very long. He began, almost for the first time in his life, to feel lonely. At first this feeling grew very gradually. And then he began to worry about the time. There was not the slightest sound. Suddenly it occurred to him that he might have been lying there for hours. Perhaps the others had gone! Perhaps they had let him wander away on purpose simply in order to leave him behind! He leaped up in a panic and began the descent.

—*The Voyage of the* **Dawn Treader**

After Eustace escapes from the hard work of repairing the damaged Dawn Treader *and finds the solitude he has been seeking, why isn't he able to enjoy himself? Have you ever sought to be alone only to find that you felt lonely? What is the difference between solitude and loneliness?*

Hunting Beasts for Sport

"THAT'S RIGHT," said Trufflehunter. "You're right, King Caspian. And as long as you will be true to Old Narnia you shall be *my* King, whatever they say. Long life to your Majesty."

"You make me sick, Badger," growled Nikabrik. "The High King Peter and the rest may have been Men, but they were a different sort of Men. This is one of the cursed Telmarines. He has *hunted* beasts for sport. Haven't you, now?" he added, rounding suddenly on Caspian.

"Well, to tell you the truth, I have," said Caspian. "But they weren't Talking Beasts."

"It's all the same thing," said Nikabrik.

"No, no, no," said Trufflehunter. "You know it isn't. You know very well that the beasts in Narnia nowadays are different and are no more than the poor dumb, witless creatures you'd find in Calormen or Telmar. They're smaller too. They're far more different from us than the half-Dwarfs are from you."

—Prince Caspian

Why would it make a difference whether the beasts Caspian hunted were Talking Beasts or dumb beasts? Would Caspian still be to blame if he hunted and killed a Talking Beast but didn't realize it?

Caring for Aslan's Body

As soon as the wood was silent again Susan and Lucy crept out onto the open hilltop. The moon was getting low and thin clouds were passing across her, but still they could see the shape of the Lion lying dead in his bonds. And down they both knelt in the wet grass and kissed his cold face and stroked his beautiful fur—what was left of it—and cried till they could cry no more. And then they looked at each other and held each other's hands for mere loneliness and cried again; and then again were silent. At last Lucy said,

"I can't bear to look at that horrible muzzle. I wonder, could we take it off?"

So they tried. And after a lot of working at it (for their fingers were cold and it was now the darkest part of the night) they succeeded. And when they saw his face without it they burst out crying again and kissed it and fondled it and wiped away the blood and the foam as well as they could. And it was all more lonely and hopeless and horrid than I know how to describe.

"I wonder, could we untie him as well?" said Susan presently. But the enemies, out of pure spitefulness, had drawn the cords so tight that the girls could make nothing of the knots.

I hope no one who reads this book has been quite as miserable as Susan and Lucy were that night; but if you have been—if you've been up all night and cried till you have no more tears left in you—you will know that there comes in the end a sort of quietness. You feel as if nothing was ever going to happen again. At any rate that was how it felt to these two. Hours and hours seemed to go by in this dead calm, and they hardly noticed that they were getting colder and colder.

—*The Lion, the Witch, and the Wardrobe*

Have you ever experienced the kind of misery followed by quietness that Lucy and Susan feel? How do we allow ourselves to feel deep grief without it over-whelming us?

The Mice and the Birds

BUT AT LAST LUCY NOTICED two other things. One was that the sky on the east side of the hill was a little less dark than it had been an hour ago. The other was some tiny movement going on in the grass at her feet. At first she took no interest in this. What did it matter? Nothing mattered now! But at last she saw that whatever-it-was had begun to move up the upright stones of the Stone Table. And now whatever-they-were were moving about on Aslan's body. She peered closer. They were little grey things.

"Ugh!" said Susan from the other side of the Table. "How beastly! There are horrid little mice crawling over him. Go away, you little beasts." And she raised her hand to frighten them away.

"Wait!" said Lucy, who had been looking at them more closely still. "Can you see what they're doing?"

Both girls bent down and stared.

"I do believe—" said Susan. "But how queer! They're nibbling away at the cords!"

"That's what I thought," said Lucy. "I think they're friendly mice. Poor little things—they don't realize he's dead. They think it'll do some good untying him."

It was quite definitely lighter by now. Each of the girls noticed for the first time the white face of the other. They could see the mice nibbling away; dozens and dozens, even hundreds, of little field mice. And at last, one by one, the ropes were all gnawed through. . . .

In the wood behind them a bird gave a chuckling sound. It had been so still for hours and hours that it startled them. Then another bird answered it. Soon there were birds singing all over the place.

It was quite definitely early morning now, not late night.

—*The Lion, the Witch, and the Wardrobe*

When have you jumped to conclusions, only to realize that what you had thought was horrifying was actually helpful?

Aslan Lives

"I'M SO COLD," said Lucy.

"So am I," said Susan. "Let's walk about a bit."

They walked to the eastern edge of the hill and looked down. The one big star had almost disappeared. The country all looked dark grey, but beyond, at the very end of the world, the sea showed pale. The sky began to turn red. They walked to and fro more times than they could count between the dead Aslan and the eastern ridge, trying to keep warm; and oh, how tired their legs felt. Then at last, as they stood for a moment looking out toward the sea and Cair Paravel (which they could now just make out) the red turned to gold along the line where the sea and the sky met and very slowly up came the edge of the sun. At that moment they heard from behind them a loud noise—a great cracking, deafening noise as if a giant had broken a giant's plate.

"What's that?" said Lucy, clutching Susan's arm.

"I—I feel afraid to turn round," said Susan; "something awful is happening."

"They're doing something worse to *Him*," said Lucy. "Come on!" And she turned, pulling Susan round with her.

The rising of the sun had made everything look so different—all colors and shadows were changed—that for a moment they didn't see the important thing. Then they did. The Stone Table was broken into two pieces by a great crack that ran down it from end to end; and there was no Aslan.

"Oh, oh, oh!" cried the two girls, rushing back to the Table.

"Oh, it's *too* bad," sobbed Lucy; "they might have left the body alone."

"Who's done it?" cried Susan. "What does it mean? Is it more magic?"

"Yes!" said a great voice behind their backs. "It is more magic." They looked round. There, shining in the sunrise, larger than they had seen him before, shaking his mane (for it had apparently grown again) stood Aslan himself.

"Oh, Aslan!" cried both the children, staring up at him, almost as much frightened as they were glad.

"Aren't you dead then, dear Aslan?" said Lucy.

"Not now," said Aslan.

"You're not—not a—?" asked Susan in a shaky voice. She couldn't bring herself to say the word *ghost*. Aslan stooped his golden head and licked her forehead. The warmth of his breath and a rich sort of smell that seemed to hang about his hair came all over her.

"Do I look it?" he said.

—*The Lion, the Witch, and the Wardrobe*

Why are the girls almost as frightened as glad? How does reading this passage make you feel?

Such a Romp

O H, YOU'RE REAL, you're real! Oh, Aslan!" cried Lucy, and both girls flung themselves upon him and covered him with kisses.

"But what does it all mean?" asked Susan when they were somewhat calmer.

"It means," said Aslan, "that though the Witch knew the Deep Magic, there is a magic deeper still which she did not know. Her knowledge goes back only to the dawn of time. But if she could have looked a little further back, into the stillness and the darkness before Time dawned, she would have read there a different incantation. She would have known that when a willing victim who had committed no treachery was killed in a traitor's stead, the Table would crack and Death itself would start working backward. And now—"

"Oh yes. Now?" said Lucy, jumping up and clapping her hands.

"Oh, children," said the Lion, "I feel my strength coming back to me. Oh, children, catch me if you can!" He stood for a second, his eyes very bright, his limbs quivering, lashing himself with his tail. Then he made a leap high over their heads and landed on the other side of the Table. Laughing, though she didn't know why, Lucy scrambled over it to reach him. Aslan leaped again. A mad chase began. Round and round the hilltop he led them, now hopelessly out of their reach, now letting them almost catch his tail, now diving between them, now tossing them in the air with his huge and beautifully velveted paws and catching them again, and now stopping unexpectedly so that all three of them rolled over together in a happy laughing heap of fur and arms and legs. It was such a romp as no one has ever had except in Narnia; and whether it was more like playing with a thunderstorm or playing with a kitten Lucy could never make up her mind.

—*The Lion, the Witch, and the Wardrobe*

Why might playing be the first thing Aslan does after coming back to life? Does this surprise you? Why or why not?

I'll Be Nobody

WHEN ARAVIS HAD FINISHED telling her story, Lasaraleen said, "But, darling, why *don't* you marry Ahoshta Tarkaan? Everyone's crazy about him. My husband says he is beginning to be one of the greatest men in Calormen. He has just been made Grand Vizier now old Axartha has died. Didn't you know?"

"I don't care. I can't stand the sight of him," said Aravis.

"But, darling, only think! Three palaces, and one of them that beautiful one down on the lake at Ilkeen. Positively ropes of pearls, I'm told. Baths of asses' milk. And you'd see such a lot of *me*."

"He can keep his pearls and palaces as far as I'm concerned," said Aravis.

"You always *were* a queer girl, Aravis," said Lasaraleen. "What more *do* you want?"

In the end, however, Aravis managed to make her friend believe that she was in earnest, and even to discuss plans [for getting Aravis to Narnia]. . . .

. . . [Lasaraleen] kept on telling Aravis that Narnia was a country of perpetual snow and ice inhabited by demons and sorcerers, and she was mad to think of going there. "And with a peasant boy, too!" said Lasaraleen. "Darling, think of it! It's not Nice." Aravis had thought of it a good deal, but she was so tired of Lasaraleen's silliness by now that, for the first time, she began to think that traveling with Shasta was really rather more fun than fashionable life in Tashbaan. So she only replied, "You forget that I'll be nobody, just like him, when we get to Narnia. And anyway, I promised."

"And to think," said Lasaraleen, almost crying, "that if only you had sense you could be the wife of a Grand Vizier!"

—*The Horse and His Boy*

What about Lasaraleen's conversation do you think makes Aravis prefer to be a nobody? What exactly do you think Aravis means by being nobody? Have you ever felt being a nobody was a good thing? Why or why not?

Your Ignorance Is Pardoned

CASPIAN ORDERED HORSES, of which there were a few in the castle, though very ill-groomed, and he, with Bern and Drinian and a few others, rode out into the town and made for the slave market. It was a long low building near the harbor and the scene which they found going on inside was very much like any other auction; that is to say, there was a great crowd and Pug, on a platform, was roaring out in a raucous voice:

"Now, gentlemen, lot twenty-three. Fine Terebinthian agricultural laborer, suitable for the mines or the galleys. Under twenty-five years of age. Not a bad tooth in his head. Good, brawny fellow. Take off his shirt, Tacks, and let the gentlemen see. There's muscle for you! Look at the chest on him. Ten crescents from the gentleman in the corner. You must be joking, sir. Fifteen! Eighteen! Eighteen is bid for lot twenty-three. Any advance on eighteen? Twenty-one. Thank you, sir. Twenty-one is bidden—"

But Pug stopped and gaped when he saw the mail-clad figures who had clanked up to the platform.

"On your knees, every man of you, to the King of Narnia," said the Duke. . . .

"Your life is forfeit, Pug, for laying hands on our royal person yesterday," said Caspian. "But your ignorance is pardoned. The slave trade was forbidden in all our dominions quarter of an hour ago. I declare every slave in this market free. . . . Every man who has bought a slave today must have his money back. Pug, bring out your takings to the last minim." (A minim is the fortieth part of a crescent.)

"Does your good Majesty mean to beggar me?" whined Pug.

"You have lived on broken hearts all your life," said Caspian, "and if you *are* beggared, it is better to be a beggar than a slave."

—*The Voyage of the* **Dawn Treader**

Despite the fact that Pug sold him as a slave only the day before, Caspian pardons him. Though he is ignorant of the law, is Pug ignorant of the results of his actions? Who in our world could be accused of "having lived on broken hearts"?

Now That I Know You

TUMNUS [SAID], "I had orders from the White Witch that if ever I saw a Son of Adam or a Daughter of Eve in the wood, I was to catch them and hand them over to her. And you are the first I ever met. And I've pretended to be your friend and asked you to tea, and all the time I've been meaning to wait till you were asleep and then go and tell *Her*."

"Oh, but you won't, Mr. Tumnus," said Lucy. "You won't, will you? Indeed, indeed you really mustn't."

"And if I don't," said he, beginning to cry again, "she's sure to find out. And she'll have my tail cut off, and my horns sawn off, and my beard plucked out, and she'll wave her wand over my beautiful cloven hoofs and turn them into horrid solid hoofs like a wretched horse's. And if she is extra and specially angry she'll turn me into stone and I shall be only a statue of a Faun in her horrible house until the four thrones at Cair Paravel are filled—and goodness knows when that will happen, or whether it will ever happen at all."

"I'm very sorry, Mr. Tumnus," said Lucy. "But please let me go home."

"Of course I will," said the Faun. "Of course I've got to. I see that now. I hadn't known what Humans were like before I met you. Of course I can't give you up to the Witch; not now that I know you. But we must be off at once. I'll see you back to the lamp-post."

—*The Lion, the Witch, and the Wardrobe*

Why does Tumnus change his mind? Have you ever thought you'd be able to do something only to realize in the face of it that you could not?

Quick!

A ND NOW, round that point there came into sight a boat. When it had cleared the point, it turned and began coming along the channel toward them. There were two people on board, one rowing, the other sitting in the stern and holding a bundle that twitched and moved as if it were alive. Both these people seemed to be soldiers. . . . The children drew back from the beach into the wood and watched without moving a finger.

"This'll do," said the soldier in the stern when the boat had come about opposite to them.

"What about tying a stone to his feet, Corporal?" said the other, resting on his oars.

"Garn!" growled the other. "We don't need that, and we haven't brought one. He'll drown sure enough without a stone, as long as we've tied the cords right." With these words he rose and lifted his bundle. Peter now saw that it was really alive and was in fact a Dwarf, bound hand and foot but struggling as hard as he could. Next moment he heard a twang just beside his ear, and all at once the soldier threw up his arms, dropping the Dwarf into the bottom of the boat, and fell over into the water. He floundered away to the far bank and Peter knew that Susan's arrow had struck his helmet. He turned and saw that she was very pale but was already fitting a second arrow to the string. But it was never used. As soon as he saw his companion fall, the other soldier, with a loud cry, jumped out of the boat on the far side, and he also floundered through the water (which was apparently just in his depth) and disappeared into the woods of the mainland.

"Quick! Before she drifts!" shouted Peter. . . . In a few seconds they had hauled [the boat] to the bank and lifted the Dwarf out, and Edmund was busily engaged in cutting his bonds with the pocket-knife.

—*Prince Caspian*

No one hesitates to step in and try to save the Dwarf. Why is such quick action warranted? When is it appropriate to stop and consider and when should we just act on instinct?

Only Noise

WHEN THE LION had first begun singing, long ago when it was still quite dark, [Uncle Andrew] had realized that the noise was a song. And he had disliked the song very much. It made him think and feel things he did not want to think and feel. Then, when the sun rose and he saw that the singer was a lion ("*only* a lion," as he said to himself) he tried his hardest to make believe that it wasn't singing and never had been singing—only roaring as any lion might in a zoo in our own world. "Of course it can't really have been singing," he thought, "I must have imagined it. I've been letting my nerves get out of order. Who ever heard of a lion singing?" And the longer and more beautifully the Lion sang, the harder Uncle Andrew tried to make himself believe that he could hear nothing but roaring. Now the trouble about trying to make yourself stupider than you really are is that you very often succeed. Uncle Andrew did. He soon did hear nothing but roaring in Aslan's song. Soon he couldn't have heard anything else even if he had wanted to. And when at last the Lion spoke and said, "Narnia, awake," he didn't hear any words: he heard only a snarl. And when the Beasts spoke in answer, he heard only barkings, growlings, baying, and howlings.

—*The Magician's Nephew*

Why would Uncle Andrew want to make himself "stupider"? How do we close ourselves off from what we do not want to experience or know? When have you closed yourself off from something right in front of you?

The Invisible Soldiers' Request

WELL, THEN, to put it in a nutshell," said the Chief Voice, "we've been waiting for ever so long for a nice little girl from foreign parts, like it might be you, Missie—that would go upstairs and go to the magic book and find the spell that takes off the invisibleness, and say it. And we all swore that the first strangers as landed on this island (having a nice little girl with them, I mean, for if they hadn't it'd be another matter) we wouldn't let them go away alive unless they'd done the needful for us. And that's why, gentlemen, if your little girl doesn't come up to scratch, it will be our painful duty to cut all your throats. Merely in the way of business, as you might say, and no offense, I hope.". . .

"But why do you want *me* to do this?" asked Lucy. "Why can't one of your own people? Haven't you got any girls?"

"We dursen't, we dursen't," said all the Voices. "We're not going upstairs again."

"In other words," said Caspian, "you are asking this lady to face some danger which you daren't ask your own sisters and daughters to face!"

"That's right, that's right," said all the Voices cheerfully. "You couldn't have said it better. Eh, you've had some education, you have. Anyone can see that."

"Well, of all the outrageous—" began Edmund, but Lucy interrupted.

"Would I have to go upstairs at night, or would it do in daylight?"

"Oh, daylight, daylight, to be sure," said the Chief Voice. "Not at night. No one's asking you to do that. Go upstairs in the dark? Ugh."

"All right, then, I'll do it," said Lucy. "No," she said, turning to the others, "don't try to stop me. Can't you see it's no use? There are dozens of them there. We can't fight them. And the other way there *is* a chance."

"But a magician!" said Caspian.

"I know," said Lucy. "But he mayn't be as bad as they make out. Don't you get the idea that these people are not very brave?"

"They're certainly not very clever," said Eustace.

"Look here, Lu," said Edmund. "We really can't let you do a thing like this. Ask Reep, I'm sure he'll say just the same."

"But it's to save my own life as well as yours," said Lucy. "I don't want to be cut to bits with invisible swords any more than anyone else."

"Her Majesty is in the right," said Reepicheep. "If we had any assurance of saving *her* by battle, our duty would be very plain. It appears to me that we have none. And the service they ask of her is in no way contrary to her Majesty's honor, but a noble and heroical act. If the Queen's heart moves her to risk the magician, I will not speak against it."

—*The Voyage of the* **Dawn Treader**

What would you say if you were in Lucy's place? In Caspian's or Edmund's? What would you think of people who asked you to help them by taking a risk they weren't willing to take themselves?

The Underground March

THE COLD LIGHT came from a large ball on top of a long pole, and the tallest of the gnomes carried this at the head of the procession. By its cheerless rays they could see that they were in a natural cavern; the walls and roof were knobbed, twisted, and gashed into a thousand fantastic shapes, and the stony floor sloped downward as they proceeded. It was worse for Jill than the others, because she hated dark, underground places. And when, as they went on, the cave got lower and narrower, and when, at last, the light-bearer stood aside, and the gnomes, one by one, stooped down (all except the very smallest ones) and stepped into a little dark crack and disappeared, she felt she could bear it no longer.

"I can't go in there, I can't! I can't! I won't!" she panted. The Earthmen said nothing but they all lowered their spears and pointed them at her.

"Steady, Pole," said Puddleglum. "Those big fellows wouldn't be crawling in there if it didn't get wider later on. And there's one thing about this underground work, we shan't get any rain."

"Oh, you don't understand. I can't," wailed Jill.

"Think how *I* felt on that cliff, Pole," said Scrubb. "You go first, Puddleglum, and I'll come after her."

"That's right," said the Marsh-wiggle, getting down on his hands and knees. "You keep a grip on my heels, Pole, and Scrubb will hold on to yours. Then we'll all be comfortable."

"Comfortable!" said Jill. But she got down and they crawled in on their elbows. It was a nasty place. You had to go flat on your face for what seemed like half an hour, though it may really have been only five minutes. It was hot. Jill felt she was being smothered. But at last a dim light showed ahead, the tunnel grew wider and higher, and they came out, hot, dirty, and shaken, into a cave so large that it scarcely seemed a cave at all.

—*The Silver Chair*

How do Puddleglum and Scrubb help Jill face her fears? What scares you in the same way that dark, confined places scare Jill? Has anyone helped you face your fears?

Let the Prince Win His Spurs

THAT, O MAN," said Aslan, "is Cair Paravel of the four thrones, in one of which you must sit as King. I show it to you because you are the firstborn and you will be High King over all the rest."

And once more Peter said nothing, for at that moment a strange noise woke the silence suddenly. It was like a bugle, but richer.

"It is your sister's horn," said Aslan to Peter in a low voice; so low as to be almost a purr, if it is not disrespectful to think of a Lion purring.

For a moment Peter did not understand. Then, when he saw all the other creatures start forward and heard Aslan say with a wave of his paw, "Back! Let the Prince win his spurs," he did understand, and set off running as hard as he could to the pavilion. And there he saw a dreadful sight.

The Naiads and Dryads were scattering in every direction. Lucy was running toward him as fast as her short legs would carry her and her face was as white as paper. Then he saw Susan make a dash for a tree, and swing herself up, followed by a huge grey beast. At first Peter thought it was a bear. Then he saw that it looked like an Alsatian, though it was far too big to be a dog. Then he realized that it was a wolf—a wolf standing on its hind legs, with its front paws against the tree-trunk, snapping and snarling. All the hair on its back stood up on end. Susan had not been able to get higher than the second big branch. One of her legs hung down so that her foot was only an inch or two above the snapping teeth. Peter wondered why she did not get higher or at least take a better grip; then he realized that she was just going to faint and that if she fainted she would fall off.

Peter did not feel very brave; indeed, he felt he was going to be sick. But that made no difference to what he had to do. He rushed straight up to the monster and aimed a slash of his sword at its side. That stroke never reached the Wolf. Quick as lightning it turned round, its eyes flaming, and its mouth wide open in a howl of anger. If it had not been so angry that it simply had to howl it would have got him by the throat at once. As it was—though all this happened too quickly for Peter to think at all—he had just time to duck down and plunge his sword, as hard as he could,

between the brute's forelegs into its heart. Then came a horrible, confused moment like something in a nightmare. He was tugging and pulling
and the Wolf seemed neither alive nor dead, and its bared teeth knocked
against his forehead, and everything was blood and heat and hair. A moment later he found that the monster lay dead and he had drawn his sword
out of it and was straightening his back and rubbing the sweat off his face
and out of his eyes. He felt tired all over.

—*The Lion, the Witch, and the Wardrobe*

*What does it mean for Peter to win his spurs? How do you think Peter acquits
himself? When in life have you had to prove yourself?*

Never Forget to Wipe Your Sword

PETER, STILL OUT OF BREATH, turned and saw Aslan close at hand.

"You have forgotten to clean your sword," said Aslan.

It was true. Peter blushed when he looked at the bright blade and saw it all smeared with the Wolf's hair and blood. He stooped down and wiped it quite clean on the grass, and then wiped it quite dry on his coat.

"Hand it to me and kneel, Son of Adam," said Aslan. And when Peter had done so he struck him with the flat of the blade and said, "Rise up, Sir Peter Wolf's-Bane. And, whatever happens, never forget to wipe your sword."

—*The Lion, the Witch, and the Wardrobe*

Peter has just killed the Wolf that was attacking his sister, and instead of a "Job well done" or similar sentiment, these are Aslan's first words to him. Why do you think Aslan chooses these words?

Ordinary People

ALL IN GOOD TIME, MY BOY," said Uncle Andrew. "They let old Mrs. Lefay out before she died and I was one of the very few people whom she would allow to see her in her last illness. She had got to dislike ordinary, ignorant people, you understand. I do myself. But she and I were interested in the same sort of things. It was only a few days before her death that she told me to go to an old bureau in her house and open a secret drawer and bring her a little box that I would find there. The moment I picked up that box I could tell by the pricking in my fingers that I held some great secret in my hands. She gave it to me and made me promise that as soon as she was dead I would burn it, unopened, with certain ceremonies. That promise I did not keep."

"Well, then, it was jolly rotten of you," said Digory.

"Rotten?" said Uncle Andrew with a puzzled look. "Oh, I see. You mean that little boys ought to keep their promises. Very true: most right and proper, I'm sure, and I'm very glad you have been taught to do it. But of course you must understand that rules of that sort, however excellent they may be for little boys—and servants—and women—and even people in general, can't possibly be expected to apply to profound students and great thinkers and sages. No, Digory. Men like me, who possess hidden wisdom, are freed from common rules just as we are cut off from common pleasures. Ours, my boy, is a high and lonely destiny."

—*The Magician's Nephew*

How does Uncle Andrew differentiate himself from the people around him? What are the dangers of thinking as he does? When have you been guilty of this attitude?

Eustace the Dragon Tells His Story

[LUCY ASKED THE DRAGON,] "Are you someone enchanted—someone human, I mean?"

It nodded violently.

And then someone said—people disputed afterward whether Lucy or Edmund said it first—"You're not—not Eustace by any chance?"

And Eustace nodded his terrible dragon head and thumped his tail in the sea and everyone skipped back (some of the sailors with ejaculations I will not put down in writing) to avoid the enormous and boiling tears which flowed from his eyes.

Lucy tried hard to console him and even screwed up her courage to kiss the scaly face, and nearly everyone said "Hard luck" and several assured Eustace that they would all stand by him and many said there was sure to be some way of disenchanting him and they'd have him as right as rain in a day or two. And of course they were all very anxious to hear his story, but he couldn't speak. More than once in the days that followed he attempted to write it for them on the sand. But this never succeeded. In the first place Eustace (never having read the right books) had no idea how to tell a story straight. And for another thing, the muscles and nerves of the dragon-claws that he had to use had never learned to write and were not built for writing anyway. As a result he never got nearly to the end before the tide came in and washed away all the writing except the bits he had already trodden on or accidentally swished out with his tail. And all that anyone had seen would be something like this—the dots are for the bits he had smudged out—

I WNET TO SLEE . . . RGOS AGRONS I MEAN DRANGONS CAVE CAUSE ITWAS DEAD AND AINING SO HAR . . . WOKE UP AND COU . . . GET OFFF MI ARM OH BOTHER . . .

—*The Voyage of the* **Dawn Treader**

We read several times that Eustace had not read the right sort of books to prepare himself for his adventures in Narnia. What might the right books have been? How could they have changed things for Eustace? What have the right books been for you? How have they changed things for you?

A Bit Sorry

I T WAS A GOOD DEAL DARKER NOW and very silent except for the sound of the waves on the beach, which Shasta hardly noticed because he had been hearing it day and night as long as he could remember. The cottage, as he approached it, showed no light. When he listened at the front there was no noise. When he went round to the only window, he could hear, after a second or two, the familiar noise of the old fisherman's squeaky snore. It was funny to think that if all went well he would never hear it again. Holding his breath and feeling a little bit sorry, but much less sorry than he was glad, Shasta glided away over the grass and went to the donkey's stable, groped along to a place he knew where the key was hidden, opened the door and found the Horse's saddle and bridle which had been locked up there for the night. He bent forward and kissed the donkey's nose. "I'm sorry we can't take *you*," he said.

—*The Horse and His Boy*

Despite his ill treatment at the hands of the fisherman, Shasta is a little bit sorry to know he will never hear his snore again. Why do you think this is? When have you felt nostalgia for something that you did not appreciate or enjoy at the time?

The Lion Gets Closer

ALL THIS TIME the Lion's song, and his stately prowl, to and fro, backward and forward, was going on. What was rather alarming was that at each turn he came a little nearer. Polly was finding the song more and more interesting because she thought she was beginning to see the connection between the music and the things that were happening. When a line of dark firs sprang up on a ridge about a hundred yards away she felt that they were connected with a series of deep, prolonged notes which the Lion had sung a second before. And when he burst into a rapid series of lighter notes she was not surprised to see primroses suddenly appearing in every direction. Thus, with an unspeakable thrill, she felt quite certain that all the things were coming (as she said) "out of the Lion's head." When you listened to his song you heard the things he was making up: when you looked round you, you saw them. This was so exciting that she had no time to be afraid. But Digory and the Cabby could not help feeling a bit nervous as each turn of the Lion's walk brought him nearer. As for Uncle Andrew, his teeth were chattering, but his knees were shaking so that he could not run away.

—*The Magician's Nephew*

For Digory and the Cabby at least, their sense of wonder at the amazing things going on around them is tempered with nervousness at the proximity of the creator Lion. Why would something so awe-inspiring make them afraid? When have you been excited and afraid at the same time?

Edmund Meets the Queen of Narnia

[O]N A MUCH HIGHER SEAT in the middle of the sledge sat a very different person—a great lady, taller than any woman that Edmund had ever seen. She also was covered in white fur up to her throat and held a long straight golden wand in her right hand and wore a golden crown on her head. Her face was white—not merely pale, but white like snow or paper or icing-sugar, except for her very red mouth. It was a beautiful face in other respects, but proud and cold and stern. . . .

"And what, pray, are you?" said the Lady, looking hard at Edmund.

"I'm—I'm—my name's Edmund," said Edmund rather awkwardly. He did not like the way she looked at him.

The Lady frowned. "Is that how you address a Queen?" she asked, looking sterner than ever.

"I beg your pardon, your Majesty, I didn't know," said Edmund.

"Not know the Queen of Narnia?" cried she. "Ha! You shall know us better hereafter. But I repeat—what are you?"

"Please, your Majesty," said Edmund, "I don't know what you mean. I'm at school—at least I was—it's the holidays now."

"But what *are* you?" said the Queen again. "Are you a great overgrown dwarf that has cut off its beard?"

"No, your Majesty," said Edmund, "I never had a beard, I'm a boy."

"A boy!" said she. "Do you mean you are a Son of Adam?"

Edmund stood still, saying nothing. He was too confused by this time to understand what the question meant.

"I see you are an idiot, whatever else you may be," said the Queen. "Answer me, once and for all, or I shall lose my patience. Are you human?"

"Yes, your Majesty," said Edmund.

"And how, pray, did you come to enter my dominions?"

"Please, your Majesty, I came in through a wardrobe."

"A wardrobe? What do you mean?"

"I—I opened a door and just found myself here, your Majesty," said Edmund.

"Ha!" said the Queen, speaking more to herself than to him. "A door. A door from the world of men! I have heard of such things. This may wreck all. But he is only one, and he is easily dealt with." As she spoke these words she rose from her seat and looked Edmund full in the face, her eyes flaming; at the same moment she raised her wand. Edmund felt sure that she was going to do something dreadful but he seemed unable to move. Then, just as he gave himself up for lost, she appeared to change her mind.

"My poor child," she said in quite a different voice, "how cold you look! Come and sit with me here on the sledge and I will put my mantle round you and we will talk."

—*The Lion, the Witch, and the Wardrobe*

What does this encounter tell us about the Queen? How would you have responded to her invitation?

What Would Have Happened

L UCY," [ASLAN] SAID, "we must not lie here for long. You have
work in hand, and much time has been lost today."

"Yes, wasn't it a shame?" said Lucy. "*I* saw you all right. They wouldn't
believe me. They're all so—"

From somewhere deep inside Aslan's body there came the faintest suggestion of a growl.

"I'm sorry," said Lucy, who understood some of his moods. "I didn't
mean to start slanging the others. But it wasn't my fault anyway, was it?"

The Lion looked straight into her eyes.

"Oh, Aslan," said Lucy. "You don't mean it was? How could I—
I couldn't have left the others and come up to you alone, how could
I? Don't look at me like that . . . oh well, I suppose I *could*. Yes, and I
wouldn't have been alone, I know, not if I was with you. But what would
have been the good?"

Aslan said nothing.

"You mean," said Lucy rather faintly, "that it would have turned out all
right—somehow? But how? Please, Aslan! Am I not to know?"

"To know what *would* have happened, child?" said Aslan. "No. Nobody
is ever told that."

"Oh dear," said Lucy.

"But anyone can find out what *will* happen," said Aslan. "If you go
back to the others now, and wake them up; and tell them you have seen
me again; and that you must all get up at once and follow me—what will
happen? There is only one way of finding out."

—*Prince Caspian*

*Why do we sometimes dwell on what would have happened rather than look-
ing to what* will *happen? How do you find yourself not taking risks that, deep
down, you know you should?*

Caspian's Procession

WHEN THEY REACHED the jetty at Narrowhaven, Caspian found a considerable crowd assembled to meet them. "This is what I sent word about last night," said Bern. "They are all friends of mine and honest people." And as soon as Caspian stepped ashore the crowd broke out into hurrahs and shouts of, "Narnia! Narnia! Long live the King." At the same moment—and this was also due to Bern's messengers—bells began ringing from many parts of the town. Then Caspian caused his banner to be advanced and his trumpet to be blown, and every man drew his sword and set his face into a joyful sternness, and they marched up the street so that the street shook, and their armor shone (for it was a sunny morning) so that one could hardly look at it steadily.

At first, the only people who cheered were those who had been warned by Bern's messenger and knew what was happening and wanted it to happen. But then all the children joined in because they liked a procession and had seen very few. And then all the schoolboys joined in because they also liked processions and felt that the more noise and disturbance there was, the less likely they would be to have any school that morning. And then all the old women put their heads out of doors and windows and began chattering and cheering because it was a king, and what is a governor compared with that? And all the young women joined in for the same reason and also because Caspian and Drinian and the rest were so handsome. And then all the young men came to see what the young women were looking at, so that by the time Caspian reached the castle gates, nearly the whole town was shouting; and where Gumpas sat in the castle, muddling and messing about with accounts and forms and rules and regulations, he heard the noise.

—*The Voyage of the* **Dawn Treader**

Caspian has arrived unexpectedly on this island, so most of the townspeople are not sure who is processing and for what reason. Does it matter why people join Caspian's procession? Should it?

JULY

Puddleglum Breaks the Enchantment

THE PRINCE and the two children were standing with their heads hung down, their cheeks flushed, their eyes half closed; the strength all gone from them; the enchantment almost complete. But Puddleglum, desperately gathering all his strength, walked over to the fire. Then he did a very brave thing. He knew it wouldn't hurt him quite as much as it would hurt a human; for his feet (which were bare) were webbed and hard and cold-blooded like a duck's. But he knew it would hurt him badly enough; and so it did. With his bare foot he stamped on the fire, grinding a large part of it into ashes on the flat hearth. And three things happened at once.

First, the sweet, heavy smell grew very much less. For though the whole fire had not been put out, a good bit of it had, and what remained smelled very largely of burnt Marsh-wiggle, which is not at all an enchanting smell. This instantly made everyone's brain far clearer. The Prince and the children held up their heads again and opened their eyes.

Secondly, the Witch, in a loud, terrible voice, utterly different from all the sweet tones she had been using up till now, called out, "What are you doing? Dare to touch my fire again, mud-filth, and I'll turn the blood to fire inside your veins."

Thirdly, the pain itself made Puddleglum's head for a moment perfectly clear and he knew exactly what he really thought. There is nothing like a good shock of pain for dissolving certain kinds of magic.

"One word, Ma'am," he said, coming back from the fire; limping, because of the pain. "One word. All you've been saying is quite right, I shouldn't wonder. I'm a chap who always liked to know the worst and then put the best face I can on it. So I won't deny any of what you said. But there's one thing more to be said, even so. Suppose we *have* only dreamed, or made up, all those things—trees and grass and sun and moon and stars and Aslan himself. Suppose we have. Then all I can say is that, in that case, the made-up things seem a good deal more important than the real ones. Suppose this black pit of a kingdom of yours *is* the only world. Well, it strikes me as a pretty poor one. And that's a funny thing, when you come to think of it. We're just babies making up a game, if you're right.

But four babies playing a game can make a play-world which licks your real world hollow. That's why I'm going to stand by the play-world. I'm on Aslan's side even if there isn't any Aslan to lead it. I'm going to live as like a Narnian as I can even if there isn't any Narnia. So, thanking you kindly for our supper, if these two gentlemen and the young lady are ready, we're leaving your court at once and setting out in the dark to spend our lives looking for Overland. Not that our lives will be very long, I should think; but that's a small loss if the world's as dull a place as you say."

—*The Silver Chair*

What do you think of Puddleglum's statement that even if Narnia and Aslan aren't real, he's going to be on Aslan's side and live like a Narnian? Is there anything you believe so strongly that you would continue to live by it even if it might not be true?

But You Will Be There?

AFTER A MEAL, which was taken in the open air on the hill-top (for the sun had got strong by now and dried the grass), they were busy for a while taking the pavilion down and packing things up. Before two o'clock they were on the march and set off in a northeasterly direction, walking at an easy pace for they had not far to go.

During the first part of the journey Aslan explained to Peter his plan of campaign. "As soon as she has finished her business in these parts," he said, "the Witch and her crew will almost certainly fall back to her House and prepare for a siege. You may or may not be able to cut her off and prevent her from reaching it." He then went on to outline two plans of battle—one for fighting the Witch and her people in the wood and another for assaulting her castle. And all the time he was advising Peter how to conduct the operations, saying things like, "You must put your Centaurs in such and such a place" or "You must post scouts to see that she doesn't do so-and-so," till at last Peter said,

"But you will be there yourself, Aslan."

"I can give you no promise of that," answered the Lion. And he continued giving Peter his instructions.

—*The Lion, the Witch, and the Wardrobe*

What must Peter be feeling to hear that not only must he lead a battle, he might be leading it on his own? Have you ever felt pushed into a responsibility for which you did not feel ready? If so, what was the outcome?

The Talking Horse

TWO CALORMENES were driving a horse which was harnessed to a log. Just as the King reached them, the log got stuck in a bad muddy place.

"Get on, son of sloth! Pull, you lazy pig!" cried the Calormenes, cracking their whips. The horse was already straining himself as hard as he could; his eyes were red and he was covered with foam.

"Work, lazy brute," shouted one of the Calormenes: and as he spoke he struck the horse savagely with his whip. It was then that the really dreadful thing happened.

Up till now Tirian had taken it for granted that the horses which the Calormenes were driving were their own horses; dumb, witless animals like the horses of our own world. And though he hated to see even a dumb horse overdriven, he was of course thinking more about the murder of the Trees. It had never crossed his mind that anyone would dare to harness one of the free Talking Horses of Narnia, much less to use a whip on it. But as that savage blow fell the horse reared up and said, half screaming:

"Fool and tyrant! Do you not see I am doing all I can?"

When Tirian knew that the Horse was one of his own Narnians, there came over him and over Jewel such a rage that they did not know what they were doing. The King's sword went up, the Unicorn's horn went down. They rushed forward together. Next moment both the Calormenes lay dead, the one beheaded by Tirian's sword and the other gored through the heart by Jewel's horn.

—*The Last Battle*

Why is enslaving a Talking Beast so much worse than enslaving a Calormene horse? Is it worthy of death?

If Aslan Is Not Aslan

"JEWEL," SAID THE KING. "We have done a dreadful deed."

"We were sorely provoked," said Jewel.

"But to leap on them unawares—without defying them—while they were unarmed—faugh! We are two murderers, Jewel. I am dishonored forever."

Jewel drooped his head. He too was ashamed.

"And then," said the King, "the Horse said it was by Aslan's orders. The Rat said the same. They all say Aslan is here. How if it were true?"

"But, Sire, how *could* Aslan be commanding such dreadful things?"

"He is not a *tame* lion," said Tirian. "How should we know what he would do? We, who are murderers. Jewel, I will go back. I will give up my sword and put myself in the hands of these Calormenes and ask that they bring me before Aslan. Let him do justice on me."

"You will go to your death, then," said Jewel.

"Do you think I care if Aslan dooms me to death?" said the King. "That would be nothing, nothing at all. Would it not be better to be dead than to have this horrible fear that Aslan has come and is not like the Aslan we have believed in and longed for? It is as if the sun rose one day and were a black sun."

"I know," said Jewel. "Or as if you drank water and it were *dry* water. You are in the right, Sire. This is the end of all things. Let us go and give ourselves up."

"There is no need for both of us to go."

"If ever we loved one another, let me go with you now," said the Unicorn. "If you are dead and if Aslan is not Aslan, what life is left for me?"

—The Last Battle

Why is it so crushing to the King and Jewel to believe Aslan is commanding dreadful things such as the enslavement of Talking Horses? Have you ever felt as disappointed by someone you revered?

The Witch and Aslan

A FEW MINUTES LATER the Witch herself walked out on to the top of the hill and came straight across and stood before Aslan. The three children who had not seen her before felt shudders running down their backs at the sight of her face; and there were low growls among all the animals present. Though it was bright sunshine everyone felt suddenly cold. The only two people present who seemed to be quite at their ease were Aslan and the Witch herself. It was the oddest thing to see those two faces—the golden face and the dead-white face—so close together. Not that the Witch looked Aslan exactly in his eyes; Mrs. Beaver particularly noticed this.

—*The Lion, the Witch, and the Wardrobe*

Why can't the Witch look Aslan in the eye? When have you not been able to meet someone's eyes? What was the reason?

Reepicheep Goes Overboard

[A]T THAT MOMENT two sounds were heard. One was a plop. The other was a voice from the fighting-top shouting, "Man overboard!" Then everyone was busy. Some of the sailors hurried aloft to take in the sail; others hurried below to get to the oars; and Rhince, who was on duty on the poop, began to put the helm hard over so as to come round and back to the man who had gone overboard. But by now everyone knew that it wasn't strictly a man. It was Reepicheep.

"Drat that mouse!" said Drinian. "It's more trouble than all the rest of the ship's company put together. If there is any scrape to be got into, in it will get! It ought to be put in irons—keel-hauled—marooned—have its whiskers cut off. Can anyone see the little blighter?"

All this didn't mean that Drinian really disliked Reepicheep. On the contrary he liked him very much and was therefore frightened about him, and being frightened put him in a bad temper—just as your mother is much angrier with you for running out into the road in front of a car than a stranger would be.

—*The Voyage of the* **Dawn Treader**

Have you ever responded as Drinian does when someone you cared for put themselves into danger? From what does such anger stem?

The Island of Dreams

SUDDENLY, FROM SOMEWHERE—no one's sense of direction was very clear by now—there came a cry, either of some inhuman voice or else a voice of one in such extremity of terror that he had almost lost his humanity. . . .

"Mercy!" cried the voice. "Mercy! Even if you are only one more dream, have mercy. Take me on board. Take me, even if you strike me dead. But in the name of all mercies do not fade away and leave me in this horrible land.". . .

Several [sailors] crowded to the port bulwark with ropes and one, leaning far out over the side, held the torch. A wild, white face appeared in the blackness of the water, and then, after some scrambling and pulling, a dozen friendly hands had heaved the stranger on board.

Edmund thought he had never seen a wilder-looking man. Though he did not otherwise look very old, his hair was an untidy mop of white, his face was thin and drawn and, for clothing, only a few wet rags hung about him. But what one mainly noticed were his eyes, which were so widely opened that he seemed to have no eyelids at all, and stared as if in an agony of pure fear. The moment his feet reached the deck he said:

"Fly! Fly! About with your ship and fly! Row, row, row for your lives away from this accursed shore."

"Compose yourself," said Reepicheep, "and tell us what the danger is. We are not used to flying."

The stranger started horribly at the voice of the Mouse, which he had not noticed before.

"Nevertheless you will fly from here," he gasped. "This is the Island where Dreams come true."

"That's the island I've been looking for this long time," said one of the sailors. "I reckoned I'd find I was married to Nancy if we landed here."

"And I'd find Tom alive again," said another.

"Fools!" said the man, stamping his foot with rage. "That is the sort of talk that brought me here, and I'd better have been drowned or never born. Do you hear what I say? This is where dreams—dreams, do you understand—come to life, come real. Not daydreams: dreams."

There was about half a minute's silence and then, with a great clatter of armor, the whole crew were tumbling down the main hatch as quick as they could and flinging themselves on the oars to row as they had never rowed before; and Drinian was swinging round the tiller, and the boatswain was giving out the quickest stroke that had ever been heard at sea. For it had taken everyone just that half-minute to remember certain dreams they had had—dreams that make you afraid of going to sleep again—and to realize what it would mean to land on a country where dreams come true.

—*The Voyage of the* **Dawn Treader**

Would you have been tempted by the thought of your dreams coming to life just as the stranger was? What dream (or daydream) in particular?

Never Taunt a Man

YOUR ROYAL HIGHNESS needs not to be told," said King Lune [to Rabadash], "that by the law of nations as well as by all reasons of prudent policy, we have as good right to your head as ever one mortal man had against another. Nevertheless, in consideration of your youth and the ill nurture, devoid of all gentilesse and courtesy, which you have doubtless had in the land of slaves and tyrants, we are disposed to set you free, unharmed, on these conditions: first, that—"

"Curse you for a barbarian dog!" spluttered Rabadash. "Do you think I will even hear your conditions? Faugh! You talk very largely of nurture and I know not what. It's easy, to a man in chains, ha! Take off these vile bonds, give me a sword, and let any of you who dares then debate with me."

Nearly all the lords sprang to their feet, and Corin shouted:

"Father! Can I *box* him? Please."

"Peace! Your Majesties! My Lords!" said King Lune. "Have we no more gravity among us than to be so chafed by the taunt of a pajock? Sit down, Corin, or shalt leave the table. I ask your Highness again, to hear our conditions."

"I hear no conditions from barbarians and sorcerers," said Rabadash. "Not one of you dare touch a hair of my head. Every insult you have heaped on me shall be paid with oceans of Narnian and Archenlandish blood. Terrible shall the vengeance of the Tisroc be: even now. But kill me, and the burnings and torturings in these northern lands shall become a tale to frighten the world a thousand years hence. Beware! Beware! Beware! The bolt of Tash falls from above!"

"Does it ever get caught on a hook halfway?" asked Corin.

"Shame, Corin," said the King. "Never taunt a man save when he is stronger than you: then, as you please."

—*The Horse and His Boy*

How hard would it be for you to listen to Rabadash's words and not respond in kind? What principle underlies the King's direction to Corin, never to taunt a man unless he is stronger than you?

A Clever Defense

BRING OUT THAT CREATURE," said Aslan. One of the Elephants lifted Uncle Andrew in its trunk and laid him at the Lion's feet. He was too frightened to move.

"Please, Aslan," said Polly, "could you say something to—to unfrighten him? And then could you say something to prevent him from ever coming back here again?"

"Do you think he *wants* to?" said Aslan.

"Well, Aslan," said Polly, "he might send someone else. He's so excited about the bar off the lamp-post growing into a lamp-post tree and he thinks—"

"He thinks great folly, child," said Aslan. "This world is bursting with life for these few days because the song with which I called it into life still hangs in the air and rumbles in the ground. It will not be so for long. But I cannot tell that to this old sinner, and I cannot comfort him either; he has made himself unable to hear my voice. If I spoke to him, he would hear only growlings and roarings. Oh, Adam's sons, how cleverly you defend yourselves against all that might do you good! But I will give him the only gift he is still able to receive."

He bowed his great head rather sadly, and breathed into the Magician's terrified face. "Sleep," he said. "Sleep and be separated for some few hours from all the torments you have devised for yourself." Uncle Andrew immediately rolled over with closed eyes and began breathing peacefully.

—*The Magician's Nephew*

How does it affect your thinking to see Uncle Andrew's actions called a defense? What defenses do you put up against things in your life that might do you good?

Narnians to the Rescue

[JILL] LEANED AS FAR OUT of the hole as she could, and yelled to the dancers.

"Help! Help! We're buried in the hill. Come and dig us out."

The Narnians, who had not even noticed the little hole in the hillside, were of course very surprised, and looked about in several wrong directions before they found out where the voice was coming from. But when they caught sight of Jill they all came running toward her, and as many as could scrambled up the bank, and a dozen or more hands were stretched up to help her. And Jill caught hold of them and thus got out of the hole and came slithering down the bank head first, and then picked herself up and said:

"Oh, do go and dig the others out. There are three others, besides the horses. And one of them is Prince Rilian."

She was already in the middle of a crowd when she said this, for besides the dancers all sorts of people who had been watching the dance, and whom she had not seen at first, came running up. Squirrels came out of the trees in showers, and so did Owls. Hedgehogs came waddling as fast as their short legs would carry them. Bears and Badgers followed at a slower pace. A great Panther, twitching its tail in excitement, was the last to join the party.

But as soon as they understood what Jill was saying, they all became active. "Pick and shovel, boys, pick and shovel. Off for our tools!" said the Dwarfs, and dashed away into the woods at top speed. "Wake up some Moles, they're the chaps for digging. They're quite as good as Dwarfs," said a voice. "What was that she said about Prince Rilian?" said another. "Hush!" said the Panther. "The poor child's crazed, and no wonder after being lost inside the hill. She doesn't know what she's saying." "That's right," said an old Bear. "Why, she said Prince Rilian was a horse!"—"No, she didn't," said a Squirrel, very pert. "Yes, she did," said another Squirrel, even perter.

"It's quite t-t-t-true. D-d-don't be so silly," said Jill. She spoke like that because her teeth were now chattering with the cold.

Immediately one of the Dryads flung round her a furry cloak which some Dwarf had dropped when he rushed to fetch his mining tools, and an obliging Faun trotted off among the trees to a place where Jill could see firelight in the mouth of a cave, to get her a hot drink.

—The Silver Chair

What does it say about Narnia that everyone is so quick to jump to Jill's help, without even understanding who she is and how she has gotten in this situation? How might this same scenario have played out in our world?

Why Can't We See Aslan Properly?

[THE APE SAID,] "Now attend to me. I want—I mean, Aslan wants—some more nuts. These you've brought aren't anything like enough. You must bring some more, do you hear? Twice as many. And they've got to be here by sunset tomorrow, and there mustn't be any bad ones or any small ones among them."

A murmur of dismay ran through the other squirrels, and the Head Squirrel plucked up courage to say:

"Please, would Aslan himself speak to us about it? If we might be allowed to see him—"

"Well, you won't," said the Ape. "He may be very kind (though it's a lot more than most of you deserve) and come out for a few minutes tonight. Then you can all have a look at him. But he will *not* have you all crowding round him and pestering him with questions. Anything you want to say to him will be passed on through me: if I think it's worth bothering him about. In the meantime all you squirrels had better go and see about the nuts. And make sure they are here by tomorrow evening or, my word! you'll catch it!"

The poor squirrels all scampered away as if a dog were after them. This new order was terrible news for them. The nuts they had carefully hoarded for the winter had nearly all been eaten by now; and of the few that were left they had already given the Ape far more than they could spare.

Then a deep voice—it belonged to a great tusked and shaggy Boar—spoke from another part of the crowd.

"But *why* can't we see Aslan properly and talk to him?" it said. "When he used to appear in Narnia in the old days everyone could talk to him face to face."

"Don't you believe it," said the Ape. "And even if it was true, times have changed. Aslan says he's been far too soft with you before, do you see? Well, he isn't going to be soft any more. He's going to lick you into shape this time. He'll teach you to think he's a tame lion!"

A low moaning and whimpering was heard among the Beasts; and after that, a dead silence which was more miserable still.

"And now there's another thing you got to learn," said the Ape. "I hear some of you are saying I'm an Ape. Well, I'm not. I'm a Man. If I look like an Ape, that's because I'm so very old: hundreds and hundreds of years old. And it's because I'm so old that I'm so wise. And it's because I'm so wise that I'm the only one Aslan is ever going to speak to. He can't be bothered talking to a lot of stupid animals. He'll tell me what you've got to do, and I'll tell the rest of you. And take my advice, and see you do it in double quick time, for he doesn't mean to stand any nonsense."

—*The Last Battle*

Why do the animals want to speak face to face with Aslan? Why are they reluctant to challenge the Ape further? What are the dangers of receiving information secondhand?

The Wonderful Mystery

"HAVE NONE OF YOU guessed where we are?" said Peter.
"Go on, go on," said Lucy. "I've felt for hours that there was some wonderful mystery hanging over this place."

"Fire ahead, Peter," said Edmund. "We're all listening."

"We are in the ruins of Cair Paravel itself," said Peter.

"But, I say," replied Edmund. "I mean, how do you make that out? This place has been ruined for ages. Look at all those big trees growing right up to the gates. Look at the very stones. Anyone can see that nobody has lived here for hundreds of years."

"I know," said Peter. "That is the difficulty. But let's leave that out for the moment. I want to take the points one by one. First point: this hall is exactly the same shape and size as the hall at Cair Paravel. Just picture a roof on this, and a colored pavement instead of grass, and tapestries on the walls, and you get our royal banqueting hall."

No one said anything.

"Second point," continued Peter. "The castle well is exactly where our well was, a little to the south of the great hall; and it is exactly the same size and shape.". . .

"Third point: Susan has just found one of our old chessmen—or something as like one of them as two peas.". . .

"Fourth point. Don't you remember—it was the very day before the ambassadors came from the King of Calormen—don't you remember planting the orchard outside the north gate of Cair Paravel? . . . Can you have forgotten that funny old Lilygloves, the chief mole, leaning on his spade and saying, 'Believe me, your Majesty, you'll be glad of these fruit trees one day.' And by Jove he was right."

"I do! I do!" said Lucy, and clapped her hands.

—*Prince Caspian*

Would you take as much pleasure as Lucy does in the wonderful mystery? Why might the others feel reluctant to recognize the ruined castle as their former home?

Reepicheep Corrects Eustace

EUSTACE CAME RUSHING IN, wringing his hands and shouting out:

"That little brute has half killed me. I insist on it being kept under control. I could bring an action against you, Caspian. I could order you to have it destroyed."

At the same moment Reepicheep appeared. His sword was drawn and his whiskers looked very fierce but he was as polite as ever.

"I ask your pardons all," he said, "and especially her Majesty's. If I had known that he would take refuge here I would have awaited a more reasonable time for his correction."

"What on earth's up?" asked Edmund.

What had really happened was this. Reepicheep, who never felt that the ship was getting on fast enough, loved to sit on the bulwarks far forward just beside the dragon's head, gazing out at the eastern horizon and singing softly in his little chirruping voice the song the Dryad had made for him. He never held on to anything, however the ship pitched, and kept his balance with perfect ease; perhaps his long tail, hanging down to the deck inside the bulwarks, made this easier. . . . [A]s soon as [Eustace] saw that long tail hanging down—and perhaps it was rather tempting— he thought it would be delightful to catch hold of it, swing Reepicheep round by it once or twice upside-down, then run away and laugh. At first the plan seemed to work beautifully. The Mouse was not much heavier than a very large cat. Eustace had him off the rail in a trice and very silly he looked (thought Eustace) with his little limbs all splayed out and his mouth open. But unfortunately Reepicheep, who had fought for his life many a time, never lost his head even for a moment. Nor his skill. It is not very easy to draw one's sword when one is swinging round in the air by one's tail, but he did. And the next thing Eustace knew was two agonizing jabs in his hand which made him let go of the tail; and the next thing after that was that the Mouse had picked itself up again as if it were a ball bouncing off the deck, and there it was facing him, and a horrid long, bright, sharp thing like a skewer was waving to and fro within an inch of his stomach. . . .

"Stop it," spluttered Eustace, "go away. Put that thing away. It's not safe. Stop it, I say. I'll tell Caspian. I'll have you muzzled and tied up."

"Why do you not draw your own sword, poltroon!" cheeped the Mouse. "Draw and fight or I'll beat you black and blue with the flat."

"I haven't got one," said Eustace. "I'm a pacifist. I don't believe in fighting."

"Do I understand," said Reepicheep, withdrawing his sword for a moment and speaking very sternly, "that you do not intend to give me satisfaction?"

"I don't know what you mean," said Eustace, nursing his hand. "If you don't know how to take a joke I shan't bother my head about you."

"Then take that," said Reepicheep, "and that—to teach you manners—and the respect due to a knight—and a Mouse—and a Mouse's tail—" and at each word he gave Eustace a blow with the side of his rapier.

—*The Voyage of the* **Dawn Treader**

Would you characterize Reepicheep's actions as a correction to Eustace? Why or why not? Do either Reepicheep or Eustace overreact?

When I'm King

IT WAS PRETTY BAD when [Edmund] reached the far side. It was growing darker every minute and what with that and the snowflakes swirling all round him he could hardly see three feet ahead. And then too there was no road. He kept slipping into deep drifts of snow, and skidding on frozen puddles, and tripping over fallen tree-trunks, and sliding down steep banks, and barking his shins against rocks, till he was wet and cold and bruised all over. The silence and the loneliness were dreadful. In fact I really think he might have given up the whole plan and gone back and owned up and made friends with the others, if he hadn't happened to say to himself, "When I'm King of Narnia the first thing I shall do will be to make some decent roads." And of course that set him off thinking about being a King and all the other things he would do and this cheered him up a good deal. He had just settled in his mind what sort of palace he would have and how many cars and all about his private cinema and where the principal railways would run and what laws he would make against beavers and dams and was putting the finishing touches to some schemes for keeping Peter in his place, when the weather changed.

—The Lion, the Witch, and the Wardrobe

What about the idea of being King keeps Edmund from giving up on trying to find the Witch? What about being a King or Queen would tempt you?

The Helpful Dragon

IT WAS, HOWEVER, clear to everyone that Eustace's character had been rather improved by becoming a dragon. He was anxious to help. He flew over the whole island and found it was all mountainous and inhabited only by wild goats and droves of wild swine. Of these he brought back many carcasses as provisions for the ship. He was a very humane killer too, for he could dispatch a beast with one blow of his tail so that it didn't know (and presumably still doesn't know) it had been killed. He ate a few himself, of course, but always alone, for now that he was a dragon he liked his food raw but he could never bear to let others see him at his messy meals. And one day, flying slowly and wearily but in great triumph, he bore back to camp a great tall pine tree which he had torn up by the roots in a distant valley and which could be made into a capital mast. And in the evening if it turned chilly, as it sometimes did after the heavy rains, he was a comfort to everyone, for the whole party would come and sit with their backs against his hot sides and get well warmed and dried; and one puff of his fiery breath would light the most obstinate fire. Sometimes he would take a select party for a fly on his back, so that they could see wheeling below them the green slopes, the rocky heights, the narrow pit-like valleys and far out over the sea to the eastward a spot of darker blue on the blue horizon which might be land.

The pleasure (quite new to him) of being liked and, still more, of liking other people, was what kept Eustace from despair. For it was very dreary being a dragon.

—*The Voyage of the* **Dawn Treader**

Why might being turned into a dragon finally make the sulky and reluctant Eustace a help to the rest of the sailing party? How must Eustace feel to be liked and to like others for the first time?

I Must Have Her

"BUT I *WANT HER*," cried the Prince. "I must have her. I shall die if I do not get her—false, proud, black-hearted daughter of a dog that she is! I cannot sleep and my food has no savor and my eyes are darkened because of her beauty. I must have the barbarian queen."

"How well it was said by a gifted poet," observed the Vizier, raising his face (in a somewhat dusty condition) from the carpet, "that deep drafts from the fountain of reason are desirable in order to extinguish the fire of youthful love."

This seemed to exasperate the Prince. "Dog," he shouted, directing a series of well-aimed kicks at the hindquarters of the Vizier, "do not dare to quote the poets to me. I have had maxims and verses flung at me all day and I can endure them no more."

—*The Horse and His Boy*

Why do you think the Prince wants Queen Susan so badly, even though he just described her in unflattering terms? When have you wanted someone or something so much? What was your desire based on?

The Voyage's Goal

"AND WHERE ARE WE HEADING FOR?" asked Edmund. "Well," said Caspian, "that's rather a long story. Perhaps you remember that when I was a child my usurping uncle Miraz got rid of seven friends of my father's (who might have taken my part) by sending them off to explore the unknown Eastern Seas beyond the Lone Islands."

"Yes," said Lucy, "and none of them ever came back."

"Right. Well, on my coronation day, with Aslan's approval, I swore an oath that, if once I established peace in Narnia, I would sail east myself for a year and a day to find my father's friends or to learn of their deaths and avenge them if I could. . . . That is my main intention. But Reepicheep here has an even higher hope." Everyone's eyes turned to the Mouse.

"As high as my spirit," it said. "Though perhaps as small as my stature. Why should we not come to the very eastern end of the world? And what might we find there? I expect to find Aslan's own country. It is always from the east, across the sea, that the great Lion comes to us."

"I say, that *is* an idea," said Edmund in an awed voice.

"But do you think," said Lucy, "Aslan's country would be that sort of country—I mean, the sort you could ever *sail* to?"

"I do not know, Madam," said Reepicheep. "But there is this. When I was in my cradle, a wood woman, a Dryad, spoke this verse over me:

Where sky and water meet,
Where the waves grow sweet,
Doubt not, Reepicheep,
To find all you seek,
There is the utter East.

"I do not know what it means. But the spell of it has been on me all my life."

—*The Voyage of the* Dawn Treader

What does it mean that Aslan's country might be one you cannot sail to?

Jill's Dream

THE RAIN FELL STEADILY all the evening and all the night, dashing against the windows of the castle, and Jill never heard it but slept deeply, past supper time and past midnight. And then came the deadest hour of the night and nothing stirred but mice in the house of the giants. At that hour there came to Jill a dream. It seemed to her that she awoke in the same room and saw the fire, sunk low and red, and in the firelight the great wooden horse. And the horse came of its own will, rolling on its wheels across the carpet, and stood at her head. And now it was no longer a horse, but a lion as big as the horse. And then it was not a toy lion, but a real lion, The Real Lion, just as she had seen him on the mountain beyond the world's end. And a smell of all sweet-smelling things there are filled the room. But there was some trouble in Jill's mind, though she could not think what it was, and the tears streamed down her face and wet the pillow. The Lion told her to repeat the signs, and she found that she had forgotten them all. At that, a great horror came over her. And Aslan took her up in his jaws (she could feel his lips and his breath but not his teeth) and carried her to the window and made her look out. The moon shone bright; and written in great letters across the world or the sky (she did not know which) were the words UNDER ME. After that, the dream faded away, and when she woke, very late next morning, she did not remember that she had dreamed at all.

—*The Silver Chair*

How does the dream-Aslan respond when Jill fails to remember the signs? When have you let someone down? How did he or she respond?

The Slave No One Would Buy

[CASPIAN ASKED,] "But where is my other friend?"

"Oh, *him*?" said Pug. "Oh, take *him* and welcome. Glad to have him off my hands. I've never seen such a drug in the market in all my born days. Priced him at five crescents in the end and even so nobody'd have him. Threw him in free with other lots and still no one would have him. Wouldn't touch him. Wouldn't look at him. Tacks, bring out Sulky."

Thus Eustace was produced, and sulky he certainly looked; for though no one would want to be sold as a slave, it is perhaps even more galling to be a sort of utility slave whom no one will buy. He walked up to Caspian and said, "I see. As usual. Been enjoying yourself somewhere while the rest of us were prisoners. I suppose you haven't even found out about the British Consul. Of course not."

—*The Voyage of the* Dawn Treader

Poor Eustace. No one even wants him as a slave. How would you feel if you were in his shoes? Would you respond the way he does to the one who had freed you?

Grief in Narnia

[D]IGORY] THOUGHT OF HIS MOTHER, and he thought of the great hopes he had had, and how they were all dying away, and a lump came into his throat and tears in his eyes, and he blurted out:

"But please, please—won't you—can't you give me something that will cure Mother?" Up till then he had been looking at the Lion's great feet and the huge claws on them; now, in his despair, he looked up at its face. What he saw surprised him as much as anything in his whole life. For the tawny face was bent down near his own and (wonder of wonders) great shining tears stood in the Lion's eyes. They were such big, bright tears compared with Digory's own that for a moment he felt as if the Lion must really be sorrier about his Mother than he was himself.

"My son, my son," said Aslan. "I know. Grief is great. Only you and I in this land know that yet. Let us be good to one another."

—*The Magician's Nephew*

Why would Aslan have such empathy for Digory's mother but still not grant his wish? What is the power of empathy in a situation like Digory's?

JULY 21

Finding the Battle

A T THIS POINT Aslan clapped his paws together and called for silence.

"Our day's work is not yet over," he said, "and if the Witch is to be finally defeated before bedtime we must find the battle at once."

"And join in, I hope, sir!" added the largest of the Centaurs.

"Of course," said Aslan. "And now! Those who can't keep up—that is, children, dwarfs, and small animals—must ride on the backs of those who can—that is, lions, centaurs, unicorns, horses, giants and eagles. Those who are good with their noses must come in the front with us lions to smell out where the battle is. Look lively and sort yourselves."

And with a great deal of bustle and cheering they did. The most pleased of the lot was the other lion who kept running about everywhere pretending to be very busy but really in order to say to everyone he met, "Did you hear what he said? *Us Lions.* That means him and me. *Us Lions.* That's what I like about Aslan. No side, no stand-off-ishness. *Us Lions.* That meant him and me." At least he went on saying this till Aslan had loaded him up with three dwarfs, one dryad, two rabbits, and a hedgehog. That steadied him a bit.

—*The Lion, the Witch, and the Wardrobe*

What does it mean for the lion to feel put on the same level as Aslan himself? What does this reveal about Aslan's leadership style?

Caspian Continues His Journey

CASPIAN MISSED NO CHANCE of questioning all the oldest sea captains whom he could find in Narrowhaven to learn if they had any knowledge or even any rumors of land further to the east. He poured out many a flagon of the castle ale to weather-beaten men with short grey beards and clear blue eyes, and many a tall yarn he heard in return. But those who seemed the most truthful could tell of no lands beyond the Lone Islands, and many thought that if you sailed too far east you would come into the surges of a sea without lands that swirled perpetually round the rim of the world—"And that, I reckon, is where your Majesty's friends went to the bottom." The rest had only wild stories of islands inhabited by headless men, floating islands, waterspouts, and a fire that burned along the water. Only one, to Reepicheep's delight, said, "And beyond that, Aslan's country. But that's beyond the end of the world and you can't get there." But when they questioned him he could only say that he'd heard it from his father.

Bern could only tell them that he had seen his six companions sail away eastward and that nothing had ever been heard of them again. He said this when he and Caspian were standing on the highest point of Avra looking down on the eastern ocean. "I've often been up here of a morning," said the Duke, "and seen the sun come up out of the sea, and sometimes it looked as if it were only a couple of miles away. And I've wondered about my friends and wondered what there really is behind that horizon. Nothing, most likely, yet I am always half ashamed that I stayed behind. But I wish your Majesty wouldn't go. . . ."

"I have an oath, my lord Duke," said Caspian. "And anyway, what *could* I say to Reepicheep?"

—*The Voyage of the* Dawn Treader

Despite what seems like almost no chance of success, Caspian chooses to continue his voyage rather than stay in Narrowhaven. Is his decision foolhardy? Why or why not? Do you think he is placing too much importance on his oath to find the other six lords who supported his father when he was King? When have you had to make a difficult choice in order to keep a promise?

The Ape in Its Glory

A T THE CENTER OF THE CLEARING, which was also the highest point of the hill, there was a little hut like a stable, with a thatched roof. Its door was shut. On the grass in front of the door there sat an Ape. Tirian and Jewel, who had been expecting to see Aslan and had heard nothing about an Ape yet, were very bewildered when they saw it. The Ape was of course Shift himself, but he looked ten times uglier than when he lived by Caldron Pool, for he was now dressed up. He was wearing a scarlet jacket which did not fit him very well, having been made for a dwarf. He had jeweled slippers on his hind paws which would not stay on properly because, as you know, the hind paws of an Ape are really like hands. He wore what seemed to be a paper crown on his head. There was a great pile of nuts beside him and he kept cracking nuts with his jaws and spitting out the shells. And he also kept on pulling up the scarlet jacket to scratch himself. A great number of Talking Beasts stood facing him, and nearly every face in that crowd looked miserably worried and bewildered. When they saw who the prisoners were they all groaned and whimpered.

"O Lord Shift, mouthpiece of Aslan," said the chief Calormene. "We bring you prisoners. By our skill and courage and by the permission of the great god Tash we have taken alive these two desperate murderers."

"Give me that man's sword," said the Ape. So they took the King's sword and handed it, with the sword-belt and all, to the monkey. And he hung it round his own neck: and it made him look sillier than ever.

—*The Last Battle*

Why does the Ape look silly? How does the Ape think he looks? Have you ever put on a front you thought was impressive, only to realize later that you looked more ridiculous than remarkable?

The Treasure in the Dragon's Lair

THE CLIMATE of this island was a very unpleasant one. In less than a minute Eustace was wet to the skin and half blinded with such rain as one never sees in Europe. There was no use trying to climb out of the valley as long as this lasted. He bolted for the only shelter in sight—the dragon's cave. There he lay down and tried to get his breath.

Most of us know what we should expect to find in a dragon's lair but, as I said before, Eustace had read only the wrong books. They had a lot to say about exports and imports and governments and drains, but they were weak on dragons. That is why he was so puzzled at the surface on which he was lying. Parts of it were too prickly to be stones and too hard to be thorns, and there seemed to be a great many round, flat things, and it all clinked when he moved. There was light enough at the cave's mouth to examine it by. And of course Eustace found it to be what any of us could have told him in advance—treasure. There were crowns (those were the prickly things), coins, rings, bracelets, ingots, cups, plates and gems.

Eustace (unlike most boys) had never thought much of treasure but he saw at once the use it would be in this new world which he had so foolishly stumbled into through the picture in Lucy's bedroom at home. "They don't have any tax here," he said. "And you don't have to give treasure to the government. With some of this stuff I could have quite a decent time here—perhaps in Calormen. It sounds the least phony of these countries. I wonder how much I can carry? That bracelet now—those things in it are probably diamonds—I'll slip that on my own wrist. Too big, but not if I push it right up here above my elbow. Then fill my pockets with diamonds—that's easier than gold. I wonder when this infernal rain's going to let up?" He got into a less uncomfortable part of the pile, where it was mostly coins, and settled down to wait. But a bad fright, when once it is over, and especially a bad fright following a mountain walk, leaves you very tired. Eustace fell asleep.

—*The Voyage of the* **Dawn Treader**

Until this point, Eustace's main concern has been getting back to the others and the Dawn Treader. *Why does finding treasure make him change his mind? What promises do treasure and riches hold for you?*

What If We Get Killed Here?

THIS TIME JILL AND EUSTACE walked together. They had been feeling very brave when they were begging to be allowed to come with the others, but now they didn't feel brave at all.

"Pole," said Eustace in a whisper. "I may as well tell you I've got the wind up."

"Oh, *you're* all right, Scrubb," said Jill. "You can fight. But I—I'm just shaking, if you want to know the truth."

"Oh, shaking's nothing," said Eustace. "I'm feeling I'm going to be sick. . . .

"Pole," said Eustace presently.

"What?" said she.

"What'll happen if we get killed here?"

"Well we'll be dead, I suppose."

"But I mean, what will happen in our own world? Shall we wake up and find ourselves back in that train? Or shall we just vanish and never be heard of any more? Or shall we be dead in England?"

"Gosh. I never thought of that."

"It'll be rum for Peter and the others if they saw me waving out of the window and then when the train comes in we're nowhere to be found! Or if they found two—I mean, if we're dead over there in England."

"Ugh!" said Jill. "What a horrid idea."

"It wouldn't be horrid for *us*," said Eustace. "We shouldn't be there."

"I almost wish—no I don't, though," said Jill.

"What were you going to say?"

"I *was* going to say I wished we'd never come. But I don't, I don't, I don't. Even if we *are* killed. I'd rather be killed fighting for Narnia than grow old and stupid at home and perhaps go about in a bath-chair and then die in the end just the same."

—*The Last Battle*

What about Jill has changed that she'd rather "be killed fighting for Narnia than grow old and stupid at home"? Do you agree with her?

Governor Gumpas

CASPIAN THEN ORDERED most of his own men to remain in the courtyard. He, with Bern and Drinian and four others, went into the hall.

Behind a table at the far end with various secretaries about him sat his Sufficiency, the Governor of the Lone Islands. Gumpas was a bilious-looking man with hair that had once been red and was now mostly grey. He glanced up as the strangers entered and then looked down at his papers saying automatically, "No interviews without appointments except between nine and ten P.M. on second Saturdays."

Caspian nodded to Bern and then stood aside. Bern and Drinian took a step forward and each seized one end of the table. They lifted it, and flung it on one side of the hall where it rolled over, scattering a cascade of letters, dossiers, ink-pots, pens, sealing-wax and documents. Then, not roughly but as firmly as if their hands were pincers of steel, they plucked Gumpas out of his chair and deposited him, facing it, about four feet away. Caspian at once sat down in the chair and laid his naked sword across his knees.

"My Lord," said he, fixing his eyes on Gumpas, "you have not given us quite the welcome we expected. We are the King of Narnia."

"Nothing about it in the correspondence," said the governor. "Nothing in the minutes. We have not been notified of any such thing. All irregular. Happy to consider any applications—"

"And we are come to inquire into your Sufficiency's conduct of your office," continued Caspian. "There are two points especially on which I require an explanation. Firstly I find no record that the tribute due from these islands to the crown of Narnia has been received for about a hundred and fifty years."

"That would be a question to raise at the Council next month," said Gumpas. "If anyone moves that a commission of inquiry be set up to report on the financial history of the islands at the first meeting next year, why then . . ."

"I also find it very clearly written in our laws," Caspian went on, "that if the tribute is not delivered, the whole debt has to be paid by the Governor of the Lone Islands out of his private purse."

At this Gumpas began to pay real attention. "Oh, that's quite out of the question," he said. "It is an economic impossibility—er—your Majesty must be joking."

Inside, he was wondering if there were any way of getting rid of these unwelcome visitors. Had he known that Caspian had only one ship and one ship's company with him, he would have spoken soft words for the moment, and hoped to have them all surrounded and killed during the night. But he had seen a ship of war sail down the straits yesterday and seen it signaling, as he supposed, to its consorts. He had not then known it was the King's ship for there was not wind enough to spread the flag out and make the golden lion visible, so he had waited further developments. Now he imagined that Caspian had a whole fleet at Bernstead. It would never have occurred to Gumpas that anyone would walk into Narrowhaven to take the islands with fewer than fifty men; it was certainly not at all the kind of thing he could imagine doing himself.

—*The Voyage of the* **Dawn Treader**

How does this passage illustrate the differences between Gumpas and Caspian as leaders? Why does Gumpas hardly react at all to Caspian, at least at first? Have you ever known people who were so wrapped up in order and method that they failed to see what was in front of their eyes? When have you been guilty of this?

Other Powers

[NIKABRIK SAID,] "The stories tell of other powers besides the ancient Kings and Queens. How if we could call *them* up?"

"If you mean Aslan," said Trufflehunter, "it's all one calling on him and on the Kings. They were his servants. If he will not send them (but I make no doubt he will), is he more likely to come himself?"

"No. You're right there," said Nikabrik. "Aslan and the Kings go together. Either Aslan is dead, or he is not on our side. Or else something stronger than himself keeps him back. And if he did come—how do we know he'd be our friend? He was not always a good friend to Dwarfs by all that's told. Not even to all beasts. Ask the Wolves. And anyway, he was in Narnia only once that I ever heard of, and he didn't stay long. You may drop Aslan out of the reckoning. I was thinking of someone else. . . . I mean a power so much greater than Aslan's that it held Narnia spellbound for years and years, if the stories are true."

"The White Witch!" cried three voices all at once, and from the noise Peter guessed that three people had leaped to their feet.

"Yes," said Nikabrik very slowly and distinctly, "I mean the Witch. Sit down again. Don't all take fright at a name as if you were children. We want power: and we want a power that will be on our side. As for power, do not the stories say that the Witch defeated Aslan, and bound him, and killed him on that very Stone which is over there, just beyond the light?"

"But they also say that he came to life again," said the Badger sharply.

"Yes, they *say*," answered Nikabrik, "but you'll notice that we hear precious little about anything he did afterward. He just fades out of the story. How do you explain that, if he really came to life? Isn't it much more likely that he didn't, and that the stories say nothing more about him because there was nothing more to say? . . . But it's very different with the Witch. They say she ruled for a hundred years: a hundred years of winter. There's power, if you like. There's something practical."

"But, heaven and earth!" said the King, "haven't we always been told that she was the worst enemy of all? Wasn't she a tyrant ten times worse than Miraz?"

"Perhaps," said Nikabrik in a cold voice. "Perhaps she *was* for you humans, if there were any of you in those days. Perhaps she was for some of the beasts. She stamped out the Beavers, I dare say; at least there are none of them in Narnia now. But she got on all right with us Dwarfs. I'm a Dwarf and I stand by my own people. *We're* not afraid of the Witch."

—*Prince Caspian*

Why does Nikabrik want to bring back the White Witch? What kind of power does he seem to be seeking?

No Longer a Friend of Narnia

"SIRE," SAID TIRIAN, when he had greeted all these. "If I have read the chronicle aright, there should be another. Has not your Majesty two sisters? Where is Queen Susan?"

"My sister Susan," answered Peter shortly and gravely, "is no longer a friend of Narnia."

"Yes," said Eustace, "and whenever you've tried to get her to come and talk about Narnia or do anything about Narnia, she says 'What wonderful memories you have! Fancy your still thinking about all those funny games we used to play when we were children.'"

"Oh Susan!" said Jill. "She's interested in nothing nowadays except nylons and lipstick and invitations. She always was a jolly sight too keen on being grown-up."

"Grown-up, indeed," said the Lady Polly. "I wish she *would* grow up. She wasted all her school time wanting to be the age she is now, and she'll waste all the rest of her life trying to stay that age. Her whole idea is to race on to the silliest time of one's life as quick as she can and then stop there as long as she can."

"Well, don't let's talk about that now," said Peter.

—*The Last Battle*

Do you find yourself trying to rush ahead or stay in one phase of life? How is that a waste?

Lucy and the Dragon

BUT WHEN [THE DRAGON] SAW THEM, instead of rising up and blowing fire and smoke, the dragon retreated—you could almost say it waddled—back into the shallows of the bay.

"What's it wagging its head like that for?" said Edmund.

"And now it's nodding," said Caspian.

"And there's something coming from its eyes," said Drinian.

"Oh, can't you see?" said Lucy. "It's crying. Those are tears."

"I shouldn't trust to that, Ma'am," said Drinian. "That's what crocodiles do, to put you off your guard."

"It wagged its head when you said that," remarked Edmund. "Just as if it meant No. Look, there it goes again."

"Do you think it understands what we're saying?" asked Lucy.

The dragon nodded its head violently.

Reepicheep slipped off Lucy's shoulder and stepped to the front.

"Dragon," came his shrill voice, "can you understand speech?"

The dragon nodded.

"Can you speak?"

It shook its head.

"Then," said Reepicheep, "it is idle to ask you your business. But if you will swear friendship with us raise your left foreleg above your head."

It did so, but clumsily because that leg was sore and swollen with the golden bracelet.

"Oh look," said Lucy, "there's something wrong with its leg. The poor thing—that's probably what it was crying about. Perhaps it came to us to be cured like in Androcles and the lion."

"Be careful, Lucy," said Caspian. "It's a very clever dragon but it may be a liar."

Lucy had, however, already run forward. . . .

—*The Voyage of the* **Dawn Treader**

Why do you think Lucy runs forward? Should she have heeded Caspian's warning? Would you be more inclined to advise caution, as Caspian does, or to run forward, as Lucy does?

Unnatural Habits

[EUSTACE ASKED,] "If this owls' parliament, as you call it, is all fair and above board and means no mischief, why does it have to be so jolly secret—meeting in a ruin in dead of night, and all that?"

"Tu-whoo! Tu-whoo!" hooted several owls. "Where should we meet? When would anyone meet except at night?"

"You see," explained Glimfeather, "most of the creatures in Narnia have such unnatural habits. They do things by day, in broad blazing sunlight (ugh!) when everyone ought to be asleep. And, as a result, at night they're so blind and stupid that you can't get a word out of them. So we owls have got into the habit of meeting at sensible hours, on our own, when we want to talk about things."

—*The Silver Chair*

Why do we expect others to conform to what's normal for us?

Deep Magic

Y OU HAVE A TRAITOR THERE, Aslan," said the Witch. Of course everyone present knew that she meant Edmund. But Edmund had got past thinking about himself after all he'd been through and after the talk he'd had that morning. He just went on looking at Aslan. It didn't seem to matter what the Witch said.

"Well," said Aslan. "His offense was not against you."

"Have you forgotten the Deep Magic?" asked the Witch.

"Let us say I have forgotten it," answered Aslan gravely. "Tell us of this Deep Magic."

"Tell you?" said the Witch, her voice growing suddenly shriller. "Tell you what is written on that very Table of Stone which stands beside us? Tell you what is written in letters deep as a spear is long on the fire-stones on the Secret Hill? Tell you what is engraved on the scepter of the Emperor-beyond-the-Sea? You at least know the Magic which the Emperor put into Narnia at the very beginning. You know that every traitor belongs to me as my lawful prey and that for every treachery I have a right to a kill. . . .

"And so," continued the Witch, "that human creature is mine. His life is forfeit to me. His blood is my property."

"Come and take it then," said the Bull with the man's head in a great bellowing voice.

"Fool," said the Witch with a savage smile that was almost a snarl, "do you really think your master can rob me of my rights by mere force? He knows the Deep Magic better than that. He knows that unless I have blood as the Law says all Narnia will be overturned and perish in fire and water."

"It is very true," said Aslan, "I do not deny it."

—*The Lion, the Witch, and the Wardrobe*

What makes betrayal, or treachery, worthy of such a punishment in Narnia? Is betrayal worse than other crimes, such as murder? Why or why not?

AUGUST

Back to Narnia

IT WAS AN EMPTY, SLEEPY, country station and there was hardly anyone on the platform except themselves. Suddenly Lucy gave a sharp little cry, like someone who has been stung by a wasp.

"What's up, Lu?" said Edmund—and then suddenly broke off and made a noise like "Ow!"

"What on earth—" began Peter, and then he too suddenly changed what he had been going to say. Instead, he said, "Susan, let go! What are you doing? Where are you dragging me to?"

"I'm not touching you," said Susan. "Someone is pulling *me*. Oh—oh—oh—stop it!"

Everyone noticed that all the others' faces had gone very white.

"I felt just the same," said Edmund in a breathless voice. "As if I were being dragged along. A most frightful pulling—ugh! it's beginning again."

"Me too," said Lucy. "Oh, I can't bear it."

"Look sharp!" shouted Edmund. "All catch hands and keep together. This is magic—I can tell by the feeling. Quick!"

"Yes," said Susan. "Hold hands. Oh, I do wish it would stop—oh!"

Next moment the luggage, the seat, the platform, and the station had completely vanished. The four children, holding hands and panting, found themselves standing in a woody place—such a woody place that branches were sticking into them and there was hardly room to move. They all rubbed their eyes and took a deep breath.

"Oh, Peter!" exclaimed Lucy. "Do you think we can possibly have got back to Narnia?"

—*Prince Caspian*

Edmund identifies the feeling they all share as magic. Do you believe in magic? When have you felt something so powerful it seemed magical?

A Very Good Answer

"COME HERE," SAID THE LION. And she had to. She was almost between its front paws now, looking straight into its face. But she couldn't stand that for long; she dropped her eyes.

"Human Child," said the Lion. "Where is the Boy?"

"He fell over the cliff," said Jill, and added, "Sir." She didn't know what else to call him, and it sounded cheek to call him nothing.

"How did he come to do that, Human Child?"

"He was trying to stop me from falling, Sir."

"Why were you so near the edge, Human Child?"

"I was showing off, Sir."

"That is a very good answer, Human Child. Do so no more."

—*The Silver Chair*

Why is Jill's response such a good answer? Could you have admitted to your weakness so quickly?

A Crazy Idea

BUT AS THE SUN SLOWLY, slowly climbed up to the top of the sky and then slowly, slowly began going downward to the West, and no one came and nothing at all happened, [Shasta] began to get more and more anxious. And of course he now realized that when they arranged to wait for one another at the Tombs no one had said anything about How Long. He couldn't wait here for the rest of his life! And soon it would be dark again, and he would have another night just like last night. A dozen different plans went through his head, all wretched ones, and at last he fixed on the worst plan of all. He decided to wait till it was dark and then go back to the river and steal as many melons as he could carry and set out for Mount Pire alone, trusting for his direction to the line he had drawn that morning in the sand. It was a crazy idea and if he had read as many books as you have about journeys over deserts he would never have dreamed of it. But Shasta had read no books at all.

—*The Horse and His Boy*

What drives Shasta to settle on the worst plan? When have you made a poor decision because no one else was there for you to talk to or bounce ideas off? Do you tend to make better decisions with another's input or when you decide by yourself?

Eustace Is Lost

SUDDENLY IT OCCURRED TO [EUSTACE] that he might have been lying there for hours. Perhaps the others had gone! Perhaps they had let him wander away on purpose simply in order to leave him behind! He leaped up in a panic and began the descent.

At first he tried to do it too quickly, slipped on the steep grass, and slid for several feet. Then he thought this had carried him too far to the left—and as he came up he had seen precipices on that side. So he clambered up again, as near as he could guess to the place he had started from, and began the descent afresh, bearing to his right. After that things seemed to be going better. He went very cautiously, for he could not see more than a yard ahead, and there was still perfect silence all around him. It is very unpleasant to have to go cautiously when there is a voice inside you saying all the time, "Hurry, hurry, hurry." For every moment the terrible idea of being left behind grew stronger. If he had understood Caspian and the Pevensies at all he would have known, of course, that there was not the least chance of their doing any such thing. But he had persuaded himself that they were all fiends in human form.

"At last!" said Eustace as he came slithering down a slide of loose stones (*scree,* they call it) and found himself on the level. "And now, where are those trees? There *is* something dark ahead. Why, I do believe the fog is clearing."

It was. The light increased every moment and made him blink. The fog lifted. He was in an utterly unknown valley and the sea was nowhere in sight.

—*The Voyage of the* **Dawn Treader**

Eustace realizes that he might have been left behind by the other passengers of the Dawn Treader, *those whom he had so happily escaped only a short time ago. How must he feel? When have you felt the panic that comes with being left behind?*

Doctor Cornelius's True Identity

B UT, DOCTOR," SAID CASPIAN, "why do you say *my* race? After all, I suppose you're a Telmarine too."

"Am I?" said the Doctor.

"Well, you're a Man anyway," said Caspian.

"Am I?" repeated the Doctor in a deeper voice, at the same moment throwing back his hood so that Caspian could see his face clearly in the moonlight.

All at once Caspian realized the truth and felt that he ought to have realized it long before. Doctor Cornelius was so small, and so fat, and had such a very long beard. Two thoughts came into his head at the same moment. One was a thought of terror—"He's not a real man, not a man at all, he's a *Dwarf,* and he's brought me up here to kill me." The other was sheer delight—"There are real Dwarfs still, and I've seen one at last."

"So you've guessed it in the end," said Doctor Cornelius. "Or guessed it nearly right. I'm not a pure Dwarf. I have human blood in me too. Many Dwarfs escaped in the great battles and lived on, shaving their beards and wearing high-heeled shoes and pretending to be men. They have mixed with your Telmarines. I am one of those, only a half-Dwarf, and if any of my kindred, the true Dwarfs, are still alive anywhere in the world, doubtless they would despise me and call me a traitor. But never in all these years have we forgotten our own people and all the other happy creatures of Narnia, and the long-lost days of freedom."

—*Prince Caspian*

Why would a true Dwarf hate Doctor Cornelius? What is an example of a similar situation from our world? In light of the feelings of the true Dwarfs, is it surprising that Doctor Cornelius still longs for the restoration of the Old Things? Why or why not?

Jill Discovers the False Aslan

"WHAT?" SAID TIRIAN. "Where have you been? What have you done?"

"Well, Sire," said Jill. "As soon as I saw that you'd got the sentry out of the way I thought hadn't I better have a look inside the stable and see what really *is* there? So I crawled along. It was as easy as anything to draw the bolt. Of course it was pitch black inside and smelled like any other stable. Then I struck a light and—would you believe it?—there was nothing at all there but this old donkey with a bundle of lion-skin tied onto his back. So I drew my knife and told him he'd have to come along with me. As a matter of fact I needn't have threatened him with the knife at all. He was very fed up with the stable and quite ready to come—weren't you, Puzzle dear?"

"Great Scott!" said Eustace. "Well I'm—jiggered. I was jolly angry with you a moment ago, and I still think it was mean of you to sneak off without the rest of us: but I must admit—well, I mean to say—well it was a perfectly gorgeous thing to do. If she was a boy she'd have to be knighted, wouldn't she, Sire?"

"If she was a boy," said Tirian, "she'd be whipped for disobeying orders." And in the dark no one could see whether he said this with a frown or a smile. Next minute there was a sound of rasping metal.

"What are you doing, Sire?" asked Jewel sharply.

"Drawing my sword to smite off the head of the accursed Ass," said Tirian in a terrible voice. "Stand clear, girl."

"Oh don't, please don't," said Jill. "Really, you mustn't. It wasn't his fault. It was all the Ape. He didn't know any better. And he's very sorry. He's a nice Donkey. His name's Puzzle. And I've got my arms round his neck."

"Jill," said Tirian, "you are the bravest and most wood-wise of all my subjects, but also the most malapert and disobedient. Well: let the Ass live. What have you to say for yourself, Ass?"

"Me, Sire?" came the Donkey's voice. "I'm sure I'm very sorry if I've done wrong. The Ape said Aslan *wanted* me to dress up like that. And I thought he'd know. I'm not clever like him. I only did what I was told. It wasn't any fun for me living in that stable. I don't even know what's been going on outside. He never let me out except for a minute or two at night. Some days they forgot to give me any water too."

—*The Last Battle*

Despite the fact that King Tirian says Jill should be whipped for slipping away from her post and calls her "malapert and disobedient," he still allows her opinion to alter his decision about Puzzle's fate. Why do you think he changes his mind? Is this kind of flexibility a good quality in a King? Why or why not?

Of All the Poisonous Little Beasts

[PETER] BEGAN LEADING the way forward into the forest. There were heavy darkish clouds overhead and it looked as if there might be more snow before night.

"I say," began Edmund presently, "oughtn't we to be bearing a bit more to the left, that is, if we are aiming for the lamp-post?" He had forgotten for the moment that he must pretend never to have been in the wood before. The moment the words were out of his mouth he realized that he had given himself away. Everyone stopped; everyone stared at him. Peter whistled.

"So you really were here," he said, "that time Lu said she'd met you in here—and you made out she was telling lies."

There was a dead silence. "Well, of all the poisonous little beasts—" said Peter, and shrugged his shoulders and said no more. There seemed, indeed, no more to say, and presently the four resumed their journey; but Edmund was saying to himself, "I'll pay you all out for this, you pack of stuck-up, self-satisfied prigs."

—The Lion, the Witch, and the Wardrobe

Why do you think Edmund lied? What motivates you to tell untruths? Is lying sometimes easier than telling the truth?

Lucy Searches for the Magic Book

W HEN LUCY WOKE UP the next morning it was like waking up on the day of an examination or a day when you are going to the dentist. It was a lovely morning with bees buzzing in and out of her open window and the lawn outside looking very like somewhere in England. She got up and dressed and tried to talk and eat ordinarily at breakfast. Then, after being instructed by the Chief Voice about what she was to do upstairs, she bid good-bye to the others, said nothing, walked to the bottom of the stairs, and began going up them without once looking back.

It was quite light, that was one good thing. There was, indeed, a window straight ahead of her at the top of the first flight. As long as she was on that flight she could hear the *tick-tock-tick-tock* of a grandfather clock in the hall below. Then she came to the landing and had to turn to her left up the next flight; after that she couldn't hear the clock any more.

Now she had come to the top of the stairs. Lucy looked and saw a long, wide passage with a large window at the far end. Apparently the passage ran the whole length of the house. It was carved and paneled and carpeted and very many doors opened off it on each side. She stood still and couldn't hear the squeak of a mouse, or the buzzing of a fly, or the swaying of a curtain, or anything—except the beating of her own heart.

"The last doorway on the left," she said to herself. It did seem a bit hard that it should be the last. To reach it she would have to walk past room after room. And in any room there might be the magician—asleep, or awake, or invisible, or even dead. But it wouldn't do to think about that. She set out on her journey. The carpet was so thick that her feet made no noise. . . .

Before she reached the last door on the left, Lucy was beginning to wonder whether the corridor had grown longer since she began her journey and whether this was part of the magic of the house. But she got to it at last. And the door was open.

It was a large room with three big windows, and it was lined from floor to ceiling with books; more books than Lucy had ever seen before, tiny little books, fat and dumpy books, and books bigger than any church

Bible you have ever seen, all bound in leather and smelling old and learned and magical. But she knew from her instructions that she need not bother about any of these. For *the* Book, the Magic Book, was lying on a reading-desk in the very middle of the room. She saw she would have to read it standing (and anyway there were no chairs) and also that she would have to stand with her back to the door while she read it. So at once she turned to shut the door.

It wouldn't shut.

—*The Voyage of the* Dawn Treader

What do you think is the hardest part of Lucy's solitary journey? Why does having her back to an open door make her even more apprehensive? What makes you anxious the way Lucy is anxious about this task?

The Stars Never Lie

"Now, Roonwit," said the King. "Do you bring us more news of Aslan?"

Roonwit looked very grave, frowning a little.

"Sire," he said. "You know how long I have lived and studied the stars; for we Centaurs live longer than you Men, and even longer than your kind, Unicorn. Never in all my days have I seen such terrible things written in the skies as there have been nightly since this year began. The stars say nothing of the coming of Aslan, nor of peace, nor of joy. I know by my art that there have not been such disastrous conjunctions of the planets for five hundred years. It was already in my mind to come and warn your Majesty that some great evil hangs over Narnia. But last night the rumor reached me that Aslan is abroad in Narnia. Sire, do not believe this tale. It cannot be. The stars never lie, but Men and Beasts do. If Aslan were really coming to Narnia the sky would have foretold it. If he were really come, all the most gracious stars would be assembled in his honor. It is all a lie."

"A lie!" said the King fiercely. "What creature in Narnia or all the world would dare to lie on such a matter?" And, without knowing it, he laid his hand on his sword hilt.

"That I know not, Lord King," said the Centaur. "But I know there are liars on earth; there are none among the stars."

"I wonder," said Jewel, "whether Aslan might not come though all the stars foretold otherwise. He is not the slave of the stars but their Maker. Is it not said in all the old stories that He is not a tame lion?"

"Well said, well said, Jewel," cried the King. "Those are the very words: *not a tame lion*. It comes in many tales."

—*The Last Battle*

Why are Jewel and King Tirian reluctant to believe Roonwit, as certain as Roonwit sounds? Is there something you trust, as Roonwit trusts the stars?

Edmund Returns

WHEN THE OTHER CHILDREN woke up next morning (they had been sleeping on piles of cushions in the pavilion) the first thing they heard—from Mrs. Beaver—was that their brother had been rescued and brought into camp late last night; and was at that moment with Aslan. As soon as they had breakfasted they all went out, and there they saw Aslan and Edmund walking together in the dewy grass, apart from the rest of the court. There is no need to tell you (and no one ever heard) what Aslan was saying, but it was a conversation which Edmund never forgot. As the others drew nearer Aslan turned to meet them, bringing Edmund with him.

"Here is your brother," he said, "and—there is no need to talk to him about what is past."

Edmund shook hands with each of the others and said to each of them in turn, "I'm sorry," and everyone said, "That's all right." And then everyone wanted very hard to say something which would make it quite clear that they were all friends with him again—something ordinary and natural—and of course no one could think of anything in the world to say.

—*The Lion, the Witch, and the Wardrobe*

Why is there no need for us to know what Aslan said to Edmund? Would Edmund's apology be enough for you? Why or why not? Despite his apology, and their forgiveness, why is there still awkwardness?

Take of My Fruit for Others

WHEN [DIGORY] HAD COME CLOSE UP to [the gates] he saw words written on the gold with silver letters; something like this:

> Come in by the gold gates or not at all,
> Take of my fruit for others or forbear,
> For those who steal or those who climb my wall
> Shall find their heart's desire and find despair.

"*Take of my fruit for others*," said Digory to himself. "Well, that's what I'm going to do. It means I mustn't eat any myself, I suppose. . . .

He knew which was the right tree at once, partly because it stood in the very center and partly because the great silver apples with which it was loaded shone so and cast a light of their own down on the shadowy places where the sunlight did not reach. He walked straight across to it, picked an apple, and put it in the breast pocket of his Norfolk jacket. But he couldn't help looking at it and smelling it before he put it away.

It would have been better if he had not. A terrible thirst and hunger came over him and a longing to taste that fruit. He put it hastily into his pocket; but there were plenty of others. Could it be wrong to taste one? After all, he thought, the notice on the gate might not have been exactly an order; it might have been only a piece of advice—and who cares about advice? Or even if it were an order, would he be disobeying it by eating an apple? He had already obeyed the part about taking one "for others."

—*The Magician's Nephew*

Why do you think taking for others is okay but taking for oneself is stealing? When have you found yourself running through a list of rationales as Digory does when considering doing something you knew deep down was wrong?

What May Be Watching You

WHILE HE WAS thinking of all this he happened to look up through the branches toward the top of the tree. There, on a branch above his head, a wonderful bird was roosting. I say "roosting" because it seemed almost asleep; perhaps not quite. The tiniest slit of one eye was open. It was larger than an eagle, its breast saffron, its head crested with scarlet, and its tail purple.

"And it just shows," said Digory afterward when he was telling the story to others, "that you can't be too careful in these magical places. You never know what may be watching you." But I think Digory would not have taken an apple for himself in any case. Things like Do Not Steal were, I think, hammered into boys' heads a good deal harder in those days than they are now. Still, we can never be certain.

—The Magician's Nephew

Even though the sign says it is forbidden, Digory is tempted to take an apple for himself, at least until he sees the bird watching him. If you were in Digory's place, would the watchful eyes of the bird make a difference for you? Why are we more likely to do the right thing when someone (or something) is watching?

Waking the Statues

W HAT AN EXTRAORDINARY place!" cried Lucy. "All those stone animals—and people too! It's—it's like a museum."

"Hush," said Susan, "Aslan's doing something."

He was indeed. He had bounded up to the stone lion and breathed on him. Then without waiting a moment he whisked round—almost as if he had been a cat chasing its tail—and breathed also on the stone dwarf, which (as you remember) was standing a few feet from the lion with his back to it. Then he pounced on a tall stone dryad which stood beyond the dwarf, turned rapidly aside to deal with a stone rabbit on his right, and rushed on to two centaurs. But at that moment Lucy said,

"Oh, Susan! Look! Look at the lion."

I expect you've seen someone put a lighted match to a bit of newspaper which is propped up in a grate against an unlit fire. And for a second nothing seems to have happened; and then you notice a tiny streak of flame creeping along the edge of the newspaper. It was like that now. For a second after Aslan had breathed upon him the stone lion looked just the same. Then a tiny streak of gold began to run along his white marble back—then it spread—then the color seemed to lick all over him as the flame licks all over a bit of paper—then, while his hindquarters were still obviously stone, the lion shook his mane and all the heavy, stone folds rippled into living hair. Then he opened a great red mouth, warm and living, and gave a prodigious yawn. And now his hind legs had come to life. He lifted one of them and scratched himself. Then, having caught sight of Aslan, he went bounding after him and frisked round him whimpering with delight and jumping up to lick his face.

Of course the children's eyes turned to follow the lion; but the sight they saw was so wonderful that they soon forgot about *him*. Everywhere the statues were coming to life. The courtyard looked no longer like a museum; it looked more like a zoo. Creatures were running after Aslan and dancing round him till he was almost hidden in the crowd. Instead of all that deadly white the courtyard was now a blaze of colors; glossy chestnut sides of centaurs, indigo horns of unicorns, dazzling plumage of birds, reddy-brown of foxes, dogs and satyrs, yellow stockings and crimson hoods of dwarfs; and the birch-girls in silver, and the beech-girls in fresh, transparent green, and the larch-girls in green so bright that it was almost yellow. And instead of the deadly silence the whole place rang with the sound of happy roarings, brayings, yelpings, barkings, squealings, cooings, neighings, stampings, shouts, hurrahs, songs and laughter.

—*The Lion, the Witch, and the Wardrobe*

What do you like about the image of the lion coming to life? What have you experienced that comes close to the joyful noises and bright colors described here?

Puzzle Fears to Meet Aslan

L OOK!" SAID JILL SUDDENLY. Someone was coming, rather timidly, to meet them; a graceful creature on four feet, all silvery-grey. And they stared at him for a whole ten seconds before five or six voices said all at once, "Why, it's old Puzzle!" They had never seen him by daylight with the lion-skin off, and it made an extraordinary difference. He was himself now: a beautiful donkey with such a soft, grey coat and such a gentle, honest face that if you had seen him you would have done just what Jill and Lucy did—rushed forward and put your arms round his neck and kissed his nose and stroked his ears.

When they asked him where he had been he said he had come in at the door along with all the other creatures but he had—well, to tell the truth, he had been keeping out of their way as much as he could; and out of Aslan's way. For the sight of the real Lion had made him so ashamed of all that nonsense about dressing up in a lion-skin that he did not know how to look anyone in the face. But when he saw that all his friends were going away Westward, and after he had had a mouthful or so of grass ("And I've never tasted such good grass in my life," said Puzzle), he plucked up his courage and followed. "But what I'll do if I really have to meet Aslan, I'm sure I don't know," he added.

"You'll find it will be all right when you really do," said Queen Lucy.

—The Last Battle

Why is Puzzle so scared of meeting Aslan? Why do you think Lucy feels so strongly it will be all right? What would be the drawbacks of never meeting Aslan?

The Mystery of the Table

CASPIAN . . . began shaking the nearest of the three sleepers. For a moment everyone thought he was going to be successful, for the man breathed hard and muttered, "I'll go eastward no more. Out oars for Narnia." But he sank back almost at once into a yet deeper sleep than before: that is, his heavy head sagged a few inches lower toward the table and all efforts to rouse him again were useless. With the second it was much the same. "Weren't born to live like animals. Get to the east while you've a chance—lands behind the sun," and sank down. And the third only said, "Mustard, please," and slept hard.

"*Out oars for Narnia,* eh?" said Drinian.

"Yes," said Caspian, "you are right, Drinian. I think our quest is at an end. Let's look at their rings. Yes, these are their devices. This is the Lord Revilian. This is the Lord Argoz: and this, the Lord Mavramorn."

"But we can't wake them," said Lucy. "What are we to do?"

"Begging your Majesties' pardons all," said Rhince, "but why not fall to while you're discussing it? We don't see a dinner like this every day."

"Not for your life!" said Caspian.

"That's right, that's right," said several of the sailors. "Too much magic about here. The sooner we're back on board the better."

"Depend upon it," said Reepicheep, "it was from eating this food that these three lords came by a seven years' sleep."

"I wouldn't touch it to save my life," said Drinian.

"The light's going uncommon quick," said Rynelf.

"Back to ship, back to ship," muttered the men.

"I really think," said Edmund, "they're right. We can decide what to do with the three sleepers tomorrow. We daren't eat the food and there's no point in staying here for the night. The whole place smells of magic—and danger."

"I am entirely of King Edmund's opinion," said Reepicheep, "as far as concerns the ship's company in general. But I myself will sit at this table till sunrise."

"Why on earth?" said Eustace.

"Because," said the Mouse, "this is a very great adventure, and no danger seems to me so great as that of knowing when I get back to Narnia that I left a mystery behind me through fear."

"I'll stay with you, Reep," said Edmund.

"And I too," said Caspian.

"And me," said Lucy. And then Eustace volunteered also. This was very brave of him because never having read of such things or even heard of them till he joined the *Dawn Treader* made it worse for him than for the others.

—*The Voyage of the* Dawn Treader

Why does Reepicheep want to stay? Why do you think the others agree to stay with him? How might having read about or experienced danger and adventure make us more brave?

The Girl with the Yellow Hair

AND NOW A DOOR OPENED in the hillside, and light appeared in the doorway, and a figure came out, and the door shut behind it. The figure carried a light, and this light was really all that they could see distinctly. It came slowly nearer and nearer till at last it stood right at the table opposite to them. Now they could see that it was a tall girl, dressed in a single long garment of clear blue which left her arms bare. She was bareheaded and her yellow hair hung down her back. And when they looked at her they thought they had never before known what beauty meant. . . .

No one had yet spoken a word. Then—Reepicheep first, and Caspian next—they all rose to their feet, because they felt that she was a great lady.

"Travelers who have come from far to Aslan's table," said the girl. "Why do you not eat and drink?"

"Madam," said Caspian, "we feared the food because we thought it had cast our friends into an enchanted sleep."

"They have never tasted it," she said. . . .

Edmund, who had been looking more and more uncomfortable for the last few minutes, now spoke.

"Look here," he said, "I hope I'm not a coward—about eating this food, I mean—and I'm sure I don't mean to be rude. But we have had a lot of queer adventures on this voyage of ours and things aren't always what they seem. When I look in your face I can't help believing all you say: but then that's just what might happen with a witch too. How are we to know you're a friend?"

"You can't know," said the girl. "You can only believe—or not."

—*The Voyage of the* Dawn Treader

How would you make the decision whether to eat at what the girl calls Aslan's table? When have you had a difficult time deciding whether to believe someone?

The Knife of Stone

P LEASE," SAID LUCY, "what happened to [the sleepers]?"

"Seven years ago," said the girl, "they came here in a ship whose sails were rags and her timbers ready to fall apart. There were a few others with them, sailors, and when they came to this table one said, 'Here is the good place. Let us set sail and reef sail and row no longer but sit down and end our days in peace!' And the second said, 'No, let us re-embark and sail for Narnia and the west; it may be that Miraz is dead.' But the third, who was a very masterful man, leaped up and said, 'No, by heaven. We are men and Telmarines, not brutes. What should we do but seek adventure after adventure? We have not long to live in any event. Let us spend what is left in seeking the unpeopled world behind the sunrise.' And as they quarreled he caught up the Knife of Stone which lies there on the table and would have fought with his comrades. But it is a thing not right for him to touch. And as his fingers closed upon the hilt, deep sleep fell upon all the three. And till the enchantment is undone they will never wake."

"What is this Knife of Stone?" asked Eustace.

"Do none of you know it?" said the girl.

"I—I think," said Lucy, "I've seen something like it before. It was a knife like it that the White Witch used when she killed Aslan at the Stone Table long ago."

"It was the same," said the girl, "and it was brought here to be kept in honor while the world lasts."

—*The Voyage of the* **Dawn Treader**

Why would the knife that killed Aslan be held in honor? Why is it not right for anyone to touch?

The Lion Appears

FAR AWAY THERE APPEARED A RED LIGHT. Then it disappeared for a moment and came back again, bigger and stronger. Then he could see dark shapes going to and fro on this side of the light and carrying bundles and throwing them down. He knew now what he was looking at. It was a bonfire, newly lit, and people were throwing bundles of brushwood onto it. Presently it blazed up and Tirian could see that it was on the very top of the hill. He could see quite clearly the stable behind it, all lit up in the red glow, and a great crowd of Beasts and Men between the fire and himself. A small figure, hunched up beside the fire, must be the Ape. It was saying something to the crowd, but he could not hear what. Then it went and bowed three times to the ground in front of the door of the stable. Then he got up and opened the door. And something on four legs—something that walked rather stiffly—came out of the stable and stood facing the crowd.

A great wailing or howling went up, so loud that Tirian could hear some of the words.

"Aslan! Aslan! Aslan!" cried the Beasts. "Speak to us. Comfort us. Be angry with us no more."

From where Tirian was he could not make out very clearly what the thing was; but he could see that it was yellow and hairy. He had never seen the Great Lion. He had never seen a common lion. He couldn't be sure that what he saw was not the real Aslan. He had not expected Aslan to look like that stiff thing which stood and said nothing. But how could one be sure? For a moment horrible thoughts went through his mind: then he remembered the nonsense about Tash and Aslan being the same and knew that the whole thing must be a cheat.

—*The Last Battle*

Why is it hard for Tirian and the others to dismiss this creature the Ape claims is Aslan, despite the discrepancies between it and what they've always understood of Aslan? When has what you imagined in your head not lived up to what was presented to you as the real thing?

Caspian Gets Past the Guard

AT THE CASTLE GATE Caspian's trumpeter blew a blast and cried, "Open for the King of Narnia, come to visit his trusty and well-beloved servant the governor of the Lone Islands." In those days everything in the islands was done in a slovenly, slouching manner. Only the little postern opened, and out came a tousled fellow with a dirty old hat on his head instead of a helmet, and a rusty old pike in his hand. He blinked at the flashing figures before him. "Carn—seez—fishansy," he mumbled (which was his way of saying, "You can't see His Sufficiency"). "No interviews without 'pointments 'cept 'tween nine 'n' ten P.M. second Saturday every month."

"Uncover before Narnia, you dog," thundered the Lord Bern, and dealt him a rap with his gauntleted hand which sent his hat flying from his head.

"'Ere? Wot's it all about?" began the door-keeper, but no one took any notice of him. Two of Caspian's men stepped through the postern and after some struggling with bars and bolts (for everything was rusty), flung both wings of the gate wide open. Then the King and his followers strode into the courtyard. Here a number of the governor's guards were lounging about and several more (they were mostly wiping their mouths) came tumbling out of various doorways. Though their armor was in a disgraceful condition, these were fellows who might have fought if they had been led or had known what was happening; so this was the dangerous moment. Caspian gave them no time to think.

"Where is the captain?" he asked.

"I am, more or less, if you know what I mean," said a languid and rather dandified young person without any armor at all.

"It is our wish," said Caspian, "that our royal visitation to our realm of the Lone Islands should, if possible, be an occasion of joy and not of terror to our loyal subjects. If it were not for that, I should have something to say about the state of your men's armor and weapons. As it is, you are pardoned. Command a cask of wine to be opened that your men may drink our health. But at noon tomorrow I wish to see them here in this courtyard looking like men-at-arms and not like vagabonds. See to it on pain of our extreme displeasure."

The captain gaped but Bern immediately cried, "Three cheers for the King," and the soldiers, who had understood about the cask of wine even if they understood nothing else, joined in.

—*The Voyage of the* **Dawn Treader**

How does Caspian so effectively defuse this dangerous situation? How does swift action command authority?

At Our Bidding

Y OU MUST THINK we're blooming soft in the head, that you must," said Griffle. "We've been taken in once and now you expect us to be taken in again the next minute. We've no more use for stories about Aslan, see! Look at him! An old moke with long ears!"

"By heaven, you make me mad," said Tirian. "Which of us said *that* was Aslan? That is the Ape's imitation of the real Aslan. Can't you understand?"

"And you've got a better imitation, I suppose!" said Griffle. "No thanks. We've been fooled once and we're not going to be fooled again."

"I have not," said Tirian angrily, "I serve the real Aslan."

"Where's he? Who's he? Show him to us!" said several Dwarfs.

"Do you think I keep him in my wallet, fools?" said Tirian. "Who am I that I could make Aslan appear at my bidding? He's not a tame lion."

—*The Last Battle*

Why do we so often need to see to believe? What does it mean that Aslan is not at our bidding? How do we sometimes try to claim control over things we have no control over?

Reepicheep Comforts the Dragon

[I]T WAS VERY DREARY being a dragon. He shuddered whenever he caught sight of his own reflection as he flew over a mountain lake. He hated the huge bat-like wings, the saw-edged ridge on his back, and the cruel, curved claws. He was almost afraid to be alone with himself and yet he was ashamed to be with the others. On the evenings when he was not being used as a hot-water bottle he would slink away from the camp and lie curled up like a snake between the wood and the water. On such occasions, greatly to his surprise, Reepicheep was his most constant comforter. The noble Mouse would creep away from the merry circle at the camp fire and sit down by the dragon's head, well to the windward to be out of the way of his smoky breath. There he would explain that what had happened to Eustace was a striking illustration of the turn of Fortune's wheel, and that if he had Eustace at his own house in Narnia (it was really a hole not a house and the dragon's head, let alone his body, would not have fitted in) he could show him more than a hundred examples of emperors, kings, dukes, knights, poets, lovers, astronomers, philosophers, and magicians, who had fallen from prosperity into the most distressing circumstances, and of whom many had recovered and lived happily ever afterward. It did not, perhaps, seem so very comforting at the time, but it was kindly meant and Eustace never forgot it.

—*The Voyage of the* **Dawn Treader**

Why might Reepicheep the Mouse, who was previously targeted so cruelly by Eustace, be the one to understand and comfort Eustace about the cruelties of his distressing circumstances? When have you experienced comfort from an unexpected corner?

Father Christmas's Gifts

PETER, ADAM'S SON," said Father Christmas.

"Here, sir," said Peter.

"These are your presents," was the answer, "and they are tools not toys. The time to use them is perhaps near at hand. Bear them well." With these words he handed to Peter a shield and a sword. The shield was the color of silver and across it there ramped a red lion, as bright as a ripe strawberry at the moment when you pick it. The hilt of the sword was of gold and it had a sheath and a sword belt and everything it needed, and it was just the right size and weight for Peter to use. Peter was silent and solemn as he received these gifts, for he felt they were a very serious kind of present.

"Susan, Eve's Daughter," said Father Christmas. "These are for you," and he handed her a bow and a quiver full of arrows and a little ivory horn. "You must use the bow only in great need," he said, "for I do not mean you to fight in the battle. It does not easily miss. And when you put this horn to your lips and blow it, then, wherever you are, I think help of some kind will come to you."

Last of all he said, "Lucy, Eve's Daughter," and Lucy came forward. He gave her a little bottle of what looked like glass (but people said afterward that it was made of diamond) and a small dagger. "In this bottle," he said, "there is a cordial made of the juice of one of the fire-flowers that grow in the mountains of the sun. If you or any of your friends is hurt, a few drops of this will restore them. And the dagger is to defend yourself at great need. For you also are not to be in the battle."

—*The Lion, the Witch, and the Wardrobe*

What does each gift have to say about the recipient's interior gifts? Which of these gifts would you most like to have received?

Happy All Your Life

"STAY WHERE YOU ARE," cried Digory, turning round to face her, "or we'll all vanish. Don't come an inch nearer."

"Foolish boy," said the Witch. "Why do you run from me? I mean you no harm. If you do not stop and listen to me now, you will miss some knowledge that would have made you happy all your life."

"Well, I don't want to hear it, thanks," said Digory. But he did.

"I know what errand you have come on," continued the Witch. "For it was I who was close beside you in the woods last night and heard all your counsels. You have plucked fruit in the garden yonder. You have it in your pocket now. And you are going to carry it back, untasted, to the Lion; for *him* to eat, for *him* to use. You simpleton! Do you know what that fruit is? I will tell you. It is the apple of youth, the apple of life. I know, for I have tasted it; and I feel already such changes in myself that I know I shall never grow old or die. Eat it, Boy, eat it; and you and I will both live forever and be king and queen of this whole world—or of your world, if we decide to go back there."

"No thanks," said Digory, "I don't know that I care much about living on and on after everyone I know is dead. I'd rather live an ordinary time and die and go to Heaven."

—*The Magician's Nephew*

The Witch promises Digory three things if he eats the apple: that he will never grow old, that he will never die, and that he will rule the world with her. Why do you think Digory is so quick to refuse? Which of the Witch's promises would most tempt you? If none of them, what are the greatest temptations in your life?

Bid Farewell to Hopes and Dreams

FROM THE HALL they came out into the courtyard. Jill, who went to a riding school in the holidays, had just noticed the smell of a stable (a very nice, honest, homely smell it is to meet in a place like Underland) when Eustace said, "Great Scott! Look at that!" A magnificent rocket had risen from somewhere beyond the castle walls and broken into green stars.

"Fireworks!" said Jill in a puzzled voice.

"Yes," said Eustace, "but you can't imagine those Earth people letting them off for fun! It must be a signal."

"And means no good to us, I'll be bound," said Puddleglum.

"Friends," said the Prince, "when once a man is launched on such an adventure as this, he must bid farewell to hopes and fears, otherwise death or deliverance will both come too late to save his honor and his reason."

—*The Silver Chair*

How do you interpret the Prince's statement? Have you found it to be true in your life?

The Sailors Hesitate

A T THIS POINT Caspian jumped to his feet. "Friends," he said, "I think you have not quite understood our purpose. You talk as if we had come to you with our hat in our hand, begging for shipmates. It isn't like that at all. We and our royal brother and sister and their kinsman and Sir Reepicheep, the good knight, and the Lord Drinian have an errand to the world's edge. It is our pleasure to choose from among such of you as are willing those whom we deem worthy of so high an enterprise. We have not said that any can come for the asking. That is why we shall now command the Lord Drinian and Master Rhince to consider carefully what men among you are the hardest in battle, the most skilled seamen, the purest in blood, the most loyal to our person, and the cleanest of life and manners; and to give their names to us in a schedule." He paused and went on in a quicker voice, "Aslan's mane!" he exclaimed. "Do you think that the privilege of seeing the last things is to be bought for a song? Why, every man that comes with us shall bequeath the title of Dawn Treader to all his descendants, and when we land at Cair Paravel on the homeward voyage he shall have either gold or land enough to make him rich all his life. Now—scatter over the island, all of you. In half an hour's time I shall receive the names that Lord Drinian brings me."

—*The Voyage of the* **Dawn Treader**

What are the qualities Caspian looks for in a shipmate? How could you cultivate these qualities in your life?

Pittencream Remains Behind

MEANWHILE CASPIAN'S SPEECH, helped perhaps by some magic of the island, was having just the effect he intended. A good many who had been anxious enough to *get* out of the voyage felt quite differently about being *left* out of it. And of course whenever any one sailor announced that he had made up his mind to ask for permission to sail, the ones who hadn't said this felt that they were getting fewer and more uncomfortable. So that before the half-hour was nearly over several people were positively "sucking up" to Drinian and Rhince (at least that was what they called it at my school) to get a good report. And soon there were only three left who didn't want to go, and those three were trying very hard to persuade others to stay with them. And very shortly after that there was only one left. And in the end he began to be afraid of being left behind all on his own and changed his mind.

At the end of the half-hour they all came trooping back to Aslan's Table and stood at one end while Drinian and Rhince went and sat down with Caspian and made their report; and Caspian accepted all the men but that one who had changed his mind at the last moment. His name was Pittencream and he stayed on the Island of the Star all the time the others were away looking for the World's End, and he very much wished he had gone with them. He wasn't the sort of man who could enjoy talking to Ramandu and Ramandu's daughter (nor they to him), and it rained a good deal, and though there was a wonderful feast on the Table every night, he didn't very much enjoy it. . . . And when the others returned he felt so out of things that he deserted on the voyage home at the Lone Islands, and went and lived in Calormen, where he told wonderful stories about his adventures at the End of the World, until at last he came to believe them himself. So you may say, in a sense, that he lived happily ever after.

—*The Voyage of the* **Dawn Treader**

Why is it so hard for Pittencream to be among the others when they return? When have you not done something because you were afraid? Did you regret it later? Why or why not?

Lucy's Cordial

THE BATTLE WAS ALL OVER a few minutes after their arrival. Most of the enemy had been killed in the first charge of Aslan and his companions; and when those who were still living saw that the Witch was dead they either gave themselves up or took to flight. . . .

"It was all Edmund's doing, Aslan," Peter was saying. "We'd have been beaten if it hadn't been for him. The Witch was turning our troops into stone right and left. But nothing would stop him. He fought his way through three ogres to where she was just turning one of your leopards into a statue. And when he reached her he had the sense to bring his sword smashing down on her wand instead of trying to go for her directly and simply getting made a statue himself for his pains. That was the mistake all the rest were making. Once her wand was broken we began to have some chance—if we hadn't lost so many already. He was terribly wounded. We must go and see him."

They found Edmund in charge of Mrs. Beaver a little way back from the fighting line. He was covered with blood, his mouth was open, and his face a nasty green color.

"Quick, Lucy," said Aslan.

And then, almost for the first time, Lucy remembered the precious cordial that had been given her for a Christmas present. Her hands trembled so much that she could hardly undo the stopper, but she managed it in the end and poured a few drops into her brother's mouth.

"There are other people wounded," said Aslan while she was still looking eagerly into Edmund's pale face and wondering if the cordial would have any result.

"Yes, I know," said Lucy crossly. "Wait a minute."

"Daughter of Eve," said Aslan in a graver voice, "others also are at the point of death. Must *more* people die for Edmund?"

"I'm sorry, Aslan," said Lucy, getting up and going with him.

—*The Lion, the Witch, and the Wardrobe*

What is the lesson Aslan is trying to teach Lucy?

We Can't Go Against Aslan

LORD KING! DEAR LORD KING," said their shrill voices, "we are so sorry for you. We daren't untie you because Aslan might be angry with us. But we've brought you your supper.". . .

"Here is cheese, Sire," said the first Mouse, "but not very much, for fear it would make you too thirsty." And after the cheese they fed him with oat-cakes and fresh butter, and then with some more wine.

"Now hand up the water," said the first Mouse, "and I'll wash the King's face. There is blood on it."

Then Tirian felt something like a tiny sponge dabbing his face, and it was most refreshing.

"Little friends," said Tirian, "how can I thank you for all this?"

"You needn't, you needn't," said the little voices. "What else could we do? *We* don't want any other King. We're your people. If it was only the Ape and the Calormenes who were against you we would have fought till we were cut into pieces before we'd have let them tie you up. We would, we would indeed. But we can't go against Aslan."

"Do you think it really is Aslan?" asked the King.

"Oh yes, yes," said the Rabbit. "He came out of the stable last night. We all saw him."

"What was he like?" said the King.

"Like a terrible, great Lion, to be sure," said one of the Mice.

"And you think it is really Aslan who is killing the Wood-Nymphs and making you all slaves to the King of Calormen?"

"Ah, that's bad, isn't it?" said the second Mouse. "It would have been better if we'd died before all this began. But there's no doubt about it. Everyone says it is Aslan's orders. And we've seen him. We didn't think Aslan would be like that. Why, we—we *wanted* him to come back to Narnia."

"He seems to have come back very angry this time," said the first Mouse. "We must all have done something dreadfully wrong without knowing it. He must be punishing us for something. But I do think we might be told what it was!"

"I suppose what we're doing now may be wrong," said the Rabbit.

"I don't care if it is," said one of the Moles. "I'd do it again."

But the others said, "Oh hush," and "Do be careful," and then they all said, "We're sorry, dear King, but we must go back now. It would never do for us to be caught here."

"Leave me at once, dear Beasts," said Tirian. "I would not for all Narnia bring any of you into danger."

"Goodnight, goodnight," said the Beasts, rubbing their noses against his knees. "We will come back—if we can." Then they all pattered away and the wood seemed darker and colder and lonelier than it had been before they came.

—*The Last Battle*

Why do you think the mice feel they can't go against Aslan even though they find his actions so deplorable? Why then would the creatures help the King even if they fear it might be wrong?

Aslan's Warning

WHEN YOU WERE LAST HERE," said Aslan, "that hollow was a pool, and when you jumped into it you came to the world where a dying sun shone over the ruins of Charn. There is no pool now. That world is ended, as if it had never been. Let the race of Adam and Eve take warning."

"Yes, Aslan," said both the children. But Polly added, "But we're not quite as bad as that world, are we, Aslan?"

"Not yet, Daughter of Eve," he said. "Not yet. But you are growing more like it. It is not certain that some wicked one of your race will not find out a secret as evil as the Deplorable Word and use it to destroy all living things. And soon, very soon, before you are an old man and an old woman, great nations in your world will be ruled by tyrants who care no more for joy and justice and mercy than the Empress Jadis. Let your world beware. That is the warning."

—*The Magician's Nephew*

What do you think Aslan wants Polly and Digory to do with his warning? Has his warning come true in our world?

Waiting and Wondering

EDMUND WAS ON THE OTHER SIDE of Aslan, looking all the time at Aslan's face. He felt a choking feeling and wondered if he ought to say something; but a moment later he felt that he was not expected to do anything except to wait, and do what he was told.

"Fall back, all of you," said Aslan, "and I will talk to the Witch alone." They all obeyed. It was a terrible time this—waiting and wondering while the Lion and the Witch talked earnestly together in low voices. Lucy said, "Oh, Edmund!" and began to cry. Peter stood with his back to the others looking out at the distant sea. The Beavers stood holding each other's paws with their heads bowed. The centaurs stamped uneasily with their hoofs. But everyone became perfectly still in the end, so that you noticed even small sounds like a bumble-bee flying past, or the birds in the forest down below them, or the wind rustling the leaves. And still the talk between Aslan and the White Witch went on.

At last they heard Aslan's voice, "You can all come back," he said. "I have settled the matter. She has renounced the claim on your brother's blood." And all over the hill there was a noise as if everyone had been holding their breath and had now begun breathing again, and then a murmur of talk.

—*The Lion, the Witch, and the Wardrobe*

What might Edmund have been feeling, just waiting for Aslan to talk to the Witch about his fate? What would your instinct have been if you were in his place?

Lucy and the Sea Girl

ALL MORNING on the following day they sailed in fairly shallow water and the bottom was weedy. Just before midday Lucy saw a large shoal of fishes grazing on the weed. They were all eating steadily and all moving in the same direction. "Just like a flock of sheep," thought Lucy. Suddenly she saw a little Sea Girl of about her own age in the middle of them—a quiet, lonely-looking girl with a sort of crook in her hand. Lucy felt sure that this girl must be a shepherdess—or perhaps a fish-herdess—and that the shoal was really a flock at pasture. Both the fishes and the girl were quite close to the surface. And just as the girl, gliding in the shallow water, and Lucy, leaning over the bulwark, came opposite to one another, the girl looked up and stared straight into Lucy's face. Neither could speak to the other and in a moment the Sea Girl dropped astern. But Lucy will never forget her face. It did not look frightened or angry like those of the other Sea People. Lucy had liked that girl and she felt certain the girl had liked her. In that one moment they had somehow become friends. There does not seem to be much chance of their meeting again in that world or any other. But if ever they do they will rush together with their hands held out.

—*The Voyage of the* Dawn Treader

How could the Sea Girl and Lucy be friends without even speaking? Have you ever connected immediately with someone, even before words were exchanged?

SEPTEMBER

The End of the Underworld

"WILL YOUR highness not put on armor?" asked Puddleglum. "I don't like the look of *those*"—and he pointed down to the street. Everyone looked down. Dozens of creatures (and now that they were close, they obviously were Earthmen) were coming up from the direction of the harbor. But they were not moving like an aimless crowd. They behaved like modern soldiers in an attack, making rushes and taking cover, anxious not to be seen from the castle windows.

"I dare not see the inside of that armor again," said the Prince. "I rode in it as in a movable dungeon, and it stinks of magic and slavery. But I will take the shield."

He left the room and returned with a strange light in his eyes a moment later.

"Look, friends," he said, holding out the shield toward them. "An hour ago it was black and without device; and now, this." The shield had turned bright as silver, and on it, redder than blood or cherries, was the figure of the Lion.

"Doubtless," said the Prince, "this signifies that Aslan will be our good lord, whether he means us to live or die. And all's one, for that. Now, by my counsel, we shall all kneel and kiss his likeness, and then all shake hands one with another, as true friends that may shortly be parted. And then, let us descend into the city and take the adventure that is sent us."

—*The Silver Chair*

What does it mean that Aslan is their good lord, whether he means them to live or die? Are you able to have faith in something without conditions?

Aslan's Country

[W]HEN THE THIRD DAY DAWNED—with a brightness you or I could not bear even if we had dark glasses on—they saw a wonder ahead. It was as if a wall stood up between them and the sky, a greenish-grey, trembling, shimmering wall. Then up came the sun, and at its first rising they saw it through the wall and it turned into wonderful rainbow colors. Then they knew that the wall was really a long, tall wave—a wave endlessly fixed in one place as you may often see at the edge of a waterfall. It seemed to be about thirty feet high, and the current was gliding them swiftly toward it. You might have supposed they would have thought of their danger. They didn't. I don't think anyone could have in their position. For now they saw something not only behind the wave but behind the sun. . . . What they saw—eastward, beyond the sun—was a range of mountains. It was so high that either they never saw the top of it or they forgot it. None of them remembers seeing any sky in that direction. And the mountains must really have been outside the world. For any mountains even a quarter of a twentieth of that height ought to have had ice and snow on them. But these were warm and green and full of forests and waterfalls however high you looked. And suddenly there came a breeze from the east, tossing the top of the wave into foamy shapes and ruffling the smooth water all round them. It lasted only a second or so but what it brought them in that second none of those three children will ever forget. It brought both a smell and a sound, a musical sound. Edmund and Eustace would never talk about it afterward. Lucy could only say, "It would break your heart." "Why," said I, "was it so sad?" "Sad!! No," said Lucy.

No one in that boat doubted that they were seeing beyond the End of the World into Aslan's country.

—*The Voyage of the* **Dawn Treader**

Why do you think Edmund and Eustace could not talk of what they saw that day? How could something break your heart but not of sadness?

Further Up and Further In!

ALONG VALLEY OPENED AHEAD and great snow-mountains, now much nearer, stood up against the sky.

"Further up and further in," cried Jewel and instantly they were off again.

They were out of Narnia now and up into the Western Wild which neither Tirian nor Peter nor even the Eagle had ever seen before. But the Lord Digory and the Lady Polly had. "Do you remember? Do you remember?" they said—and said it in steady voices too, without panting, though the whole party was now running faster than an arrow flies.

"What, Lord?" said Tirian. "Is it then true, as stories tell, that you two journeyed here on the very day the world was made?"

"Yes," said Digory, "and it seems to me as if it were only yesterday."

"And on a flying horse?" asked Tirian. "Is that part true?"

"Certainly," said Digory. But the dogs barked, "Faster, faster!"

So they ran faster and faster till it was more like flying than running, and even the Eagle overhead was going no faster than they. And they went through winding valley after winding valley and up the steep sides of hills and, faster than ever, down the other side, following the river and sometimes crossing it and skimming across mountain lakes as if they were living speedboats, till at last at the far end of one long lake which looked as blue as a turquoise, they saw a smooth green hill. Its sides were as steep as the sides of a pyramid and round the very top of it ran a green wall: but above the wall rose the branches of trees whose leaves looked like silver and their fruit like gold.

"Further up and further in!" roared the Unicorn, and no one held back. They charged straight at the foot of the hill and then found themselves running up it almost as water from a broken wave runs up a rock out at the point of some bay. Though the slope was nearly as steep as the roof of a house and the grass was smooth as a bowling green, no one slipped. Only when they had reached the very top did they slow up; that was because they found themselves facing great golden gates. And for a moment none of them was bold enough to try if the gates would open. They all felt just as they had felt about the fruit—"Dare we? Is it right? Can it be meant for *us*?"

But while they were standing thus a great horn, wonderfully loud and sweet, blew from somewhere inside that walled garden and the gates swung open.

—*The Last Battle*

Why is it appropriate to rush forward toward whatever the strange world holds? When have you held yourself back out of fear or pride or uncertainty? How would your life change if you adopted "Further up and further in!" as a rallying cry?

'Course We've Got a Hope

As soon as Mr. Beaver said, "There's no time to lose," everyone began bundling themselves into coats, except Mrs. Beaver, who started picking up sacks and laying them on the table and said: "Now, Mr. Beaver, just reach down that ham. And here's a packet of tea, and there's sugar, and some matches. And if someone will get two or three loaves out of the crock over there in the corner."

"What *are* you doing, Mrs. Beaver?" exclaimed Susan.

"Packing a load for each of us, dearie," said Mrs. Beaver very coolly. "You didn't think we'd set out on a journey with nothing to eat, did you?"

"But we haven't time!" said Susan, buttoning the collar of her coat. "She may be here any minute."

"That's what I say," chimed in Mr. Beaver.

"Get along with you all," said his wife. "Think it over, Mr. Beaver. She can't be here for quarter of an hour at least."

"But don't we want as big a start as we can possibly get," said Peter, "if we're to reach the Stone Table before her?"

"You've got to remember *that*, Mrs. Beaver," said Susan. "As soon as she has looked in here and finds we're gone she'll be off at top speed."

"That she will," said Mrs. Beaver. "But we can't get there before her whatever we do, for she'll be on a sledge and we'll be walking."

"Then—have we no hope?" said Susan.

"Now don't you get fussing, there's a dear," said Mrs. Beaver, "but just get half a dozen clean handkerchiefs out of the drawer. 'Course we've got a hope. We can't get there *before* her but we can keep under cover and go by ways she won't expect and perhaps we'll get through."

—*The Lion, the Witch, and the Wardrobe*

How does Mrs. Beaver's perspective on their journey differ from that of the others? How do you tend to act in emergencies?

You Needed to Know What It Felt Like

[ASLAN SAID,] "Draw near, Aravis my daughter. See! My paws are velveted. You will not be torn this time."

"This time, sir?" said Aravis.

"It was I who wounded you," said Aslan. "I am the only lion you met in all your journeyings. Do you know why I tore you?"

"No, sir."

"The scratches on your back, tear for tear, throb for throb, blood for blood, were equal to the stripes laid on the back of your stepmother's slave because of the drugged sleep you cast upon her. You needed to know what it felt like."

—The Horse and His Boy

Why is it important for Aravis to understand the sufferings of the slave who was punished because Aravis drugged her in order to escape? When have you been best able to empathize with someone else's suffering?

No Such Person

[P OGGIN THE DWARF SAID,] "One of those dreadful midnight meetings had just broken up the night before last and I'd gone a bit of the way home when I found I'd left my pipe behind. It was a real good 'un, an old favorite, so I went back to look for it. But before I got to the place where I'd been sitting (it was black as pitch there) I heard a cat's voice say *Mew* and a Calormene voice say 'here . . . speak softly,' so I just stood as still as if I was frozen. And these two were Ginger and Rishda Tarkaan as they call him. 'Noble Tarkaan,' said the Cat in that silky voice of his, 'I just wanted to know exactly what we both meant today about Aslan meaning *no more* than Tash.' 'Doubtless, most sagacious of cats,' says the other, 'you have perceived my meaning.' 'You mean,' says Ginger, 'that there's no such person as either.' 'All who are enlightened know that,' said the Tarkaan. 'Then we can understand one another,' purrs the Cat. 'Do you, like me, grow a little weary of the Ape?' 'A stupid, greedy brute,' says the other, 'but we must use him for the present. Thou and I must provide for all things in secret and make the Ape do our will.' 'And it would be better, wouldn't it,' said Ginger, 'to let some of the more enlightened Narnians into our counsels: one by one as we find them apt. For the Beasts who really believe in Aslan may turn at any moment: and will, if the Ape's folly betrays his secret. But those who care neither for Tash nor Aslan but have only an eye to their own profit and such reward as The Tisroc may give them when Narnia is a Calormene province, will be firm.' 'Excellent Cat,' said the Captain. 'But choose which ones carefully.' "

—*The Last Battle*

What's worse—believing in a false Aslan or not believing in Aslan at all? Why? Why would those who disbelieve think of themselves as enlightened?

Over the Edge

D RINIAN SAID:
   "I can't understand this. There is not a breath of wind. The sail hangs dead. The sea is as flat as a pond. And yet we drive on as fast as if there were a gale behind us."

"I've been thinking that, too," said Caspian. "We must be caught in some strong current."

"H'm," said Edmund. "That's not so nice if the World really has an edge and we're getting near it."

"You mean," said Caspian, "that we might be just—well, poured over it?"

"Yes, yes," cried Reepicheep, clapping his paws together. "That's how I've always imagined it—the World like a great round table and the waters of all the oceans endlessly pouring over the edge. The ship will tip up— stand on her head—for one moment we shall see over the edge—and then, down, down, the rush, the speed—"

"And what do you think will be waiting for us at the bottom, eh?" said Drinian.

"Aslan's country perhaps," said the Mouse, its eyes shining. "Or perhaps there isn't any bottom. Perhaps it goes down for ever and ever. But whatever it is, won't it be worth anything just to have looked for one moment beyond the edge of the world."

—*The Voyage of the* **Dawn Treader**

Could you share in Reepicheep's excitement about seeing beyond the edge of the world and then speeding over it? Do you know anyone who values adventure as he does?

Emeth's Story

I AM EMETH, THE seventh son of Harpa Tarkaan of the city of Tehishbaan, Westward beyond the desert. I came lately into Narnia with nine and twenty others under the command of Rishda Tarkaan. Now when I first heard that we should march upon Narnia I rejoiced; for I had heard many things of your Land and desired greatly to meet you in battle. But when I found that we were to go in disguised as merchants (which is a shameful dress for a warrior and the son of a Tarkaan) and to work by lies and trickery, then my joy departed from me. And most of all when I found we must wait upon a Monkey, and when it began to be said that Tash and Aslan were one, then the world became dark in my eyes. For always since I was a boy I have served Tash and my great desire was to know more of him, if it might be, to look upon his face. But the name of Aslan was hateful to me.

"And, as you have seen, we were called together outside the straw-roofed hovel, night after night, and the fire was kindled, and the Ape brought forth out of the hovel something upon four legs that I could not well see. And the people and the Beasts bowed down and did honor to it. But I thought, the Tarkaan is deceived by the Ape: for this thing that comes out of the stable is neither Tash nor any other god. But when I watched the Tarkaan's face, and marked every word that he said to the Monkey, then I changed my mind: for I saw that the Tarkaan did not believe in it himself. And then I understood that he did not believe in Tash at all: for if he had, how could he dare to mock him?

"When I understood this, a great rage fell upon me and I wondered that the true Tash did not strike down both the Monkey and the Tarkaan with fire from heaven. Nevertheless I hid my anger and held my tongue and waited to see how it would end. But last night, as some of you know, the Monkey brought not forth the yellow thing but said that all who desired to look upon Tashlan—for so they mixed the two words to pretend that they were all one—must pass one by one into the hovel. And I said to myself, Doubtless this is some other deception. But when the Cat had followed in and had come out again in a madness of terror, then I said to myself, Surely the true Tash, whom they called on without knowledge or belief, has now come among us, and will avenge himself. And though my heart was turned into water inside me because of the greatness and terror of Tash, yet my desire was stronger than my fear, and I put force upon my knees to stay them from trembling, and on my teeth that they should not chatter, and resolved to look upon the face of Tash though he should slay me. So I offered myself to go into the hovel; and the Tarkaan, though unwillingly, let me go."

—*The Last Battle*

What power did Emeth's faith in Tash give him? Have you ever wanted something so much that you were able to overcome a great fear to get it?

Seeking Tash and Finding Aslan

[L]O! IN A NARROW PLACE between two rocks there came to meet me a great Lion. . . . He was more terrible than the Flaming Mountain of Lagour, and in beauty he surpassed all that is in the world even as the rose in bloom surpasses the dust of the desert. Then I fell at his feet and thought, Surely this is the hour of death, for the Lion (who is worthy of all honor) will know that I have served Tash all my days and not him. Nevertheless, it is better to see the Lion and die than to be Tisroc of the world and live and not to have seen him. But the Glorious One bent down his golden head and touched my forehead with his tongue and said, 'Son, thou art welcome.' But I said, 'Alas, Lord, I am no son of thine but the servant of Tash.' He answered, 'Child, all the service thou hast done to Tash, I account as service done to me.' Then by reasons of my great desire for wisdom and understanding, I overcame my fear and questioned the Glorious One and said, Lord, is it then true, as the Ape said, that thou and Tash are one? The Lion growled so that the earth shook (but his wrath was not against me) and said, It is false. Not because he and I are one, but because we are opposites, I take to me the services which thou hast done to him. For I and he are of such different kinds that no service which is vile can be done to me, and none which is not vile can be done to him. Therefore if any man swear by Tash and keep his oath for the oath's sake, it is by me that he has truly sworn, though he know it not, and it is I who reward him. And if any man do a cruelty in my name, then, though he says the name Aslan, it is Tash whom he serves and by Tash his deed is accepted. Dost thou understand, Child? I said, Lord, thou knowest how much I understand. But I said also (for the truth constrained me), Yet I have been seeking Tash all my days. Beloved, said the Glorious One, unless thy desire had been for me thou wouldst not have sought so long and so truly. For all find what they truly seek."

—*The Last Battle*

How could Emeth's service in the name of Tash actually be in the name of Aslan? What do you think it means that all find what they truly seek?

What About This Mother of Yours?

BUT WHAT ABOUT this Mother of yours whom you pretend to love so?" [said the Witch.]

"What's she got to do with it?" said Digory.

"Do you not see, Fool, that one bite of that apple would heal her? You have it in your pocket. We are here by ourselves and the Lion is far away. Use your Magic and go back to your own world. A minute later you can be at your Mother's bedside, giving her the fruit. Five minutes later you will see the color coming back to her face. She will tell you the pain is gone. Soon she will tell you she feels stronger. Then she will fall asleep—think of that; hours of sweet natural sleep, without pain, without drugs. Next day everyone will be saying how wonderfully she has recovered. Soon she will be quite well again. All will be well again. Your home will be happy again. You will be like other boys."

"Oh!" gasped Digory as if he had been hurt, and put his hand to his head. For he now knew that the most terrible choice lay before him.

—*The Magician's Nephew*

The Witch is asking Digory to choose between following Aslan's directions and healing his mother. Why is that the most terrible choice? What is the hardest choice you've ever had to make?

Enchanted Turkish Delight

THE QUEEN LET another drop fall from her bottle onto the snow, and instantly there appeared a round box, tied with green silk ribbon, which, when opened, turned out to contain several pounds of the best Turkish Delight. Each piece was sweet and light to the very center and Edmund had never tasted anything more delicious. He was quite warm now, and very comfortable.

While he was eating, the Queen kept asking him questions. . . . She seemed especially interested in the fact that there were four of them, and kept on coming back to it. "You are sure there are just four of you?" she asked. "Two Sons of Adam and two Daughters of Eve, neither more nor less?" and Edmund, with his mouth full of Turkish Delight, kept on saying, "Yes, I told you that before," and forgetting to call her "Your Majesty," but she didn't seem to mind now.

At last the Turkish Delight was all finished and Edmund was looking very hard at the empty box and wishing that she would ask him whether he would like some more. Probably the Queen knew quite well what he was thinking; for she knew, though Edmund did not, that this was enchanted Turkish Delight and that anyone who had once tasted it would want more and more of it, and would even, if they were allowed, go on eating it till they killed themselves. But she did not offer him any more. Instead, she said to him,

"Son of Adam, I should so much like to see your brother and your two sisters. Will you bring them to see me?"

"I'll try," said Edmund, still looking at the empty box. . . .

"It is a lovely place, my house," said the Queen. "I am sure you would like it. There are whole rooms full of Turkish Delight, and what's more, I have no children of my own. I want a nice boy whom I could bring up as a Prince and who would be King of Narnia when I am gone. While he was Prince he would wear a gold crown and eat Turkish Delight all day long; and you are much the cleverest and handsomest young man I've ever met. I think I would like to make you the Prince—some day, when you bring the others to visit me.". . . .

"There's nothing special about *them*," said Edmund, "and, anyway, I could always bring them some other time."

"Ah, but once you were in my house," said the Queen, "you might forget all about them. You would be enjoying yourself so much that you wouldn't want the bother of going to fetch them. No. You must go back to your own country now and come to me another day, *with them,* you understand. It is no good coming without them."

—*The Lion, the Witch, and the Wardrobe*

What weaknesses of Edmund's does the Queen play upon? Looking back, when in your life has someone taken advantage of a weakness of yours to get something from you?

A Horrible Emptiness Called the Sky

I'LL BE SWORN 'TIS AN HONEST GNOME," said the Prince. "Let go of it, friend Puddleglum. As for me, good Golg, I have been enchanted like you and your fellows, and have but newly remembered myself. And now, one question more. Do you know the way to those new diggings, by which the sorceress meant to lead out an army against Overland?"

"Ee-ee-ee!" squeaked Golg. "Yes, I know that terrible road. I will show you where it begins. But it is no manner of use your Honor asking me to go with you on it. I'll die rather."

"Why?" asked Eustace anxiously. "What's so dreadful about it?"

"Too near the top, the outside," said Golg, shuddering. "That was the worst thing the Witch did to us. We were going to be led out into the open—into the outside of the world. They say there's no roof at all there; only a horrible, great emptiness called the sky. And the diggings have gone so far that a few strokes of the pick would bring you out to it. I wouldn't dare go near them."

"Hurrah! Now you're talking!" cried Eustace, and Jill said, "But it's not horrid at all up there. We like it. We live there."

"I know you Overlanders live there," said Golg. "But I thought it was because you couldn't find your way down inside. You can't really *like* it—crawling about like flies on top of the world!"

—*The Silver Chair*

Why would living on the outside be so horrible for Golg? What value is there in trying to see things from another point of view?

Trumpkin Meets Aslan

A ND NOW!" said Aslan in a much louder voice with just a hint of roar in it, while his tail lashed his flanks. "And now, where is this little Dwarf, this famous swordsman and archer, who doesn't believe in lions? Come here, Son of Earth, come HERE!"—and the last word was no longer the hint of a roar but almost the real thing.

"Wraiths and wreckage!" gasped Trumpkin in the ghost of a voice. The children, who knew Aslan well enough to see that he liked the Dwarf very much, were not disturbed; but it was quite another thing for Trumpkin, who had never seen a lion before, let alone this Lion. He did the only sensible thing he could have done; that is, instead of bolting, he tottered toward Aslan.

Aslan pounced. Have you ever seen a very young kitten being carried in the mother cat's mouth? It was like that. The Dwarf, hunched up in a little, miserable ball, hung from Aslan's mouth. The Lion gave him one shake and all his armor rattled like a tinker's pack and then—hey-presto—the Dwarf flew up in the air. He was as safe as if he had been in bed, though he did not feel so. As he came down the huge velvety paws caught him as gently as a mother's arms and set him (right way up, too) on the ground.

"Son of Earth, shall we be friends?" asked Aslan.

"Ye—he—he—hes," panted the Dwarf, for he had not yet got his breath back.

—*Prince Caspian*

What do you think it means to be friends with Aslan?

Eustace's Rescue Party

B Y THE TIME HE WAS SOUND ASLEEP and snoring the others had finished dinner and became seriously alarmed about him. They shouted, "Eustace! Eustace! Coo-ee!" till they were hoarse and Caspian blew his horn.

"He's nowhere near or he'd have heard that," said Lucy with a white face.

"Confound the fellow," said Edmund. "What on earth did he want to slink away like this for?"

"But we must do something," said Lucy. "He may have got lost, or fallen into a hole, or been captured by savages."

"Or killed by wild beasts," said Drinian.

"And a good riddance if he has, *I* say," muttered Rhince.

"Master Rhince," said Reepicheep, "you never spoke a word that became you less. The creature is no friend of mine but he is of the Queen's blood, and while he is one of our fellowship it concerns our honor to find him and to avenge him if he is dead."

"Of course we've got to find him (if we *can*)," said Caspian wearily. "That's the nuisance of it. It means a search party and endless trouble. Bother Eustace."

—*The Voyage of the* **Dawn Treader**

Why would it concern their honor to find and avenge Eustace? When have you had to care for someone you seriously disliked because you felt bound by duty?

True Colors

B UT THE PRINCE SHOUTED SUDDENLY, "'Ware! Look to the Witch."

When they did look their hair nearly stood on end.

The instrument dropped from her hands. Her arms appeared to be fastened to her sides. Her legs were intertwined with each other, and her feet had disappeared. The long green train of her skirt thickened and grew solid, and seemed to be all one piece with the writhing green pillar of her interlocked legs. And that writhing green pillar was curving and swaying as if it had no joints, or else were all joints. Her head was thrown far back and while her nose grew longer and longer, every other part of her face seemed to disappear, except her eyes. Huge flaming eyes they were now, without brows or lashes. All this takes time to write down; it happened so quickly that there was only just time to see it. Long before there was time to do anything, the change was complete, and the great serpent which the Witch had become, green as poison, thick as Jill's waist, had flung two or three coils of its loathsome body round the Prince's legs. Quick as lightning another great loop darted round, intending to pinion his sword-arm to his side. But the Prince was just in time. He raised his arms and got them clear: the living knot closed only round his chest—ready to crack his ribs like firewood when it drew tight.

The Prince caught the creature's neck in his left hand, trying to squeeze it till it choked. This held its face (if you could call it a face) about five inches from his own. The forked tongue flickered horribly in and out, but could not reach him. With his right hand he drew back his sword for the strongest blow he could give. Meanwhile Scrubb and Puddleglum had drawn their weapons and rushed to his aid. All three blows fell at once: Scrubb's (which did not even pierce the scales and did no good) on the body of the snake below the Prince's hand, but the Prince's own blow and Puddleglum's both on its neck. Even that did not quite kill it, though it began to loosen its hold on Rilian's legs and chest. With repeated blows they hacked off its head. The horrible thing went on coiling and moving like a bit of wire long after it had died; and the floor, as you may imagine, was a nasty mess.

The Prince, when he had breath, said, "Gentlemen, I thank you." Then the three conquerors stood staring at one another and panting, without another word, for a long time. Jill had very wisely sat down and was keeping quiet; she was saying to herself, "I do hope I don't faint—or blub—or do anything idiotic."

"My royal mother is avenged," said Rilian presently. "This is undoubtedly the same worm that I pursued in vain by the fountain in the forest of Narnia, so many years ago. All these years I have been the slave of my mother's slayer. Yet I am glad, gentlemen, that the foul Witch took to her serpent form at the last. It would not have suited well either with my heart or with my honor to have slain a woman."

—*The Silver Chair*

Why is it so much easier for the Prince to slay the serpent when it shows its true form? Why do we so often confuse beauty with goodness?

Into the Waterfall

FOR NOW THEY SAW before them Caldron Pool and beyond the Pool the high unclimbable cliffs and, pouring down the cliffs, thousands of tons of water every second, flashing like diamonds in some places and dark, glassy green in others, the Great Waterfall; and already the thunder of it was in their ears.

"Don't stop! Further up and further in," called Farsight, tilting his flight a little upward.

"It's all very well for *him*," said Eustace, but Jewel also cried out:

"Don't stop. Further up and further in! Take it in your stride."

His voice could only just be heard above the roar of the water but next moment everyone saw that he had plunged into the Pool. And helter-skelter behind him, with splash after splash, all the others did the same. The water was not bitingly cold as all of them (and especially Puzzle) expected, but of a delicious foamy coolness. They all found they were swimming straight for the Waterfall itself.

"This is absolutely crazy," said Eustace to Edmund.

"I know. And yet—" said Edmund.

"Isn't it wonderful?" said Lucy. "Have you noticed one can't feel afraid, even if one wants to? Try it."

"By Jove, neither one can," said Eustace after he had tried.

Jewel reached the foot of the Waterfall first, but Tirian was only just behind him. Jill was last, so she could see the whole thing better than the others. She saw something white moving steadily up the face of the Waterfall. That white thing was the Unicorn. You couldn't tell whether he was swimming or climbing, but he moved on, higher and higher. The point of his horn divided the water just above his head, and it cascaded out in two rainbow-colored streams all round his shoulders. Just behind him came King Tirian. He moved his legs and arms as if he were swimming, but he moved straight upward: as if one could swim up the wall of a house. . . .

But before Jill had time to notice all these things fully, she was going up the Waterfall herself. It was the sort of thing that would have been quite impossible in our world. Even if you hadn't been drowned, you would have been smashed to pieces by the terrible weight of water against the countless jags of rock. But in that world you could do it. You went on, up and up, with all kinds of reflected lights flashing at you from the water and all manner of colored stones flashing through it, till it seemed as if you were climbing up light itself—and always higher and higher till the sense of height would have terrified you if you could be terrified, but later it was only gloriously exciting. And then at last one came to the lovely, smooth green curve in which the water poured over the top and found that one was out on the level river above the Waterfall. The current was racing away behind you, but you were such a wonderful swimmer that you could make headway against it. Soon they were all on the bank, dripping but happy.

—*The Last Battle*

What might it feel like not to be afraid, even if you tried? Is that something you can imagine? How big a role does even unconscious fear play in your life?

The Witch's Fatal Mistake

Wᴀᴛ ʜᴀꜱ ᴛʜᴇ Lɪᴏɴ ᴇᴠᴇʀ ᴅᴏɴᴇ for you that you should be his slave?" said the Witch. "What can he do to you once you are back in your own world? And what would your Mother think if she knew that you *could* have taken her pain away and given her back her life and saved your Father's heart from being broken, and that you *wouldn't*—that you'd rather run messages for a wild animal in a strange world that is no business of yours?"

"I—I don't think he is a wild animal," said Digory in a dried-up sort of voice. "He is—I don't know—"

"Then he is something worse," said the Witch. "Look what he has done to you already; look how heartless he has made you. That is what he does to everyone who listens to him. Cruel, pitiless boy! You would let your own Mother die rather than—"

"Oh shut up," said the miserable Digory, still in the same voice. "Do you think I don't see? But I—I promised."

"Ah, but you didn't know what you were promising. And no one here can prevent you."

"Mother herself," said Digory, getting the words out with difficulty, "wouldn't like it—awfully strict about keeping promises—and not stealing—and all that sort of thing. *She'd* tell me not to do it—quick as anything—if she was here."

"But she need never know," said the Witch, speaking more sweetly than you would have thought anyone with so fierce a face could speak. "You wouldn't tell her how you'd got the apple. Your Father need never know. No one in your world need know anything about this whole story. You needn't take the little girl back with you, you know."

That was where the Witch made her fatal mistake. Of course Digory knew that Polly could get away by her own ring as easily as he could get away by his. But apparently the Witch didn't know this. And the mean-ness of the suggestion that he should leave Polly behind suddenly made all the other things the Witch had been saying to him sound false and hollow. And even in the midst of all his misery, his head suddenly cleared, and he said (in a different and much louder voice):

"Look here; where do *you* come into all this? Why are *you* so precious fond of *my* Mother all of a sudden? What's it got to do with you? What's your game?"

—*The Magician's Nephew*

What about the Witch's suggestion helps Digory to see her real motivations? How can we see through those people and things in life that try to tempt us away from what we know is right?

Back Through the Wardrobe

So these Kings and Queens entered the thicket, and before they had gone a score of paces they all remembered that the thing they had seen was called a lamp-post, and before they had gone twenty more they noticed that they were making their way not through branches but through coats. And next moment they all came tumbling out of a wardrobe door into the empty room, and they were no longer Kings and Queens in their hunting array but just Peter, Susan, Edmund and Lucy in their old clothes. It was the same day and the same hour of the day on which they had all gone into the wardrobe to hide. Mrs. Macready and the visitors were still talking in the passage; but luckily they never came into the empty room and so the children weren't caught.

And that would have been the very end of the story if it hadn't been that they felt they really must explain to the Professor why four of the coats out of his wardrobe were missing. And the Professor, who was a very remarkable man, didn't tell them not to be silly or not to tell lies, but believed the whole story. "No," he said, "I don't think it will be any good trying to go back through the wardrobe door to get the coats. You won't get into Narnia again by *that* route. Nor would the coats be much use by now if you did! Eh? What's that? Yes, of course you'll get back to Narnia again someday. Once a King in Narnia, always a King in Narnia. But don't go trying to use the same route twice. Indeed, don't *try* to get there at all. It'll happen when you're not looking for it. And don't talk too much about it even among yourselves. And don't mention it to anyone else unless you find that they've had adventures of the same sort themselves. What's that? How will you know? Oh, you'll *know* all right. Odd things they say— even their looks—will let the secret out. Keep your eyes open. Bless me, what *do* they teach them at these schools?"

—The Lion, the Witch, and the Wardrobe

Why can they only get back to Narnia when they aren't looking to do so? What else in life is like that?

Our Crowning Glory

H AIL, ASLAN!" came his shrill voice. "I have the honor—"
But then he suddenly stopped.

The fact was that he still had no tail—whether that Lucy had forgotten it or that her cordial, though it could heal wounds, could not make things grow again. Reepicheep became aware of his loss as he made his bow; perhaps it altered something in his balance. He looked over his right shoulder. Failing to see his tail, he strained his neck further till he had to turn his shoulders and his whole body followed. But by that time his hind-quarters had turned too and were out of sight. Then he strained his neck looking over his shoulder again, with the same result. Only after he had turned completely round three times did he realize the dreadful truth.

"I am confounded," said Reepicheep to Aslan. "I am completely out of countenance. I must crave your indulgence for appearing in this unseemly fashion."

"It becomes you very well, Small One," said Aslan.

"All the same," replied Reepicheep, "if anything could be done . . . Perhaps her Majesty?" and here he bowed to Lucy.

"But what do you want with a tail?" asked Aslan.

"Sir," said the Mouse, "I can eat and sleep and die for my King without one. But a tail is the honor and glory of a Mouse."

"I have sometimes wondered, friend," said Aslan, "whether you do not think too much about your honor."

"Highest of all High Kings," said Reepicheep, "permit me to remind you that a very small size has been bestowed on us Mice, and if we did not guard our dignity, some (who weigh worth by inches) would allow themselves very unsuitable pleasantries at our expense. That is why I have been at some pains to make it known that no one who does not wish to feel this sword as near his heart as I can reach shall talk in my presence about Traps or Toasted Cheese or Candles: no, Sir—not the tallest fool in Narnia!" Here he glared very fiercely up at Wimbleweather, but the Giant, who was always a stage behind everyone else, had not yet discovered what was being talked about down at his feet, and so missed the point.

"Why have your followers all drawn *their* swords, may I ask?" said Aslan.

"May it please your High Majesty," said the second Mouse, whose name was Peepiceek, "we are all waiting to cut off our own tails if our Chief must go without his. We will not bear the shame of wearing an honor which is denied to the High Mouse."

"Ah!" roared Aslan. "You have conquered me. You have great hearts. Not for the sake of your dignity, Reepicheep, but for the love that is between you and your people, and still more for the kindness your people showed me long ago when you ate away the cords that bound me on the Stone Table (and it was then, though you have long forgotten it, that you began to be *Talking* Mice), you shall have your tail again."

—*Prince Caspian*

Why does Aslan capitulate and give Reepicheep his tail back? When does being concerned about your honor keep you from thinking about what really matters?

Aslan and Tash

P LEASE," SAID THE LAMB, "I can't understand. What have we to do with the Calormenes? We belong to Aslan. They belong to Tash. They have a god called Tash. They say he has four arms and the head of a vulture. They kill Men on his altar. I don't believe there's any such person as Tash. But if there was, how could Aslan be friends with him?"

All the animals cocked their heads sideways and all their bright eyes flashed toward the Ape. They knew it was the best question anyone had asked yet.

The Ape jumped up and spat at the Lamb.

"Baby!" he hissed. "Silly little bleater! Go home to your mother and drink milk. What do you understand of such things? But the others, listen. Tash is only another name for Aslan. All that old idea of us being right and the Calormenes wrong is silly. We know better now. The Calormenes use different words but we all mean the same thing. Tash and Aslan are only two different names for you know Who. That's why there can never be any quarrel between them. Get that into your heads, you stupid brutes. Tash is Aslan: Aslan is Tash."

You know how sad your own dog's face can look sometimes. Think of that and then think of all the faces of those Talking Beasts—all those honest, humble, bewildered Birds, Bears, Badgers, Rabbits, Moles, and Mice— all far sadder than that. Every tail was down, every whisker drooped. It would have broken your heart with very pity to see their faces.

—*The Last Battle*

Why is it so horrifying to the Narnians to hear the Ape say that Aslan and Tash are the same?

His Majesty Cannot

"FRIENDS," SAID CASPIAN, "we have now fulfilled the quest on which you embarked. The seven lords are all accounted for, and as Sir Reepicheep has sworn never to return, when you reach Ramandu's land you will doubtless find the Lords Revilian and Argoz and Mavramorn awake. To you, my Lord Drinian, I entrust this ship, bidding you sail to Narnia with all the speed you may, and above all not to land on the Island of Deathwater. And instruct my regent, the Dwarf Trumpkin, to give to all these, my shipmates, the rewards I promised them. They have been earned well. And if I come not again it is my will that the Regent, and Master Cornelius, and Trufflehunter the Badger, and the Lord Drinian choose a King of Narnia with the consent—"

"But, Sire," interrupted Drinian, "are you abdicating?"

"I am going with Reepicheep to see the World's End," said Caspian.

A low murmur of dismay ran through the sailors.

"We will take the boat," said Caspian. "You will have no need of it in these gentle seas and you must build a new one on Ramandu's Island. And now—"

"Caspian," said Edmund suddenly and sternly, "you can't do this."

"Most certainly," said Reepicheep, "his Majesty cannot."

"No indeed," said Drinian.

"Can't?" said Caspian sharply, looking for a moment not unlike his uncle Miraz.

"Begging your Majesty's pardon," said Rynelf from the deck below, "but if one of us did the same it would be called deserting."

"You presume too much on your long service, Rynelf," said Caspian.

"No, Sire! He's perfectly right," said Drinian.

"By the Mane of Aslan," said Caspian, "I had thought you were all my subjects here, not my schoolmasters."

"I'm not," said Edmund, "and I say you can *not* do this."

"Can't again," said Caspian. "What do you mean?"

"If it please your Majesty, we mean *shall not*," said Reepicheep with a very low bow. "You are the King of Narnia. You break faith with all your subjects, and especially Trumpkin, if you do not return. You shall not please yourself with adventures as if you were a private person. And if your Majesty will not hear reason it will be the truest loyalty of every man on board to follow me in disarming and binding you till you come to your senses."

—*The Voyage of the* **Dawn Treader**

Why are the words from the others so hard for Caspian to hear? Why is it important that Caspian not continue to the World's End?

What Is the Good of Anything?

[C]ASPIAN] STOOD IRRESOLUTE for a moment and then shouted out to the ship in general.

"Well, have your way. The quest is ended. We all return. Get the boat up again."

"Sire," said Reepicheep, "we do not *all* return. I, as I explained before—"

"Silence!" thundered Caspian. "I've been lessoned but I'll not be baited. Will no one silence that Mouse?"

"Your Majesty promised," said Reepicheep, "to be a good lord to the Talking Beasts of Narnia."

"Talking beasts, yes," said Caspian. "I said nothing about beasts that never stop talking." And he flung down the ladder in a temper and went into the cabin, slamming the door.

But when the others rejoined him a little later they found him changed; he was white and there were tears in his eyes.

"It's no good," he said. "I might as well have behaved decently for all the good I did with my temper and swagger. Aslan has spoken to me. No—I don't mean he was actually here. He wouldn't fit into the cabin, for one thing. But that gold lion's head on the wall came to life and spoke to me. It was terrible—his eyes. Not that he was at all rough with me—only a bit stern at first. But it was terrible all the same. And he said—he said—oh, I can't bear it. The worst thing he could have said. You're to go on—Reep and Edmund, and Lucy, and Eustace; and I'm to go back. Alone. And at once. And what *is* the good of anything?"

"Caspian, dear," said Lucy. "You knew we'd have to go back to our own world sooner or later."

"Yes," said Caspian with a sob, "but this is sooner."

—*The Voyage of the* **Dawn Treader**

Why is Caspian so upset that he has to go back and the others are to go on to the End of the World? How do you sometimes want your story to look like others' stories?

Why Can't I See Him?

IT IS A TERRIBLE THING to have to wake four people, all older than yourself and all very tired, for the purpose of telling them something they probably won't believe and making them do something they certainly won't like. . . .

She went to Peter first and shook him. "Peter," she whispered in his ear, "wake up. Quick. Aslan is here. He says we've got to follow him at once."

"Certainly, Lu. Whatever you like," said Peter unexpectedly. This was encouraging, but as Peter instantly rolled round and went to sleep again it wasn't much use.

Then she tried Susan. Susan did really wake up, but only to say in her most annoying grown-up voice, "You've been dreaming, Lucy. Go to sleep again."

She tackled Edmund next. It was very difficult to wake him, but when at last she had done it he was really awake and sat up.

"Eh?" he said in a grumpy voice. "What are you talking about?"

She said it all over again. . . .

"Aslan!" said Edmund, jumping up. "Hurray! Where?". . .

"There. There. Don't you see? Just this side of the trees."

Edmund stared hard for a while and then said, "No. There's nothing there. You've got dazzled and muddled with the moonlight. One does, you know. I thought I saw something for a moment myself. It's only an optical what-do-you-call-it."

"I can see him all the time," said Lucy. "He's looking straight at us."

"Then why can't I see him?"

"He said you mightn't be able to."

"Why?"

"I don't know. That's what he said."

"Oh, bother it all," said Edmund. "I do wish you wouldn't keep on seeing things. But I suppose we'll have to wake the others."

—*Prince Caspian*

Whose attitude do you think would be closest to your own if you were woken by Lucy? What do you think Edmund means when he says he wishes she'd stop seeing things?

Help for the Journey

YES SIR," SAID DIGORY AGAIN. He hadn't the least idea of how he was to climb the cliff and find his way among all the mountains, but he didn't like to say that for fear it would sound like making excuses. But he did say, "I hope, Aslan, you're not in a hurry. I shan't be able to get there and back very quickly."

"Little son of Adam, you shall have help," said Aslan. He then turned to the Horse who had been standing quietly beside them all this time, swishing his tail to keep the flies off, and listening with his head on one side as if the conversation were a little difficult to understand.

"My dear," said Aslan to the Horse, "would you like to be a winged horse?"

—*The Magician's Nephew*

How do you think Digory feels to know that he does not have to go on his journey alone? How does having a companion help us complete certain tasks?

Giant Rumblebuffin

T HE WHOLE CROWD of liberated statues surged back into the courtyard. And it was then that someone (Tumnus, I think) first said,

"But how are we going to get out?" for Aslan had got in by a jump and the gates were still locked.

"That'll be all right," said Aslan; and then, rising on his hind-legs, he bawled up at the Giant. "Hi! You up there," he roared. "What's your name?"

"Giant Rumblebuffin, if it please your honor," said the Giant, once more touching his cap.

"Well then, Giant Rumblebuffin," said Aslan, "just let us out of this, will you?"

"Certainly, your honor. It will be a pleasure," said Giant Rumblebuffin. "Stand well away from the gates, all you little 'uns." Then he strode to the gate himself and bang—bang—bang—went his huge club. The gates creaked at the first blow, cracked at the second, and shivered at the third. Then he tackled the towers on each side of them and after a few minutes of crashing and thudding both the towers and a good bit of the wall on each side went thundering down in a mass of hopeless rubble; and when the dust cleared it was odd, standing in that dry, grim, stony yard, to see through the gap all the grass and waving trees and sparkling streams of the forest, and the blue hills beyond that and beyond them the sky.

"Blowed if I ain't all in a muck sweat," said the Giant, puffing like the largest railway engine. "Comes of being out of condition. I suppose neither of you young ladies has such a thing as a pocket-handkerchee about you?"

"Yes, I have," said Lucy, standing on tip-toes and holding her handkerchief up as far as she could reach.

"Thank you, Missie," said Giant Rumblebuffin, stooping down. Next moment Lucy got rather a fright for she found herself caught up in mid-air between the Giant's finger and thumb. But just as she was getting near his face he suddenly started and then put her gently back on the ground muttering, "Bless me! I've picked up the little girl instead. I beg your pardon, Missie, I thought you *was* the handkerchee!"

"No, no," said Lucy, laughing, "here it is!" This time he managed to get it but it was only about the same size to him that a saccharine tablet would be to you, so that when she saw him solemnly rubbing it to and fro across his great red face, she said, "I'm afraid it's not much use to you, Mr. Rumblebuffin."

"Not at all. Not at all," said the giant politely. "Never met a nicer handkerchee. So fine, so handy. So—I don't know how to describe it."

"What a nice giant he is!" said Lucy to Mr. Tumnus.

"Oh, yes," replied the Faun. "All the Buffins always were. One of the most respected of all the giant families in Narnia. Not very clever, perhaps (I never knew a giant that was), but an old family. With traditions, you know. If he'd been the other sort she'd never have turned him into stone."

—*The Lion, the Witch, and the Wardrobe*

What about being an old family with traditions might be threatening to the Witch?

The Darkness over the Sea

ABOUT NINE THAT MORNING, very suddenly, it was so close that they could see that it was not land at all, nor even, in an ordinary sense, a mist. It was a Darkness. It is rather hard to describe, but you will see what it was like if you imagine yourself looking into the mouth of a railway tunnel—a tunnel either so long or so twisty that you cannot see the light at the far end. And you know what it would be like. For a few feet you would see the rails and sleepers and gravel in broad daylight; then there would come a place where they were in twilight; and then, pretty suddenly, but of course without a sharp dividing line, they would vanish altogether into smooth, solid blackness. It was just so here. For a few feet in front of their bows they could see the swell of the bright greenish-blue water. Beyond that, they could see the water looking pale and grey as it would look late in the evening. But beyond that again, utter blackness as if they had come to the edge of moonless and starless night.

Caspian shouted to the boatswain to keep her back, and all except the rowers rushed forward and gazed from the bows. But there was nothing to be seen by gazing. Behind them was the sea and the sun, before them the Darkness.

"Do we go into this?" asked Caspian at length.

"Not by my advice," said Drinian.

"The Captain's right," said several sailors.

"I almost think he is," said Edmund.

Lucy and Eustace didn't speak but they felt very glad inside at the turn things seemed to be taking. But all at once the clear voice of Reepicheep broke in upon the silence.

"And why not?" he said. "Will someone explain to me why not?"

No one was anxious to explain, so Reepicheep continued:

"If I were addressing peasants or slaves," he said, "I might suppose that this suggestion proceeded from cowardice. But I hope it will never be told in Narnia that a company of noble and royal persons in the flower of their age turned tail because they were afraid of the dark."

"But what manner of use would it be plowing through that blackness?" asked Drinian.

"Use?" replied Reepicheep. "Use, Captain? If by use you mean filling our bellies or our purses, I confess it will be no use at all. So far as I know we did not set sail to look for things useful but to seek honor and adventure. And here is as great an adventure as ever I heard of, and here, if we turn back, no little impeachment of all our honors."

Several of the sailors said things under their breath that sounded like "Honor be blowed," but Caspian said:

"Oh, *bother* you, Reepicheep. I almost wish we'd left you at home. All right! If you put it that way, I suppose we shall have to go on. Unless Lucy would rather not?"

Lucy felt that she would very much rather not, but what she said out loud was, "I'm game."

—*The Voyage of the* Dawn Treader

Why is Reepicheep's speech so persuasive? When have you been motivated by a sense of honor and adventure?

Aslan's Orders

O MY MASTER," said one of them, "we lead these manikins to Calormen to work in the mines of The Tisroc, may-he-live-forever."

"By the great god Tash, they are very obedient," said Tirian. Then suddenly he turned to the Dwarfs themselves. About one in six of them carried a torch and by that flickering light he could see their bearded faces all looking at him with grim and dogged expressions. "Has The Tisroc fought a great battle, Dwarfs, and conquered your land?" he asked, "that thus you go patiently to die in the salt-pits of Pugrahan?"

The two soldiers glared at him in surprise but the Dwarfs all answered, "Aslan's orders, Aslan's orders. He's sold us. What can we do against *him*?"

"Tisroc indeed!" added one and spat. "I'd like to see him try it!"

"Silence, dogs!" said the chief soldier.

"Look!" said Tirian, pulling Puzzle forward into the light. "It has all been a lie. Aslan has not come to Narnia at all. You have been cheated by the Ape. This is the thing he brought out of the stable to show you. Look at it."

What the Dwarfs saw, now that they could see it close, was certainly enough to make them wonder how they had ever been taken in. The lion-skin had got pretty untidy already during Puzzle's imprisonment in the stable and it had been knocked crooked during his journey through the dark wood. Most of it was in a big lump on one shoulder. The head, besides being pushed sideways, had somehow got very far back so that anyone could now see his silly, gentle, donkeyish face gazing out of it. Some grass stuck out of one corner of his mouth, for he'd been doing a little quiet nibbling as they brought him along. And he was muttering, "It wasn't my fault, I'm not clever. I never said I *was*."

—*The Last Battle*

When have you been taken in by a poor imitation?

Ungrateful Dwarfs

[TIRIAN SAID,] "Now, Dwarfs, you are free. Tomorrow I will lead you to free all Narnia. Three cheers for Aslan!"

But the result which followed was simply wretched. There was a feeble attempt from a few dwarfs (about five) which died away all at once: from several others there were sulky growls. Many said nothing at all.

"Don't they understand?" said Jill impatiently. "What's wrong with all you Dwarfs? Don't you hear what the King says? It's all over. The Ape isn't going to rule Narnia any longer. Everyone can go back to ordinary life. You can have fun again. Aren't you glad?". . .

"Well," said the Black Dwarf (whose name was Griffle), "I don't know how all you chaps feel, but I feel I've heard as much about Aslan as I want to for the rest of my life."

"That's right, that's right," growled the other Dwarfs. "It's all a plant, all a blooming plant."

"What do you mean?" said Tirian. He had not been pale when he was fighting but he was pale now. He had thought this was going to be a beautiful moment, but it was turning out more like a bad dream. . . .

"Do you mean you don't believe in the real Aslan?" said Jill. "But I've seen him. And he has sent us two here out of a different world."

"Ah," said Griffle with a broad smile. "So *you* say. They've taught you your stuff all right. Saying your lessons, ain't you?"

"Churl," cried Tirian, "will you give a lady the lie to her very face?"

"You keep a civil tongue in your head, Mister," replied the Dwarf. "I don't think we want any more Kings—if you *are* Tirian, which you don't look like him—no more than we want any Aslans. We're going to look after ourselves from now on and touch our caps to nobody. See?"

—*The Last Battle*

Why do you think the Dwarfs react this way to their rescue from slavery? When have you tried to help someone only to receive a less-than-grateful reaction?

The Party Arrives at Harfang

[T]HE TWO CHILDREN BOTH SAID, "Come on," and began stumbling forward on the slippery tableland as quickly as their legs would carry them. The Marsh-wiggle followed them: still talking, but now that they were forcing their way into the wind again, they could not have heard him even if they had wanted to. And they didn't want. They were thinking of baths and beds and hot drinks; and the idea of coming to Harfang too late and being shut out was almost unbearable.

In spite of their haste, it took them a long time to cross the flat top of that hill. And even when they had crossed it, there were still several ledges to climb down on the far side. But at last they reached the bottom and could see what Harfang was like.

It stood on a high crag, and in spite of its many towers was more a huge house than a castle. Obviously, the Gentle Giants feared no attack. There were windows in the outside wall quite close to the ground—a thing no one would have in a serious fortress. There were even odd little doors here and there, so that it would be quite easy to get in and out of the castle without going through the courtyard. This raised the spirits of Jill and Scrubb. It made the whole place look more friendly and less forbidding.

At first the height and steepness of the crag frightened them, but presently they noticed that there was an easier way up on the left and that the road wound up toward it. It was a terrible climb, after the journey they had already had, and Jill nearly gave up. Scrubb and Puddleglum had to help her for the last hundred yards. But in the end they stood before the castle gate. The portcullis was up and the gate was open.

However tired you are, it takes some nerve to walk up to a giant's front door. In spite of all his previous warnings against Harfang, it was Puddleglum who showed the most courage.

"Steady pace, now," he said. "Don't look frightened, whatever you do. We've done the silliest thing in the world by coming at all: but now that we *are* here, we'd best put a bold face on it."

With these words he strode forward into the gateway, stood still under the arch where the echo would help his voice, and called out as loud as he could.

"Ho! Porter! Guests who seek lodging."

And while he was waiting for something to happen, he took off his hat and knocked off the heavy mass of snow which had gathered on its wide brim.

"I say," whispered Scrubb to Jill. "He may be a wet blanket, but he has plenty of pluck—and cheek."

—*The Silver Chair*

Why would the children lose heart just as they reach the place they have been longing for for days? Have you ever had a similar last-minute attack of nervousness? Why do you think Puddleglum boldly announces their arrival despite his reluctance to come to Harfang?

The New Kings and Queens of Narnia

THAT EVENING AFTER TEA the four children all managed to get down to the beach again and get their shoes and stockings off and feel the sand between their toes. But next day was more solemn. For then, in the Great Hall of Cair Paravel—that wonderful hall with the ivory roof and the west wall hung with peacock's feathers and the eastern door which looks towards the sea, in the presence of all their friends and to the sound of trumpets, Aslan solemnly crowned them and led them to the four thrones amid deafening shouts of, "Long Live King Peter! Long Live Queen Susan! Long Live King Edmund! Long Live Queen Lucy!"

"Once a king or queen in Narnia, always a king or queen. Bear it well, Sons of Adam! Bear it well, Daughters of Eve!" said Aslan.

And through the eastern door, which was wide open, came the voices of the mermen and the mermaids swimming close to the shore and singing in honor of their new Kings and Queens.

So the children sat on their thrones and scepters were put into their hands and they gave rewards and honors to all their friends, to Tumnus the Faun, and to the Beavers, and Giant Rumblebuffin, to the leopards, and the good centaurs, and the good dwarfs, and to the lion. And that night there was a great feast in Cair Paravel, and revelry and dancing, and gold flashed and wine flowed, and answering to the music inside, but stranger, sweeter and more piercing, came the music of the sea people.

—*The Lion, the Witch, and the Wardrobe*

What does it mean that once a king or queen in Narnia, always a king or queen? What do you think the children need to do to bear it well?

OCTOBER

Even a Traitor May Mend

AFTER LUNCH, which they had on the terrace (it was cold birds and cold game pie and wine and bread and cheese), King Lune ruffled up his brow and heaved a sigh and said, "Heigh-ho! We have still that sorry creature Rabadash on our hands, my friends, and must needs resolve what to do with him."

Lucy was sitting on the King's right and Aravis on his left. King Edmund sat at one end of the table and the Lord Darrin faced him at the other. Dar and Peridan and Cor and Corin were on the same side as the King.

"Your Majesty would have a perfect right to strike off his head," said Peridan. "Such an assault as he made puts him on a level with assassins."

"It is very true," said Edmund. "But even a traitor may mend. I have known one that did." And he looked very thoughtful.

—*The Horse and His Boy*

Are you willing to give people another chance?

The Apple of Life

THEN DIGORY TOOK A MINUTE to get his breath, and then went softly into his Mother's room. And there she lay, as he had seen her lie so many other times, propped up on the pillows, with a thin, pale face that would make you cry to look at it. Digory took the Apple of Life out of his pocket.

And just as the Witch Jadis had looked different when you saw her in our world instead of in her own, so the fruit of that mountain garden looked different too. There were of course all sorts of colored things in the bedroom; the colored counterpane on the bed, the wallpaper. . . . But the moment Digory took the Apple out of his pocket, all those things seemed to have scarcely any color at all. Every one of them, even the sunlight, looked faded and dingy. . . . Nothing else was worth looking at: you couldn't look at anything else. And the smell of the Apple of Youth was as if there was a window in the room that opened on Heaven.

"Oh, darling, how lovely," said Digory's Mother.

"You will eat it, won't you? Please," said Digory.

"I don't know what the Doctor would say," she answered. "But really— I almost feel as if I could."

He peeled it and cut it up and gave it to her piece by piece. And no sooner had she finished it than she smiled and her head sank back on the pillow and she was asleep: a real, natural, gentle sleep, without any of those nasty drugs, which was, as Digory knew, the thing in the whole world that she wanted most. . . . He bent down and kissed her very softly and stole out of the room with a beating heart, taking the core of the apple with him. For the rest of that day, whenever he looked at the things about him, and saw how ordinary and unmagical they were, he hardly dared to hope; but when he remembered the face of Aslan he did hope.

—*The Magician's Nephew*

Why, until he remembers the face of Aslan, does it seem harder for Digory to hope when he is back in his world? When in your life has something that seemed so real in one setting seemed harder to understand or believe in another setting? Are there things you cling to that help you believe?

The Beauty Spell

T HEN SHE CAME TO A PAGE which was such a blaze of pictures that one hardly noticed the writing. Hardly—but she *did* notice the first words. They were, *An infallible spell to make beautiful her that uttereth it beyond the lot of mortals.* Lucy peered at the pictures with her face close to the page, and though they had seemed crowded and muddlesome before, she found she could now see them quite clearly. The first was a picture of a girl standing at a reading-desk reading in a huge book. And the girl was dressed exactly like Lucy. In the next picture Lucy (for the girl in the picture was Lucy herself) was standing up with her mouth open and a rather terrible expression on her face, chanting or reciting something. In the third picture the beauty beyond the lot of mortals had come to her. It was strange, considering how small the pictures had looked at first, that the Lucy in the picture now seemed quite as big as the real Lucy; and they looked into each other's eyes and the real Lucy looked away after a few minutes because she was dazzled by the beauty of the other Lucy; though she could still see a sort of likeness to herself in that beautiful face. And now the pictures came crowding on her thick and fast. She saw herself throned on high at a great tournament in Calormen and all the Kings of the world fought because of her beauty. After that it turned from tournaments to real wars, and all Narnia and Archenland, Telmar and Calormen, Galma and Terebinthia, were laid waste with the fury of the kings and dukes and great lords who fought for her favor. Then it changed and Lucy, still beautiful beyond the lot of mortals, was back in England. And Susan (who had always been the beauty of the family) came home from America. The Susan in the picture looked exactly like the real Susan only plainer and with a nasty expression. And Susan was jealous of the dazzling beauty of Lucy, but that didn't matter a bit because no one cared anything about Susan now.

"I *will* say the spell," said Lucy. "I don't care. I will." She said *I don't care* because she had a strong feeling that she mustn't.

But when she looked back at the opening words of the spell, there in the middle of the writing, where she felt quite sure there had been no picture before, she found the great face of a lion, of The Lion, Aslan himself, staring into hers. It was painted such a bright gold that it seemed to be coming toward her out of the page; and indeed she never was quite sure afterward that it hadn't really moved a little. At any rate she knew the expression on his face quite well. He was growling and you could see most of his teeth. She became horribly afraid and turned over the page at once.

—*The Voyage of the* **Dawn Treader**

What do the pictures reveal about Lucy's weaknesses? Even as she is tempted, Lucy has a strong feeling that she shouldn't say the spell. Where do you think that feeling comes from? What quality would tempt you as beauty tempts Lucy?

Help Will Come

[Nikabrik said,] "You, you great clerk, you master magician, you know-all; are you still asking us to hang our hopes on Aslan and King Peter and all the rest of it?"

"I must confess—I cannot deny it—that I am deeply disappointed in the result of the operation," came the answer. ("That'll be Doctor Cornelius," said Trumpkin.)

"To speak plainly," said Nikabrik, "your wallet's empty, your eggs addled, your fish uncaught, your promises broken. Stand aside then and let others work. And that is why—"

"The help will come," said Trufflehunter. "I stand by Aslan. Have patience, like us beasts. The help will come. It may be even now at the door."

"Pah!" snarled Nikabrik. "You badgers would have us wait till the sky falls and we can all catch larks. I tell you we *can't* wait. Food is running short; we lose more than we can afford at every encounter; our followers are slipping away."

—Prince Caspian

Why do you think Trufflehunter remains so confident that help is on the way? How can we know, in difficult situations, when it is best to stay the course with patience and when we must drastically alter our course?

The Indescribable Fruit

TIRIAN HAD THOUGHT—or he would have thought if he had time to think at all—that they were inside a little thatched stable, about twelve feet long and six feet wide. In reality they stood on grass, the deep blue sky was overhead, and the air which blew gently on their faces was that of a day in early summer. Not far away from them rose a grove of trees, thickly leaved, but under every leaf there peeped out the gold or faint yellow or purple or glowing red of fruits such as no one has seen in our world. The fruit made Tirian feel that it must be autumn but there was something in the feel of the air that told him it could not be later than June. They all moved toward the trees.

Everyone raised his hand to pick the fruit he best liked the look of, and then everyone paused for a second. This fruit was so beautiful that each felt "It can't be meant for me . . . surely we're not allowed to pluck it."

"It's all right," said Peter. "I know what we're all thinking. But I'm sure, quite sure, we needn't. I've a feeling we've got to the country where everything is allowed."

"Here goes, then!" said Eustace. And they all began to eat.

What was the fruit like? Unfortunately no one can describe a taste. All I can say is that, compared with those fruits, the freshest grapefruit you've ever eaten was dull, and the juiciest orange was dry, and the most melting pear was hard and woody, and the sweetest wild strawberry was sour. And there were no seeds or stones, and no wasps. If you had once eaten that fruit, all the nicest things in this world would taste like medicines after it. But I can't describe it. You can't find out what it is like unless you can get to that country and taste it for yourself.

—*The Last Battle*

In what kind of place could everything be allowed? Why isn't everything allowed in Narnia or in our world?

To the Bottom of the World?

"Your Honors," said Golg (and when they turned to look at him they could see nothing but blackness for a few minutes, their eyes were so dazzled). "Your Honors, why don't you come down to Bism? You'd be happier there than in that cold, unprotected, naked country out on top. Or at least come down for a short visit."

Jill took it for granted that none of the others would listen to such an idea for a moment. To her horror she heard the Prince saying:

"Truly, friend Golg, I have half a mind to come down with you. For this is a marvelous adventure, and it may be no mortal man has ever looked into Bism before or will ever have the chance again. And I know not how, as the years pass, I shall bear to remember that it was once in my power to have probed the uttermost pit of Earth and that I forbore. But could a man live there? You do not swim in the fire-river itself?"

"Oh no, your Honor. Not we. It's only salamanders live in the fire itself."

"What kind of beast is your salamander?" asked the Prince.

"It is hard to tell their kind, your Honor," said Golg. "For they are too white-hot to look at. But they are most like small dragons. They speak to us out of the fire. They are wonderfully clever with their tongues: very witty and eloquent."

Jill glanced hastily at Eustace. She had felt sure that he would like the idea of sliding down that chasm even less than she did. Her heart sank as she saw that his face was quite changed. He looked much more like the Prince than like the old Scrubb at Experiment House. For all his adventures, and the days when he had sailed with King Caspian, were coming back to him.

"Your Highness," he said. "If my old friend Reepicheep the Mouse were here, he would say we could not now refuse the adventures of Bism without a great impeachment to our honor."

"Down there," said Golg, "I could show you real gold, real silver, real diamonds."

"Bosh!" said Jill rudely. "As if we didn't know that we're below the deepest mines even here."

"Yes," said Golg. "I have heard of those little scratches in the crust that you Topdwellers call mines. But that's where you get dead gold, dead silver, dead gems. Down in Bism we have them alive and growing. There I'll pick you bunches of rubies that you can eat and squeeze you a cupful of diamond juice. You won't care much about fingering the cold, dead treasures of your shallow mines after you have tasted the live ones in Bism."

"My father went to the world's end," said Rilian thoughtfully. "It would be a marvelous thing if his son went to the bottom of the world."

—*The Silver Chair*

Why are Eustace and Rilian tempted to travel to the bottom of the world? Would you be interested in doing so? If so, what would be the most alluring part?

He Ought to Know

WHEN AT LAST SHE WAS FREE to come back to Edmund she found him standing on his feet and not only healed of his wounds but looking better than she had seen him look—oh, for ages; in fact ever since his first term at that horrid school which was where he had begun to go wrong. He had become his real old self again and could look you in the face. And there on the field of battle Aslan made him a knight.

"Does he know," whispered Lucy to Susan, "what Aslan did for him? Does he know what the arrangement with the Witch really was?"

"Hush! No. Of course not," said Susan.

"Oughtn't he to be told?" said Lucy.

"Oh, surely not," said Susan. "It would be too awful for him. Think how you'd feel if you were he."

"All the same I think he ought to know," said Lucy. But at that moment they were interrupted.

—*The Lion, the Witch, and the Wardrobe*

Lucy and Susan are debating whether Edmund should know that Aslan gave his life at the Table in Edmund's place. Do you agree with Susan that he would rather not know or with Lucy that he ought? How would you feel if you were Edmund hearing such a thing?

Could It Be True?

I T I S A R A F T," said King Tirian.

And so it was. Half a dozen splendid tree trunks, all newly cut and newly lopped of their branches, had been lashed together to make a raft, and were gliding swiftly down the river. On the front of the raft there was a water rat with a pole to steer it.

"Hey! Water-Rat! What are you about?" cried the King.

"Taking logs down to sell to the Calormenes, Sire," said the Rat, touching his ear as he might have touched his cap if he had had one.

"Calormenes!" thundered Tirian. "What do you mean? Who gave order for these trees to be felled?"

The River flows so swiftly at that time of the year that the raft had already glided past the King and Jewel. But the Water-Rat looked back over its shoulder and shouted out:

"The Lion's orders, Sire. Aslan himself." He added something more but they couldn't hear it.

The King and the Unicorn stared at one another and both looked more frightened than they had ever been in any battle.

"Aslan," said the King at last, in a very low voice. "Aslan. Could it be true? *Could* he be felling the holy trees and murdering the Dryads?"

"Unless the Dryads have all done something dreadfully wrong—" murmured Jewel.

"But selling them to Calormenes!" said the King. "Is it possible?"

"I don't know," said Jewel miserably. "He's not a *tame* lion."

—The Last Battle

What does Aslan's not being a tame lion have to do with anything? What does it mean to be tame or not? How would you characterize yourself?

He Likes to Be Asked

I AM HUNGRY," SAID Digory.

"Well, tuck in," said Fledge, taking a big mouthful of grass. Then he raised his head, still chewing and with bits of grass sticking out on each side of his mouth like whiskers, and said, "Come on, you two. Don't be shy. There's plenty for us all."

"But we can't eat grass," said Digory.

"H'm, h'm," said Fledge, speaking with his mouth full. "Well—h'm— don't know quite what you'll do then. Very good grass too."

Polly and Digory stared at one another in dismay.

"Well, I *do* think someone might have arranged about our meals," said Digory.

"I'm sure Aslan would have, if you'd asked him," said Fledge.

"Wouldn't he know without being asked?" said Polly.

"I've no doubt he would," said the Horse (still with his mouth full). "But I've a sort of idea he likes to be asked."

—*The Magician's Nephew*

Why is it wrong for Polly and Digory to assume that someone should have provided their meals? What do we learn when we have to ask for what we need?

Poggin's Optimism

POGGIN WAS REALLY QUITE CHEERFUL about the night's work they had to do. He was sure that the Boar and the Bear, and probably all the Dogs would come over to their side at once. And he couldn't believe that all the other Dwarfs would stick to Griffle. And fighting by firelight and in and out among trees would be an advantage to the weaker side. And then, if they could win tonight, need they really throw their lives away by meeting the main Calormene army a few days later?

Why not hide in the woods, or even up in the Western Waste beyond the great waterfall and live like outlaws? And they might gradually get stronger and stronger, for Talking Beasts and Archenlanders would be joining them every day. And at last they'd come out of hiding and sweep the Calormenes (who would have got careless by then) out of the country and Narnia would be revived. After all, something very like that had happened in the time of King Miraz!

And Tirian heard all this and thought, "But what about Tash?" and felt in his bones that none of it was going to happen. But he didn't say so.

—The Last Battle

Despite the news that Narnia has been overthrown by the Calormenes, Poggin remains optimistic. Why do you think Tirian chooses not to share his own less optimistic views? If you were King Tirian, would you have spoken up? Why or why not?

Lunch with the Giants

A T LUNCHTIME something happened which made all three of them more anxious than ever to leave the castle of the Gentle Giants. They had lunch in the great hall at a little table of their own, near the fireplace. At a bigger table, about twenty yards away, half a dozen old giants were lunching. Their conversation was so noisy, and so high up in the air, that the children soon took no more notice of it than you would of hooters outside the window or traffic noises in the street. They were eating cold venison, a kind of food which Jill had never tasted before, and she was liking it.

Suddenly Puddleglum turned to them, and his face had gone so pale that you could see the paleness under the natural muddiness of his complexion. He said:

"Don't eat another bite."

"What's wrong?" asked the other two in a whisper.

"Didn't you hear what those giants were saying? 'That's a nice tender haunch of venison,' said one of them. 'Then that stag was a liar,' said another. 'Why?' said the first one. 'Oh,' said the other. 'They say that when he was caught he said, Don't kill me, I'm tough. You won't like me.'" For a moment Jill did not realize the full meaning of this. But she did when Scrubb's eyes opened wide with horror and he said:

"So we've been eating a *Talking* stag."

This discovery didn't have exactly the same effect on all of them. Jill, who was new to that world, was sorry for the poor stag and thought it rotten of the giants to have killed him. Scrubb, who had been in that world before and had at least one Talking beast as his dear friend, felt horrified; as you might feel about a murder. But Puddleglum, who was Narnian born, was sick and faint, and felt as you would feel if you found you had eaten a baby.

—*The Silver Chair*

Why do they each react so differently to the discovery that they have been eating a Talking stag? Why is it such a tragedy?

Eustace Is Visited by a Lion

WELL, ANYWAY, I looked up and saw the very last thing I expected: a huge lion coming slowly toward me. And one queer thing was that there was no moon last night, but there was moonlight where the lion was. So it came nearer and nearer. I was terribly afraid of it. You may think that, being a dragon, I could have knocked any lion out easily enough. But it wasn't that kind of fear. I wasn't afraid of it eating me, I was just afraid of *it*—if you can understand. Well, it came close up to me and looked straight into my eyes. And I shut my eyes tight. But that wasn't any good because it told me to follow it."

"You mean it spoke?"

"I don't know. Now that you mention it, I don't think it did. But it told me all the same. And I knew I'd have to do what it told me, so I got up and followed it."

—*The Voyage of the* **Dawn Treader**

After being turned into a dragon, Eustace is visited by a lion, perhaps in the night or perhaps in a dream. Why is Eustace afraid? Why does he follow the lion even though he fears it?

Eustace Sheds His Skin

[Eustace said,] "And [the lion] led me a long way into the mountains. . . . So at last we came to the top of a mountain I'd never seen before and on the top of this mountain there was a garden. . . . In the middle of it there was a well.

"I knew it was a well because you could see the water bubbling up from the bottom of it: but it was a lot bigger than most wells—like a very big, round bath with marble steps going down into it. The water was as clear as anything and I thought if I could get in there and bathe, it would ease the pain in my leg. But the lion told me I must undress first. Mind you, I don't know if he said any words out loud or not.

"I was just going to say that I couldn't undress because I hadn't any clothes on when I suddenly thought that dragons are snaky sort of things and snakes can cast their skins. Oh, of course, thought I, that's what the lion means. So I started scratching myself and my scales began coming off all over the place. And then I scratched a little deeper and, instead of just scales coming off here and there, my whole skin started peeling off beautifully, like it does after an illness, or as if I was a banana. In a minute or two I just stepped out of it. I could see it lying there beside me, looking rather nasty. It was a most lovely feeling. So I started to go down into the well for my bathe.

"But just as I was going to put my feet into the water I looked down and saw that they were all hard and rough and wrinkled and scaly just as they had been before. Oh, that's all right, said I, it only means I had another smaller suit on underneath the first one, and I'll have to get out of it too. So I scratched and tore again and this underskin peeled off beautifully. . . .

"Well, exactly the same thing happened again. And I thought to myself, oh dear, how ever many skins have I got to take off? For I was longing to bathe my leg. So I scratched away for the third time and got off a third skin, just like the two others, and stepped out of it. But as soon as I looked at myself in the water I knew it had been no good."

—*The Voyage of the* **Dawn Treader**

Why do you think Eustace is unable to effectively remove his own skin? When and why have you wanted to step out of your skin?

The Lion Removes Eustace's Skin

THEN THE LION said—but I don't know if it spoke—'You will have to let me undress you.' I was afraid of his claws, I can tell you, but I was pretty nearly desperate now. So I just lay flat down on my back to let him do it.

"The very first tear he made was so deep that I thought it had gone right into my heart. And when he began pulling the skin off, it hurt worse than anything I've ever felt. The only thing that made me able to bear it was just the pleasure of feeling the stuff peel off. You know—if you've ever picked the scab off a sore place. It hurts like billy-oh but it *is* fun to see it coming away."

"I know exactly what you mean," said Edmund.

"Well, he peeled the beastly stuff right off—just as I thought I'd done it myself the other three times, only they hadn't hurt—and there it was, lying on the grass, only ever so much thicker, and darker, and more knobbly-looking than the others had been. And there was I as smooth and soft as a peeled switch and smaller than I had been. Then he caught hold of me—I didn't like that much for I was very tender underneath now that I'd no skin on—and threw me into the water. It smarted like anything but only for a moment. After that it became perfectly delicious and as soon as I started swimming and splashing I found that all the pain had gone from my arm. And then I saw why. I'd turned into a boy again. You'd think me simply phony if I told you how I felt about my own arms. I know they've no muscle and are pretty mouldy compared with Caspian's, but I was so glad to see them."

—*The Voyage of the* Dawn Treader

What about having his dragon skin removed do you think hurts and feels good at the same time? What have you experienced that was painful at the time but in the end made you feel much better?

I Think You've Seen Aslan

AFTER A BIT the lion took me out and dressed me—"
"Dressed you? With his paws?"

"Well, I don't exactly remember that bit. But he did somehow or other, in new clothes—the same I've got on now, as a matter of fact. And then suddenly I was back here. Which is what makes me think it must have been a dream."

"No. It wasn't a dream," said Edmund.

"Why not?"

"Well, there are the clothes, for one thing. And you have been—well, un-dragoned, for another."

"What do you think it was, then?" asked Eustace.

"I think you've seen Aslan," said Edmund.

"Aslan!" said Eustace. "I've heard that name mentioned several times since we joined the *Dawn Treader*. And I felt—I don't know what—I hated it. But I was hating everything then. And by the way, I'd like to apologize. I'm afraid I've been pretty beastly."

"That's all right," said Edmund. "Between ourselves, you haven't been as bad as I was on my first trip to Narnia. You were only an ass, but I was a traitor." . . .

It would be nice, and fairly nearly true, to say that "from that time forth Eustace was a different boy." To be strictly accurate, he began to be a different boy. He had relapses. There were still many days when he could be very tiresome. But most of those I shall not notice. The cure had begun.

—*The Voyage of the* **Dawn Treader**

Have you ever seen a transformation like Eustace's? How are you likely to focus on the relapses rather than the overall cure?

The Cat Enters the Stable

THE APE WAS CALLING THE CAT to come forward. "Ho-ho!" said the Ape. "So you, a pert Puss, would look upon him face to face. Come on, then! I'll open the door for you. Don't blame me if he scares the whiskers off your face. That's your affair."

And the Cat got up and came out of its place in the crowd, walking primly and daintily, with its tail in the air, not one hair on its sleek coat out of place. It came on till it had passed the fire and was so close that Tirian, from where he stood with his shoulder against the end-wall of the stable, could look right into its face. Its big green eyes never blinked. ("Cool as a cucumber," muttered Eustace. "*It* knows it has nothing to fear.") The Ape, chuckling and making faces, shuffled across beside the Cat: put up his paw: drew the bolt and opened the door. Tirian thought he could hear the Cat purring as it walked into the dark doorway.

"Aii-aii-aouwee!—" The most horrible caterwaul you ever heard made everyone jump. You have been wakened yourself by cats quarreling or making love on the roof in the middle of the night: you know the sound.

This was worse. The Ape was knocked head over heels by Ginger coming back out of the stable at top speed. If you had not known he was a cat, you might have thought he was a ginger-colored streak of lightning. He shot across the open grass, back into the crowd. No one wants to meet a cat in that state. You could see animals getting out of his way to left and right. He dashed up a tree, whisked round, and hung head downward. His tail was bristled out till it was nearly as thick as his whole body: his eyes were like saucers of green fire: along his back every single hair stood on end. . . .

"Now, Ginger," said the Captain. "Enough of that noise. Tell them what thou hast seen."

"Aii—Aii—Aaow—Awah," screamed the Cat.

"Art thou not called a *Talking* Beast?" said the Captain. "Then hold thy devilish noise and talk."

What followed was rather horrible. Tirian felt quite certain (and so did the others) that the Cat was trying to say something: but nothing came out of his mouth except the ordinary, ugly cat-noises you might hear from any angry or frightened old Tom in a backyard in England. And the longer he caterwauled the less like a Talking Beast he looked. Uneasy whimperings and little sharp squeals broke out from among the other Animals.

"Look, look!" said the voice of the Bear. "It can't talk. It has forgotten how to talk! It has gone back to being a dumb beast. Look at its face." Everyone saw that it was true. And then the greatest terror of all fell upon those Narnians. For every one of them had been taught—when only a chick or a puppy or a cub—how Aslan at the beginning of the world had turned the beasts of Narnia into Talking Beasts and warned them that if they weren't good they might one day be turned back again and be like the poor witless animals one meets in other countries. "And now it is coming upon us," they moaned.

"Mercy! Mercy!" wailed the Beasts. "Spare us, Lord Shift, stand between us and Aslan, you must always go in and speak to him for us. We daren't, we daren't."

Ginger disappeared further up into the tree. No one ever saw him again.

—The Last Battle

After the Cat enters the stable where Shift the Ape claims Aslan is waiting, he is changed back into a dumb beast. Why is seeing that the greatest terror of all for the other Narnians? What might being changed from a Talking Beast to a dumb beast be equivalent to in our world?

Jill and Eustace Return

THEN ASLAN EXPLAINED to Caspian what Jill and Eustace were going back to and all about Experiment House: he seemed to know it quite as well as they did.

"Daughter," said Aslan to Jill, "pluck a switch off that bush." She did; and as soon as it was in her hand it turned into a fine new riding crop.

"Now, Sons of Adam, draw your swords," said Aslan. "But use only the flat, for it is cowards and children, not warriors, against whom I send you."

"Are you coming with us, Aslan?" said Jill.

"They shall see only my back," said Aslan.

He led them rapidly through the wood, and before they had gone many paces, the wall of Experiment House appeared before them. Then Aslan roared so that the sun shook in the sky and thirty feet of the wall fell down before them. They looked through the gap, down into the school shrubbery and on to the roof of the gym, all under the same dull autumn sky which they had seen before their adventures began. Aslan turned to Jill and Eustace and breathed upon them and touched their foreheads with his tongue. Then he lay down amid the gap he had made in the wall and turned his golden back to England, and his lordly face toward his own lands. At the same moment Jill saw figures whom she knew only too well running up through the laurels toward them. Most of the gang were there—Adela Pennyfather and Cholmondely Major, Edith Winterblott, "Spotty" Sorner, big Bannister, and the two loathsome Garrett twins. But suddenly they stopped. Their faces changed, and all the meanness, conceit, cruelty, and sneakishness almost disappeared in one single expression of terror. For they saw the wall fallen down, and a lion as large as a young elephant lying in the gap, and three figures in glittering clothes with weapons in their hands rushing down upon them. For, with the strength of Aslan in them, Jill plied her crop on the girls and Caspian and Eustace plied the flats of their swords on the boys so well that in two minutes all the bullies were running like mad, crying out, "Murder! Fascists! Lions! It isn't *fair*." And then the Head (who was, by the way, a woman) came running out to see what was happening. And when she saw the lion and the broken wall and Caspian and Jill and Eustace (whom she quite failed to recognize) she had hysterics and went back to the house and began ringing up the police with stories about a lion escaped from a circus, and escaped convicts who broke down walls and carried drawn swords. In the midst of all this fuss Jill and Eustace slipped quietly indoors and changed out of their bright clothes into ordinary things, and Caspian went back into his own world. And the wall, at Aslan's word, was made whole again. When the police arrived and found no lion, no broken wall, and no convicts, and the Head behaving like a lunatic, there was an inquiry into the whole thing. And in the inquiry all sorts of things about Experiment House came out, and about ten people got expelled. After that, the Head's friends saw that the Head was no use as a Head, so they got her made an Inspector to interfere with other Heads. And when they found she wasn't much good even at that, they got her into Parliament where she lived happily ever after.

—*The Silver Chair*

Have you ever imagined a revenge on bullies or others? If so, how might yours go? How would revenge make or not make a difference?

The Feasters Are Turned to Stone

A LITTLE WAY OFF at the foot of a tree sat a merry party, a squirrel and his wife with their children and two satyrs and a dwarf and an old dog-fox, all on stools round a table. Edmund couldn't quite see what they were eating, but it smelled lovely and there seemed to be decorations of holly and he wasn't at all sure that he didn't see something like a plum pudding. At the moment when the sledge stopped, the Fox, who was obviously the oldest person present, had just risen to its feet, holding a glass in its right paw as if it was going to say something. But when the whole party saw the sledge stopping and who was in it, all the gaiety went out of their faces. The father squirrel stopped eating with his fork halfway to his mouth and one of the satyrs stopped with its fork actually in its mouth, and the baby squirrels squeaked with terror.

"What is the meaning of this?" asked the Witch Queen. Nobody answered.

"Speak, vermin!" she said again. "Or do you want my dwarf to find you a tongue with his whip? What is the meaning of all this gluttony, this waste, this self-indulgence? Where did you get all these things?"

"Please, your Majesty," said the Fox, "we were given them. And if I might make so bold as to drink your Majesty's very good health—"

"Who gave them to you?" said the Witch.

"F-F-F-Father Christmas," stammered the Fox.

"What?" roared the Witch, springing from the sledge and taking a few strides nearer to the terrified animals. "He has not been here! He cannot have been here! How dare you—but no. Say you have been lying and you shall even now be forgiven."

At that moment one of the young squirrels lost its head completely.

"He has—he has—he has!" it squeaked, beating its little spoon on the table. Edmund saw the Witch bite her lips so that a drop of blood appeared on her white cheek. Then she raised her wand. "Oh, don't, don't, please don't," shouted Edmund, but even while he was shouting she had waved her wand and instantly where the merry party had been there were only statues of creatures (one with its stone fork fixed forever halfway to its stone mouth) seated round a stone table on which there were stone plates and a stone plum pudding.

"As for you," said the Witch, giving Edmund a stunning blow on the face as she remounted the sledge, "let that teach you to ask favor for spies and traitors. Drive on!" And Edmund, for the first time in this story, felt sorry for someone besides himself. It seemed so pitiful to think of those little stone figures sitting there all the silent days and all the dark nights, year after year, till the moss grew on them and at last even their faces crumbled away.

—The Lion, the Witch, and the Wardrobe

Why is a celebratory feast so repugnant to the Witch? Why do you think this scene finally awakens empathy in Edmund?

Eustace Slays a Calormene Soldier

"GIVE THE PASSWORD," said the chief soldier.
"This is my password," said the King as he drew his sword.
"*The light is dawning, the lie broken.* Now guard thee, miscreant, for I am Tirian of Narnia."

He flew upon the chief soldier like lightning. Eustace, who had drawn his sword when he saw the King draw his, rushed at the other one: his face was deadly pale, but I wouldn't blame him for that. And he had the luck that beginners sometimes do have. He forgot all that Tirian had tried to teach him that afternoon, slashed wildly (indeed I'm not sure his eyes weren't shut) and suddenly found, to his own great surprise, that the Calormene lay dead at his feet. And though that was a great relief, it was, at the moment, rather frightening. The King's fight lasted a second or two longer: then he too had killed his man and shouted to Eustace, "'Ware the other two."

But the Dwarfs had settled the two remaining Calormenes. There was no enemy left.

"Well struck, Eustace!" cried Tirian, clapping him on the back.

—*The Last Battle*

Why is Eustace frightened to realize he has prevailed over the Calormene? How do you think you would react in the same situation?

Remember the Signs

B UT LONG BEFORE she had got anywhere near the edge, the voice behind her said, "Stand still. In a moment I will blow. But, first, remember, remember, remember the signs. Say them to yourself when you wake in the morning and when you lie down at night, and when you wake in the middle of the night. And whatever strange things may happen to you, let nothing turn your mind from following the signs. And secondly, I give you a warning. Here on the mountain I have spoken to you clearly: I will not often do so down in Narnia. Here on the mountain, the air is clear and your mind is clear; as you drop down into Narnia, the air will thicken. Take great care that it does not confuse your mind. And the signs which you have learned here will not look at all as you expect them to look, when you meet them there. That is why it is so important to know them by heart and pay no attention to appearances. Remember the signs and believe the signs. Nothing else matters. And now, daughter of Eve, farewell—"

—*The Silver Chair*

Why wouldn't Aslan speak clearly to Jill in Narnia as he does on the mountain? Are there any signs you watch for in life to help you keep your priorities straight? If so, what are they?

Seeing Is Believing

THE APE WAS SPEAKING AGAIN.

"And after a horrid thing like that, Aslan—Tashlan—is angrier than ever. He says he's been a great deal too good to you, coming out every night to be looked at, see! Well, he's not coming out any more."

Howls and mewings and squeals and grunts were the Animals' answer to this, but suddenly a quite different voice broke in with a loud laugh.

"Hark what the monkey says," it shouted. "We know why he isn't going to bring his precious Aslan out. I'll tell you why: because he hasn't got him. He never had anything except an old donkey with a lion-skin on its back. Now he's lost *that* and he doesn't know what to do."

Tirian could not see the faces on the other side of the fire very well but he guessed this was Griffle the Chief Dwarf. And he was quite certain of it when, a second later, all the Dwarfs' voices joined in, singing: "Don't know what to do! Don't know what to do! Don't know what to do-o-o!"

"Silence!" thundered Rishda Tarkaan. "Silence, children of mud! Listen to me, you other Narnians, lest I give command to my warriors to fall upon you with the edge of the sword. The Lord Shift has already told you of that wicked Ass. Do you think, because of him that there is no *real* Tashlan in the stable! Do you? Beware, beware!"

"No, no," shouted most of the crowd. But the Dwarfs said, "That's right, Darkie, you've got it. Come on, Monkey, show us what's in the stable, seeing is believing."

—The Last Battle

The Donkey that the Ape dressed up as Aslan has escaped, leaving the Ape in an awkward position. When the Narnians can no longer see the false Aslan, they may no longer believe. Why is seeing Aslan so important to believing? When have you had trouble believing without seeing?

Going It Alone

ALL ROUND THE VERY TOP of the hill ran a high wall of green turf. Inside the wall, trees were growing. Their branches hung out over the wall; their leaves showed not only green but also blue and silver when the wind stirred them. When the travelers reached the top they walked nearly all the way round it outside the green wall before they found the gates: high gates of gold, fast shut, facing due east.

Up till now I think Fledge and Polly had had the idea that they would go in with Digory. But they thought so no longer. You never saw a place which was so obviously private. You could see at a glance that it belonged to someone else. Only a fool would dream of going in unless he had been sent there on very special business. Digory himself understood at once that the others wouldn't and couldn't come in with him. He went forward to the gates alone.

—*The Magician's Nephew*

How do you think Digory feels about proceeding by himself? What are some things in life that we must do alone?

The Return of the Prince

FOR NOW THEY SAW THE PRINCE.
No one doubted for a moment who he was. There were plenty of Beasts and Dryads and Dwarfs and Fauns who remembered him from the days before his enchanting. There were some old ones who could just remember how his father, King Caspian, had looked when he was a young man, and saw the likeness. But I think they would have known him anyway. Pale though he was from long imprisonment in the Deep Lands, dressed in black, dusty, disheveled, and weary, there was something in his face and air which no one could mistake. That look is in the face of all true Kings of Narnia, who rule by the will of Aslan and sit at Cair Paravel on the throne of Peter the High King. Instantly every head was bared and every knee was bent; a moment later such cheering and shouting, such jumps and reels of joy, such hand-shakings and kissings and embracings of everybody by everybody else broke out that the tears came into Jill's eyes. Their quest had been worth all the pains it cost.

—*The Silver Chair*

What makes the entire journey worth it to Jill? When have you had to struggle through difficulties to find it was all worth it in the end?

Too Old for Narnia

"COME ON," said Peter suddenly to Edmund and Lucy. "Our time's up."

"What do you mean?" said Edmund.

"This way," said Susan, who seemed to know all about it. "Back into the trees. We've got to change."

"Change what?" asked Lucy.

"Our clothes, of course," said Susan. "Nice fools we'd look on the platform of an English station in *these*."

"But our other things are at Caspian's castle," said Edmund.

"No, they're not," said Peter, still leading the way into the thickest wood. "They're all here. They were brought down in bundles this morning. It's all arranged."

"Was that what Aslan was talking to you and Susan about this morning?" asked Lucy.

"Yes—that and other things," said Peter, his face very solemn. "I can't tell it all to you. There were things he wanted to say to Su and me because we're not coming back to Narnia."

"Never?" cried Edmund and Lucy in dismay.

"Oh, you two are," answered Peter. "At least, from what he said, I'm pretty sure he means you to get back some day. But not Su and me. He says we're getting too old."

"Oh, Peter," said Lucy. "What awful bad luck. Can you bear it?"

"Well, I think I can," said Peter. "It's all rather different from what I thought. You'll understand when it comes to your last time. But, quick, here are our things."

—Prince Caspian

Why would their age prevent Peter and Susan from returning to Narnia? What qualities do we have as children that many of us lose as we get older? Are you ever too old for Narnia?

The Talking Horses Join the Battle

L ISTEN!" SAID JEWEL: and then, "Look!" said Farsight. A moment later there was no doubt what it was. With a thunder of hoofs, with tossing heads, widened nostrils, and waving manes, over a score of Talking Horses of Narnia came charging up the hill. The gnawers and nibblers had done their work.

Poggin the Dwarf and the children opened their mouths to cheer but that cheer never came. Suddenly the air was full of the sound of twanging bow-strings and hissing arrows. It was the Dwarfs who were shooting and—for a moment Jill could hardly believe her eyes—they were shooting the Horses. Dwarfs are deadly archers. Horse after Horse rolled over. Not one of those noble Beasts ever reached the King.

"Little *Swine,*" shrieked Eustace, dancing in his rage. "Dirty, filthy, treacherous little brutes." Even Jewel said, "Shall I run after those Dwarfs, Sire, and spit ten of them on my horn at each plunge?" But Tirian with his face as stern as stone, said, "Stand fast, Jewel. If you must weep, sweetheart" (this was to Jill), "turn your face aside and see you wet not your bowstring. And peace, Eustace. Do not scold, like a kitchen-girl. No warrior scolds. Courteous words or else hard knocks are his only language."

But the Dwarfs jeered back at Eustace. "That was a surprise for you, little boy, eh? Thought we were on *your* side, did you? No fear. We don't want any Talking Horses. We don't want you to win any more than the other gang. You can't take *us* in. The Dwarfs are for the Dwarfs."

—*The Last Battle*

What does the Dwarfs' purpose seem to be in killing the Talking Horses? What do you think Tirian means by saying that courteous words or hard knocks are the only language of the warrior?

The Most Wonderful Ride

THEN [ASLAN] SAID,
"We have a long journey to go. You must ride on me." And he crouched down and the children climbed onto his warm, golden back, and Susan sat first, holding on tightly to his mane and Lucy sat behind holding on tightly to Susan. And with a great heave he rose underneath them and then shot off, faster than any horse could go, down hill and into the thick of the forest.

That ride was perhaps the most wonderful thing that happened to them in Narnia. Have you ever had a gallop on a horse? Think of that; and then take away the heavy noise of the hoofs and the jingle of the bits and imagine instead the almost noiseless padding of the great paws. Then imagine instead of the black or grey or chestnut back of the horse the soft roughness of golden fur, and the mane flying back in the wind. And then imagine you are going about twice as fast as the fastest racehorse. But this is a mount that doesn't need to be guided and never grows tired. He rushes on and on, never missing his footing, never hesitating, threading his way with perfect skill between tree trunks, jumping over bush and briar and the smaller streams, wading the larger, swimming the largest of all. And you are riding not on a road nor in a park nor even on the downs, but right across Narnia, in spring, down solemn avenues of beech and across sunny glades of oak, through wild orchards of snow-white cherry trees, past roaring waterfalls and mossy rocks and echoing caverns, up windy slopes alight with gorse bushes, and across the shoulders of heathery mountains and along giddy ridges and down, down, down again into wild valleys and out into acres of blue flowers.

—The Lion, the Witch, and the Wardrobe

Why is this ride the most wonderful thing that has happened to Susan and Lucy? When have you come closest to experiencing what Lucy and Susan feel on this ride?

The Reluctant First King and Queen

"MY CHILDREN," SAID ASLAN, fixing his eyes on both of them, "you are to be the first King and Queen of Narnia."

The Cabby opened his mouth in astonishment, and his wife turned very red.

"You shall rule and name all these creatures, and do justice among them, and protect them from our enemies when enemies arise. And enemies will arise, for there is an evil Witch in this world."

The Cabby swallowed hard two or three times and cleared his throat.

"Begging your pardon, sir," he said, "and thanking you very much I'm sure (which my Missus does the same) but I ain't no sort of a chap for a job like that. I never 'ad much eddycation, you see."

—*The Magician's Nephew*

What does the Cabby's initial reluctance say about the kind of person he is? How would you react if someone selected you for an honor of this magnitude?

I Should Frighten Them

LUCY FOLLOWED THE GREAT LION out into the passage and at once she saw coming toward them an old man, barefoot, dressed in a red robe. His white hair was crowned with a chaplet of oak leaves, his beard fell to his girdle, and he supported himself with a curiously carved staff. When he saw Aslan he bowed low and said,

"Welcome, Sir, to the least of your houses."

"Do you grow weary, Coriakin, of ruling such foolish subjects as I have given you here?"

"No," said the Magician, "they are very stupid but there is no real harm in them. I begin to grow rather fond of the creatures. Sometimes, perhaps, I am a little impatient, waiting for the day when they can be governed by wisdom instead of this rough magic."

"All in good time, Coriakin," said Aslan.

"Yes, all in very good time, Sir," was the answer. "Do you intend to show yourself to them?"

"Nay," said the Lion, with a little half-growl that meant (Lucy thought) the same as a laugh. "I should frighten them out of their senses. Many stars will grow old and come to take their rest in islands before your people are ripe for that."

—*The Voyage of the* **Dawn Treader**

Why would seeing Aslan frighten Coriakin's people (the Duffers) out of their senses? What might it take for the Duffers to be "ripe" to see him? Do you think you'd be ready to see Aslan?

A Beast Like the Rest of Us

BREE," SAID ARAVIS, who was not very interested in the cut of his tail, "I've been wanting to ask you something for a long time. Why do you keep on swearing *By the Lion* and *By the Lion's Mane*? I thought you hated lions."

"So I do," answered Bree. "But when I speak of *the* Lion, of course I mean Aslan, the great deliverer of Narnia who drove away the Witch and the Winter. All Narnians swear by *him*."

"But is he a lion?"

"No, no, of course not," said Bree in a rather shocked voice.

"All the stories about him in Tashbaan say he is," replied Aravis. "And if he isn't a lion why do you call him a lion?"

"Well, you'd hardly understand that at your age," said Bree. "And I was only a little foal when I left so I don't quite fully understand it myself."

(Bree was standing with his back to the green wall while he said this, and the other two were facing him. He was talking in rather a superior tone with his eyes half shut; that was why he didn't see the changed expression in the faces of Hwin and Aravis. They had good reason to have open mouths and staring eyes, because while Bree spoke they saw an enormous lion leap up from outside and balance itself on the top of the green wall; only it was a brighter yellow and it was bigger and more beautiful and more alarming than any lion they had ever seen. And at once it jumped down inside the wall and began approaching Bree from behind. It made no noise at all. And Hwin and Aravis couldn't make any noise themselves, no more than if they were frozen.)

"No doubt," continued Bree, "when they speak of him as a Lion, they only mean he's as strong as a lion or (to our enemies, of course) as fierce as a lion. Or something of that kind. Even a little girl like you, Aravis, must see that it would be quite absurd to suppose he is a *real* lion. Indeed it would be disrespectful. If he was a lion he'd have to be a Beast just like the rest of us. Why!" (and here Bree began to laugh) "If he was a lion he'd have four paws, and a tail, and *Whiskers*!... Aie, ooh, hoo-hoo! Help!"

For just as he said the word *Whiskers* one of Aslan's had actually tickled his ear. Bree shot away like an arrow to the other side of the enclosure and there turned; the wall was too high for him to jump and he could fly no further. Aravis and Hwin both started back. There was about a second of intense silence. Then Hwin, though shaking all over, gave a strange little neigh, and trotted across to the Lion.

"Please," she said, "you're so beautiful. You may eat me if you like. I'd sooner be eaten by you than fed by anyone else."

"Dearest daughter," said Aslan, planting a lion's kiss on her twitching, velvet nose, "I knew you would not be long in coming to me. Joy shall be yours."

Then he lifted his head and spoke in a louder voice:

"Now, Bree," he said, "you poor, proud frightened Horse, draw near. Nearer still, my son. Do not dare not to dare. Touch me. Smell me. Here are my paws, here is my tail, these are my whiskers. I am a true Beast."

—*The Horse and His Boy*

Why is it so hard for Bree to view Aslan as a true beast? Why would Aslan want to show him the truth this way? When have you asserted something so confidently only to be proven wrong?

Tirian's Worst Nightmare

TIRIAN AND JEWEL walked sadly together in the rear. The King had his arm on the Unicorn's shoulder and sometimes the Unicorn nuzzled the King's cheek with his soft nose. They did not try to comfort one another with words. It wasn't very easy to think of anything to say that would be comforting. Tirian had never dreamed that one of the results of an Ape's setting up a false Aslan would be to stop people from believing in the real one. He had felt quite sure that the Dwarfs would rally to his side the moment he showed them how they had been deceived. And then next night he would have led them to Stable Hill and shown Puzzle to all the creatures and everyone would have turned against the Ape and, perhaps after a scuffle with the Calormenes, the whole thing would have been over. But now, it seemed, he could count on nothing. How many other Narnians might turn the same way as the Dwarfs?

—*The Last Battle*

After seeing the false Aslan (Puzzle the Donkey wearing a lion-skin), the Dwarfs announce that they have had enough of Aslan and of Kings. Why would realizing they've been fooled by a false Aslan cause the Dwarfs and other Narnians to disbelieve in the true Aslan? Have you ever been so dis-appointed after being let down that it affected your ability to believe or trust the next time around?

A Doddering Old Man

I SAY, SCRUBB, isn't it all simply too exciting and scrumptious for words?"...

"Oh! That's what you think, is it?" said Scrubb: and then, after a pause, "I wish to goodness we'd never come."

"Why on earth?"

"I can't bear it," said Scrubb. "Seeing the King—Caspian—a doddering old man like that. It's—it's frightful."

"Why, what harm does it do you?"

"Oh, you don't understand. Now that I come to think of it, you couldn't. I didn't tell you that this world has a different time from ours."

"How do you mean?"

"The time you spend here doesn't take up any of our time. Do you see? I mean, however long we spend here, we shall still get back to Experiment House at the moment we left it—"

"That won't be much fun—"

"Oh, dry up! Don't keep interrupting. And when you're back in England—in our world—you can't tell how time is going here. It might be any number of years in Narnia while we're having one year at home. The Pevensies explained it all to me, but, like a fool, I forgot about it. And now apparently it's been about seventy years—Narnian years—since I was here last. Do you see now? And I come back and find Caspian an old, old man."

"Then the King *was* an old friend of yours!" said Jill. A horrid thought had struck her.

"I should jolly well think he was," said Scrubb miserably. "About as good a friend as a chap could have. And last time he was only a few years older than me. And to see that old man with a white beard, and to remember Caspian as he was the morning we captured the Lone Islands, or in the fight with the Sea Serpent—oh, it's frightful. It's worse than coming back and finding him dead."

—*The Silver Chair*

Why is Scrubb so upset to see King Caspian as an old man?

November

The Creatures Come to Aslan

THE LIGHT FROM BEHIND THEM (and a little to their right) was so strong that it lit up even the slopes of the Northern Moors. Something was moving there. Enormous animals were crawling and sliding down into Narnia: great dragons and giant lizards and featherless birds with wings like bats' wings. They disappeared into the woods and for a few minutes there was a silence. Then there came—at first from very far off—sounds of wailing and then, from every direction, a rustling and a pattering and a sound of wings. It came nearer and nearer. Soon one could distinguish the scamper of little feet from the padding of big paws, and the clack-clack of light little hoofs from the thunder of great ones. And then one could see thousands of pairs of eyes gleaming. And at last, out of the shadow of the trees, racing up the hill for dear life, by thousands and by millions, came all kinds of creatures—Talking Beasts, Dwarfs, Satyrs, Fauns, Giants, Calormenes, men from Archenland, Monopods, and strange unearthly things from the remote islands or the unknown Western lands. And all these ran up to the doorway where Aslan stood. . . .

The creatures came rushing on, their eyes brighter and brighter as they drew nearer and nearer to the standing Stars. But as they came right up to Aslan one or other of two things happened to each of them. They all looked straight in his face, I don't think they had any choice about that. And when some looked, the expression of their faces changed terribly— it was fear and hatred: except that, on the faces of Talking Beasts, the fear and hatred lasted only for a fraction of a second. You could see that they suddenly ceased to be *Talking* Beasts. They were just ordinary animals. And all the creatures who looked at Aslan in that way swerved to their right, his left, and disappeared into his huge black shadow, which (as you have heard) streamed away to the left of the doorway. The children never saw them again. I don't know what became of them. But the others looked in the face of Aslan and loved him, though some of them were very frightened at the same time. And all these came in at the Door, in on Aslan's right. There were some queer specimens among them. Eustace even recognized one of those very Dwarfs who had helped to shoot the

Horses. But he had no time to wonder about that sort of thing (and anyway it was no business of his) for a great joy put everything else out of his head. Among the happy creatures who now came crowding round Tirian and his friends were all those whom they had thought dead. There was Roonwit the Centaur and Jewel the Unicorn and the good Boar and the good Bear, and Farsight the Eagle, and the dear Dogs and the Horses, and Poggin the Dwarf.

—*The Last Battle*

What makes the creatures react to Aslan either with fear and hatred or with love? Why were they divided not by how Aslan treated them, but by how they reacted to Aslan?

Think No More of That

I WISH I WAS AT HOME," said Jill.

Eustace nodded, saying nothing, and bit his lip.

"I have come," said a deep voice behind them. They turned and saw the Lion himself, so bright and real and strong that everything else began at once to look pale and shadowy compared with him. And in less time than it takes to breathe Jill forgot about the dead King of Narnia and remembered only how she had made Eustace fall over the cliff, and how she had helped to muff nearly all the signs, and about all the snappings and quarrelings. And she wanted to say "I'm sorry" but she could not speak. Then the Lion drew them toward him with his eyes, and bent down and touched their pale faces with his tongue, and said:

"Think of that no more. I will not always be scolding. You have done the work for which I sent you into Narnia."

"Please, Aslan," said Jill, "may we go home now?"

"Yes. I have come to bring you Home," said Aslan.

—*The Silver Chair*

Do you think of Aslan as always scolding? How must it feel for Jill and Eustace to hear Aslan dismiss their mistakes? Do you think Aslan would have reacted differently if Jill had not been feeling sorrow for her mistakes?

Narnia or a New Home

NEXT DAY MESSENGERS (who were chiefly squirrels and birds) were sent all over the country with a proclamation to the scattered Telmarines—including, of course, the prisoners in Beruna. They were told that Caspian was now King and that Narnia would henceforth belong to the Talking Beasts and the Dwarfs and Dryads and Fauns and other creatures quite as much as to the men. Any who chose to stay under the new conditions might do so; but for those who did not like the idea, Aslan would provide another home. Anyone who wished to go there must come to Aslan and the Kings at the Ford of Beruna by noon on the fifth day. You may imagine that this caused plenty of head-scratching among the Telmarines. Some of them, chiefly the young ones, had, like Caspian, heard stories of the Old Days and were delighted that they had come back. They were already making friends with the creatures. These all decided to stay in Narnia. But most of the older men, especially those who had been important under Miraz, were sulky and had no wish to live in a country where they could not rule the roost. "Live here with a lot of blooming performing animals! No fear," they said. "And ghosts too," some added with a shudder. "That's what those there Dryads really are. It's not canny." They were also suspicious. "I don't trust 'em," they said. "Not with that awful Lion and all. He won't keep his claws off us long, *you'll* see." But then they were equally suspicious of his offer to give them a new home. "Take us off to his den and eat us one by one most likely," they muttered. And the more they talked to one another the sulkier and more suspicious they became. But on the appointed day more than half of them turned up.

—*Prince Caspian*

Why do you think the young ones were more likely to want to stay in Narnia under new rule? Would your younger self have decided differently on such a matter than you might today? Why or why not?

Wild Aslan

But amid all these rejoicings Aslan himself quietly slipped away. And when the Kings and Queens noticed that he wasn't there they said nothing about it. For Mr. Beaver had warned them, "He'll be coming and going," he had said. "One day you'll see him and another you won't. He doesn't like being tied down—and of course he has other countries to attend to. It's quite all right. He'll often drop in. Only you mustn't press him. He's wild, you know. Not like a *tame* lion."

—*The Lion, the Witch, and the Wardrobe*

What does it mean that Aslan is wild? Do you know anyone who is wild in the same way?

Me? Me?

Y OU WILL KEEP ON LOOKING at everything from the wrong point of view," said Uncle Andrew with a look of impatience. "Can't you understand that the thing is a great experiment? The whole point of sending anyone into the Other Place is that I want to find out what it's like."

"Well why didn't you go yourself then?"

Digory had hardly ever seen anyone look so surprised and offended as his Uncle did at this simple question. "Me? Me?" he exclaimed. "The boy must be mad! A man at my time of life, and in my state of health, to risk the shock and the dangers of being flung suddenly into a different universe? I never heard anything so preposterous in my life! Do you realize what you're saying? Think what Another World means—you might meet anything—anything."

"And I suppose you've sent Polly into it then," said Digory. His cheeks were flaming with anger now. "And all I can say," he added, "even if you are my Uncle—is that you've behaved like a coward, sending a girl to a place you're afraid to go to yourself."

"Silence, sir!" said Uncle Andrew, bringing his hand down on the table. "I will not be talked to like that by a little, dirty, schoolboy. You don't understand. I am the great scholar, the magician, the adept, who is *doing* the experiment. Of course I need subjects to do it *on*. Bless my soul, you'll be telling me next that I ought to have asked the guinea-pigs' permission before I used *them*! No great wisdom can be reached without sacrifice. But the idea of my going myself is ridiculous. It's like asking a general to fight as a common soldier. Supposing I got killed, what would become of my life's work?"

—*The Magician's Nephew*

Why is Uncle Andrew so horrified at the idea of going to the Other Place himself? Can you relate to his point of view? How can we know when self-interest is healthy and when it crosses the dangerous line into narcissism?

Great Trees Are Falling

ROONWIT HAD JUST RAISED HIS HAND and was leaning forward to say something very earnestly to the King when all three of them turned their heads to listen to a wailing sound that was quickly drawing nearer. The wood was so thick to the West of them that they could not see the newcomer yet. But they could soon hear the words.

"Woe, woe, woe!" called the voice. "Woe for my brothers and sisters! Woe for the holy trees! The woods are laid waste. The axe is loosed against us. We are being felled. Great trees are falling, falling, falling."

With the last "falling" the speaker came in sight. She was like a woman but so tall that her head was on a level with the Centaur's yet she was like a tree too. It is hard to explain if you have never seen a Dryad but quite unmistakable once you have—something different in the color, the voice, and the hair. King Tirian and the two Beasts knew at once that she was the nymph of a beech tree.

"Justice, Lord King!" she cried. "Come to our aid. Protect your people. They are felling us in Lantern Waste. Forty great trunks of my brothers and sisters are already on the ground."

"What, Lady! Felling Lantern Waste? Murdering the talking trees?" cried the King, leaping to his feet and drawing his sword. "How dare they? And who dares it? Now by the Mane of Aslan—"

"A-a-a-h," gasped the Dryad, shuddering as if in pain—shuddering time after time as if under repeated blows. Then all at once she fell sideways as suddenly as if both her feet had been cut from under her. For a second they saw her lying dead on the grass and then she vanished. They knew what had happened. Her tree, miles away, had been cut down.

For a moment the King's grief and anger were so great that he could not speak. Then he said:

"Come, friends. We must go up river and find the villains who have done this, with all the speed we may. I will leave not one of them alive."

"Sire, with a good will," said Jewel.

But Roonwit said, "Sire, be wary in your just wrath. There are strange doings on foot. If there should be rebels in arms further up the valley, we three are too few to meet them. If it would please you to wait while—"

"I will not wait the tenth part of a second," said the King. "But while Jewel and I go forward, do you gallop as hard as you may to Cair Paravel. Here is my ring for your token. Get me a score of men-at-arms, all well mounted, and a score of Talking Dogs, and ten Dwarfs (let them all be fell archers), and a Leopard or so, and Stonefoot the Giant. Bring all these after us as quickly as can be."

"With a good will, Sire," said Roonwit. And at once he turned and galloped Eastward down the valley.

—*The Last Battle*

Why do you think the King is so impatient to rush off? Is he right to go immediately even though he has little backup and there is great danger?

Making Do

DIGORY SAID that Polly had better take herself home by ring and get something to eat there; he couldn't himself because he had promised to go straight on his message for Aslan, and, if once he showed up again at home, anything might happen to prevent his getting back. But Polly said she wouldn't leave him, and Digory said it was jolly decent of her.

"I say," said Polly, "I've still got the remains of that bag of toffee in my jacket. It'll be better than nothing."

"A lot better," said Digory. "But be careful to get your hand into your pocket without touching your ring."

This was a difficult and delicate job but they managed it in the end. The little paper bag was very squashy and sticky when they finally got it out, so that it was more a question of tearing the bag off the toffees than of getting the toffees out of the bag. Some grown-ups (you know how fussy they can be about that sort of thing) would rather have gone without supper altogether than eaten those toffees. There were nine of them all told. It was Digory who had the bright idea of eating four each and planting the ninth; for, as he said, "if the bar off the lamp-post turned into a little light-tree, why shouldn't this turn into a toffee-tree?" So they dibbled a small hole in the turf and buried the piece of toffee. Then they ate the other pieces, making them last as long as they could. It was a poor meal, even with all the paper they couldn't help eating as well.

—*The Magician's Nephew*

Polly could return home for a real meal or keep the toffees to herself. After all, the task of picking an apple from the special tree has been given to Digory. Why do you think she chooses to stay and to share? When have you set aside your own physical needs to accomplish something important?

Clearing the Door

THERE'S ONE THING," said Lucy. "If this is Cair Paravel there ought to be a door at this end of the dais. In fact we ought to be sitting with our backs against it at this moment. You know—the door that led down to the treasure chamber."

"I suppose there *isn't* a door," said Peter, getting up.

The wall behind them was a mass of ivy.

"We can soon find out," said Edmund, taking up one of the sticks that they had laid ready for putting on the fire. He began beating the ivied wall. Tap-tap went the stick against the stone; and again, tap-tap; and then, all at once, boom-boom, with a quite different sound, a hollow, wooden sound.

"Great Scott!" said Edmund.

"We must clear this ivy away," said Peter.

"Oh, do let's leave it alone," said Susan. "We can try it in the morning. If we've got to spend the night here I don't want an open door at my back and a great big black hole that anything might come out of, besides the draft and the damp. And it'll soon be dark."

"Susan! How can you?" said Lucy with a reproachful glance. But both the boys were too much excited to take any notice of Susan's advice. They worked at the ivy with their hands and with Peter's pocket-knife till the knife broke. After that they used Edmund's. Soon the whole place where they had been sitting was covered with ivy; and at last they had the door cleared.

"Locked, of course," said Peter.

"But the wood's all rotten," said Edmund. "We can pull it to bits in no time, and it will make extra firewood. Come on."

It took them longer than they expected and, before they had done, the great hall had grown dusky and the first star or two had come out overhead. Susan was not the only one who felt a slight shudder as the boys stood above the pile of splintered wood, rubbing the dirt off their hands and staring into the cold, dark opening they had made.

"Now for a torch," said Peter.

"Oh, what *is* the good?" said Susan. "And as Edmund said—"

"I'm not saying it now," Edmund interrupted. "I still don't understand, but we can settle that later. I suppose you're coming down, Peter?"

"We must," said Peter. "Cheer up, Susan. It's no good behaving like kids now that we are back in Narnia. You're a Queen here. And anyway no one could go to sleep with a mystery like this on their minds."

—*Prince Caspian*

Susan advises caution, but the others proceed without listening. Do you agree with Peter that not proceeding would be behaving like kids? What do you think he is saying about adulthood, or at least royal adulthood?

Well Done

[T]HE EARTH TREMBLED. The sweet air grew suddenly sweeter. A brightness flashed behind them. All turned. Tirian turned last because he was afraid. There stood his heart's desire, huge and real, the golden Lion, Aslan himself, and already the others were kneeling in a circle round his forepaws and burying their hands and faces in his mane as he stooped his great head to touch them with his tongue. Then he fixed his eyes upon Tirian, and Tirian came near, trembling, and flung himself at the Lion's feet, and the Lion kissed him and said, "Well done, last of the Kings of Narnia who stood firm at the darkest hour."

—*The Last Battle*

Why is Tirian afraid when seeing Aslan is his heart's desire? Why does Tirian throw himself at Aslan's feet? Can you imagine a more powerful pronouncement than the one Aslan makes to Tirian?

The Lights Go Out

MEANWHILE, the land was changing. The roof of Underland was so near that even by that dull light they could now see it quite distinctly. And the great, rugged walls of Underland could be seen drawing closer on each side. The road, in fact, was leading them up into a steep tunnel. They began to pass picks and shovels and barrows and other signs that the diggers had recently been at work. If only one could be sure of getting out, all this was very cheering. But the thought of going on into a hole that would get narrower and narrower, and harder to turn back in, was very unpleasant.

At last the roof was so low that Puddleglum and the Prince knocked their heads against it. The party dismounted and led the horses. The road was uneven here and one had to pick one's steps with some care. That was how Jill noticed the growing darkness. There was no doubt about it now. The faces of the others looked strange and ghastly in the green glow. Then all at once (she couldn't help it) Jill gave a little scream. One light, the next one ahead, went out altogether. The one behind them did the same. Then they were in absolute darkness.

"Courage, friends," came Prince Rilian's voice. "Whether we live or die Aslan will be our good lord."

"That's right, Sir," said Puddleglum's voice. "And you must always remember there's one good thing about being trapped down here: it'll save funeral expenses."

Jill held her tongue. (If you don't want other people to know how frightened you are, this is always a wise thing to do; it's your voice that gives you away.)

"We might as well go on as stand here," said Eustace; and when she heard the tremble in *his* voice, Jill knew how wise she'd been not to trust her own.

—*The Silver Chair*

Why doesn't Jill want her companions to know how frightened she is? When is owning up to fear wise and when is it best to keep it hidden?

No Rest for the Weary

THE WHOLE SHIP'S company went ashore in two boatloads and everyone drank and washed deliciously in the river and had a meal and a rest before Caspian sent four men back to keep the ship, and the day's work began. There was everything to be done. The casks must be brought ashore and the faulty ones mended if possible and all refilled; a tree—a pine if they could get it—must be felled and made into a new mast; sails must be repaired; a hunting party organized to shoot any game the land might yield; clothes to be washed and mended; and countless small breakages on board to be set right. For the *Dawn Treader* herself— and this was more obvious now that they saw her at a distance—could hardly be recognized as the same gallant ship which had left Narrow-haven. She looked a crippled, discolored hulk which anyone might have taken for a wreck. And her officers and crew were no better—lean, pale, red-eyed from lack of sleep, and dressed in rags.

As Eustace lay under a tree and heard all these plans being discussed, his heart sank. Was there going to be no rest? It looked as if their first day on the longed-for land was going to be quite as hard work as a day at sea. Then a delightful idea occurred to him. Nobody was looking—they were all chattering about their ship as if they actually liked the beastly thing. Why shouldn't he simply slip away? He would take a stroll inland, find a cool, airy place up in the mountains, have a good long sleep, and not rejoin the others till the day's work was over. He felt it would do him good. But he would take great care to keep the bay and the ship in sight so as to be sure of his way back. He wouldn't like to be left behind in this country.

—*The Voyage of the* **Dawn Treader**

Why do you think the others don't seem to want to get out of the work? When have you been tempted to try to get out of shared work? Did you follow through with your impulse? Why or why not?

True Freedom

Aᴺᴰ ɴᴏᴡ ʜᴇʀᴇ'ꜱ ᴀɴᴏᴛʜᴇʀ ᴛʜɪɴɢ," the Ape went on, fitting a fresh nut into its cheek, "I hear some of the horses are saying, Let's hurry up and get this job of carting timber over as quickly as we can, and then we'll be free again. Well, you can get that idea out of your heads at once. And not only the Horses either. Everybody who can work is going to be made to work in future. Aslan has it all settled with the King of Calormen—The Tisroc, as our dark faced friends the Calormenes call him. All you Horses and Bulls and Donkeys are to be sent down into Calormen to work for your living—pulling and carrying the way horses and such-like do in other countries. And all you digging animals like Moles and Rabbits and Dwarfs are going down to work in The Tisroc's mines. And—"

"No, no, no," howled the Beasts. "It can't be true. Aslan would never sell us into slavery to the King of Calormen."

"None of that! Hold your noise!" said the Ape with a snarl. "Who said anything about slavery? You won't be slaves. You'll be paid—very good wages too. That is to say, your pay will be paid into Aslan's treasury and he will use it all for everybody's good. . . . We'll be able, with the money you earn, to make Narnia a country worth living in. There'll be oranges and bananas pouring in—and roads and big cities and schools and offices and whips and muzzles and saddles and cages and kennels and prisons— Oh, everything."

"But we don't want all those things," said an old Bear. "We want to be free. And we want to hear Aslan speak himself."

"Now don't you start arguing," said the Ape, "for it's a thing I won't stand. I'm a Man: you're only a fat, stupid old Bear. What do you know about freedom? You think freedom means doing what you like. Well, you're wrong. That isn't true freedom. True freedom means doing what I tell you."

—*The Last Battle*

What is true freedom? Is there any truth to either of the Ape's definitions— doing what you like or doing what someone tells you?

Good-bye to Puddleglum

"GOOD-BYE, DEAR PUDDLEGLUM," said Jill, going over to the Marsh-wiggle's bed. "I'm sorry we called you a wet blanket."

"So'm I," said Eustace. "You've been the best friend in the world."

"And I do hope we'll meet again," added Jill.

"Not much chance of that, I should say," replied Puddleglum. "I don't reckon I'm very likely to see my old wigwam again, either. And that Prince—he's a nice chap—but do you think he's very strong? Constitution ruined with living underground, I shouldn't wonder. Looks the sort that might go off any day."

"Puddleglum!" said Jill. "You're a regular old humbug. You sound as doleful as a funeral and I believe you're perfectly happy. And you talk as if you were afraid of everything, when you're really as brave as—as a lion."

"Now, speaking of funerals," began Puddleglum, but Jill, who heard the Centaurs tapping with their hoofs behind her, surprised him very much by flinging her arms round his thin neck and kissing his muddy-looking face, while Eustace wrung his hand. Then they both rushed away to the Centaurs, and the Marsh-wiggle, sinking back on his bed, remarked to himself, "Well, I wouldn't have dreamt of her doing that. Even though I *am* a good-looking chap."

—The Silver Chair

Do you find it surprising that Puddleglum can be both doleful and happy? That he can sound afraid and at the same time be brave as a lion? Why or why not? Who have you known who has demonstrated such apparent inconsistencies? What dualities are in your own nature?

An Apple from Aslan

I—I NEARLY ATE ONE MYSELF, ASLAN," said Digory. "Would I—"

"You would, child," said Aslan. "For the fruit always works—it must work—but it does not work happily for any who pluck it at their own will. If any Narnian, unbidden, had stolen an apple and planted it here to protect Narnia, it would have protected Narnia. But it would have done so by making Narnia into another strong and cruel empire like Charn, not the kindly land I mean it to be. And the Witch tempted you to do another thing, my son, did she not?"

"Yes, Aslan. She wanted me to take an apple home to Mother."

"Understand, then, that it would have healed her; but not to your joy or hers. The day would have come when both you and she would have looked back and said it would have been better to die in that illness."

—*The Magician's Nephew*

What could be worse than the death of someone you love? Why do we some-times view death as the worst of all things when there are other things that might be even more terrible?

The Gift

AND DIGORY COULD SAY NOTHING, for tears choked him and he gave up all hopes of saving his Mother's life; but at the same time he knew that the Lion knew what would have happened, and that there might be things more terrible even than losing someone you love by death. But now Aslan was speaking again, almost in a whisper:

"That is what *would* have happened, child, with a stolen apple. It is not what will happen now. What I give you now will bring joy. It will not, in your world, give endless life, but it will heal. Go. Pluck her an apple from the Tree."

For a second Digory could hardly understand. It was as if the whole world had turned inside out and upside down. And then, like someone in a dream, he was walking across to the Tree, and the King and Queen were cheering him and all the creatures were cheering too. He plucked the apple and put it in his pocket. Then he came back to Aslan.

"Please," he said, "may we go home now?" He had forgotten to say "Thank you," but he meant it, and Aslan understood.

—*The Magician's Nephew*

What is the significance of the difference between a stolen apple and an apple given by Aslan? What have you received that meant so much more because someone had given it to you?

Never Desert a Companion

SUDDENLY FROM SOMEWHERE behind him there came a terrible sound. Shasta's heart gave a great jump and he had to bite his tongue to keep himself from screaming. Next moment he realized what it was: the horns of Tashbaan blowing for the closing of the gates. "Don't be a silly little coward," said Shasta to himself. "Why, it's only the same noise you heard this morning." But there is a great difference between a noise heard letting you in with your friends in the morning, and a noise heard alone at nightfall, shutting you out. And now that the gates were shut he knew there was no chance of the others joining him that evening. "Either they're shut up in Tashbaan for the night," thought Shasta, "or else they've gone on without me. It's just the sort of thing that Aravis would do. But Bree wouldn't. Oh, he wouldn't—now, would he?"

In this idea about Aravis Shasta was once more quite wrong. She was proud and could be hard enough but she was as true as steel and would never have deserted a companion, whether she liked him or not.

—*The Horse and His Boy*

Aravis has made it clear that she views Shasta as inferior. Is that any excuse for his assuming she would have deserted him? What does it mean that Aravis is proud but also true? How could her pride prevent Shasta from seeing her true character?

Drink Your Own Medicine!

THE APE HAD NOT REALIZED his danger as quickly as the Tarkaan. For a second or so he remained squatting beside the fire staring at the newcomers. Then Tirian rushed upon the wretched creature, picked it up by the scruff of the neck, and dashed back to the stable shouting, "Open the door!" Poggin opened it. "Go and drink your own medicine, Shift!" said Tirian and hurled the Ape through into the darkness. But as the Dwarf banged the door shut again, a blinding greenish-blue light shone out from the inside of the stable, the earth shook, and there was a strange noise—a clucking and screaming as if it was the hoarse voice of some monstrous bird. The Beasts moaned and howled and called out "Tashlan! Hide us from him!" and many fell down, and many hid their faces in their wings or paws. No one except Farsight the Eagle, who has the best eyes of all living things, noticed the face of Rishda Tarkaan at that moment. And from what Farsight saw there he knew at once that Rishda was just as surprised, and nearly as frightened, as everyone else. "There goes one," thought Farsight, "who has called on gods he does not believe in. How will it be with him if they have really come?"

—*The Last Battle*

Shift the Ape and Rishda Tarkaan boldly presented a false Aslan and claimed he was the same as the god Tash. Now there seems to be something they did not anticipate in the stable where they had hidden the false Aslan. In what way do you think they called on gods they did not believe in? What do you think is the worse crime: impersonating Aslan or not believing in him?

The Lion's Kiss

[ASLAN SAID,] "The Witch whom you have brought into this world will come back to Narnia again. But it need not be yet. It is my wish to plant a tree that she will not dare to approach, and that tree will protect Narnia from her for many years. So the land shall have a long, bright morning before any clouds come over the sun. You must get me the seed from which that tree is to grow."

"Yes, sir," said Digory. He didn't know how it was to be done but he felt quite sure now that he would be able to do it. The Lion drew a deep breath, stooped its head even lower and gave him a Lion's kiss. And at once Digory felt that new strength and courage had gone into him.

—*The Magician's Nephew*

Do you think the fact that Aslan places this trust in Digory gives Digory confidence? Who in your life has had such faith in you?

What Lies Beyond the Hill

SHASTA WAS NOT AT ALL INTERESTED in anything that lay south of his home because he had once or twice been to the village with Arsheesh and he knew that there was nothing very interesting there. In the village he only met other men who were just like his father—men with long, dirty robes, and wooden shoes turned up at the toe, and turbans on their heads, and beards, talking to one another very slowly about things that sounded dull. But he was very interested in everything that lay to the North because no one ever went that way and he was never allowed to go there himself. When he was sitting out of doors mending the nets, and all alone, he would often look eagerly to the North. One could see nothing but a grassy slope running up to a level ridge and beyond that the sky with perhaps a few birds in it.

Sometimes if Arsheesh was there Shasta would say, "O my Father, what is there beyond that hill?" And then if the fisherman was in a bad temper he would box Shasta's ears and tell him to attend to his work. Or if he was in a peaceable mood he would say, "O my son, do not allow your mind to be distracted by idle questions. For one of the poets has said, 'Application to business is the root of prosperity, but those who ask questions that do not concern them are steering the ship of folly toward the rock of indigence.'"

Shasta thought that beyond the hill there must be some delightful secret which his father wished to hide from him. In reality, however, the fisherman talked like this because he didn't know what lay to the North. Neither did he care. He had a very practical mind.

—*The Horse and His Boy*

Why does the North appeal so much to Shasta? Why is the opposite true for his father? Have you ever felt yourself drawn to a place as Shasta is drawn to the North?

Eustace Offends Reepicheep

"OH! UGH! What on earth's *that*? Take it away, the horrid thing."

[Eustace] really had some excuse this time for feeling a little surprised. Something very curious indeed had come out of the cabin in the poop and was slowly approaching them. You might call it—and indeed it was—a Mouse. But then it was a Mouse on its hind legs and stood about two feet high. A thin band of gold passed round its head under one ear and over the other and in this was stuck a long crimson feather. . . . Its left paw rested on the hilt of a sword very nearly as long as its tail. Its balance, as it paced gravely along the swaying deck, was perfect, and its manners courtly. Lucy and Edmund recognized it at once—Reepicheep, the most valiant of all the Talking Beasts of Narnia, and the Chief Mouse. . . . Lucy longed, as she had always done, to take Reepicheep up in her arms and cuddle him. But this, as she well knew, was a pleasure she could never have: it would have offended him deeply. Instead, she went down on one knee to talk to him.

Reepicheep put forward his left leg, drew back his right, bowed, kissed her hand, straightened himself, twirled his whiskers, and said in his shrill, piping voice:

"My humble duty to your Majesty. And to King Edmund, too." (Here he bowed again.). . .

"Ugh, take it away," wailed Eustace. "I hate mice. And I never could bear performing animals. They're silly and vulgar and—and sentimental."

"Am I to understand," said Reepicheep to Lucy after a long stare at Eustace, "that this singularly discourteous person is under your Majesty's protection? Because, if not—"

—*The Voyage of the* **Dawn Treader**

Why is Eustace's description of Reepicheep as a performing animal so hurtful to Reepicheep? How does Lucy's greeting of getting down on one knee differ? What is the most courteous or least courteous way you've ever been greeted?

Good, Ordinary Times

"OH, THIS *IS* NICE!" said Jill. "Just walking along like this. I wish there could be more of *this* sort of adventure. It's a pity there's always so much happening in Narnia."

But the Unicorn explained to her that she was quite mistaken. He said that the Sons and Daughters of Adam and Eve were brought out of their own strange world into Narnia only at times when Narnia was stirred and upset, but she mustn't think it was always like that. In between their visits there were hundreds and thousands of years when peaceful King followed peaceful King till you could hardly remember their names or count their numbers, and there was really hardly anything to put into the History Books. And he went on to talk of old Queens and heroes whom she had never heard of. He spoke of Swanwhite the Queen who had lived before the days of the White Witch and the Great Winter, who was so beautiful that when she looked into any forest pool the reflection of her face shone out of the water like a star by night for a year and a day afterward. He spoke of Moonwood the Hare who had such ears that he could sit by Caldron Pool under the thunder of the great waterfall and hear what men spoke in whispers at Cair Paravel. He told how King Gale, who was ninth in descent from Frank the first of all Kings, had sailed far away into the Eastern seas and delivered the Lone Islanders from a dragon and how, in return, they had given him the Lone Islands to be part of the royal lands of Narnia forever. He talked of whole centuries in which all Narnia was so happy that notable dances and feasts, or at most tournaments, were the only things that could be remembered, and every day and week had been better than the last. And as he went on, the picture of all those happy years, all the thousands of them, piled up in Jill's mind till it was rather like looking down from a high hill onto a rich, lovely plain full of woods and waters and cornfields, which spread away and away till it got thin and misty from distance. And she said:

"Oh, I do hope we can soon settle the Ape and get back to those good, ordinary times. And then I hope they'll go on forever and ever and ever. *Our* world is going to have an end some day. Perhaps this one won't. Oh

Jewel—wouldn't it be lovely if Narnia just went on and on—like what you said it has been?"

"Nay, sister," answered Jewel, "all worlds draw to an end, except Aslan's own country."

"Well, at least," said Jill, "I hope the end of this one is millions of millions of millions of years away."

—*The Last Battle*

Do you share Jill's idea that Narnia is a place where there is always a crisis? Why do you think we as a culture and as individuals tend to remember the difficult times instead of the happy, ordinary ones? Is this true of you? If so, could you do anything to help yourself better remember the ordinary times?

Now or Never

THE TRUMPET AT LAST! On the move now—now trotting—the banner streaming out in the wind. They had topped a low ridge now, and below them the whole scene suddenly opened out; a little, many-towered castle with its gate toward them. No moat, unfortunately, but of course the gate shut and the portcullis down. On the walls they could see, like little white dots, the faces of the defenders. Down below, about fifty of the Calormenes, dismounted, were steadily swinging a great tree trunk against the gate. But at once the scene changed. The main bulk of Rabadash's men had been on foot ready to assault the gate. But now he had seen the Narnians sweeping down from the ridge. There is no doubt those Calormenes are wonderfully trained. It seemed to Shasta only a second before a whole line of the enemy were on horseback again, wheeling round to meet them, swinging toward them.

And now a gallop. The ground between the two armies grew less every moment. Faster, faster. All swords out now, all shields up to the nose, all prayers said, all teeth clenched. Shasta was dreadfully frightened. But it suddenly came into his head, "If you funk this, you'll funk every battle all your life. Now or never."

—*The Horse and His Boy*

Why does this moment become Shasta's proving ground? When in your life have you known that your chance was now or never?

Return to Your Own Place

FOR A LONG TIME they could not speak nor even shed a tear. Then the Unicorn stamped the ground with his hoof, and shook his mane, and spoke.

"Sire," he said, "there is now no need of counsel. We see that the Ape's plans were laid deeper than we dreamed of. Doubtless he has been long in secret traffic with The Tisroc, and as soon as he had found the lion-skin he sent him word to make ready his navy for the taking of Cair Paravel and all Narnia. Nothing now remains for us seven but to go back to Stable Hill, proclaim the truth, and take the adventure that Aslan sends us. And if, by a great marvel, we defeat those thirty Calormenes who are with the Ape, then to turn again and die in battle with the far greater host of them that will soon march from Cair Paravel."

Tirian nodded. But he turned to the children and said: "Now, friends, it is time for you to go hence into your own world. Doubtless you have done all that you were sent to do."

"B—but we've done nothing," said Jill who was shivering, not with fear exactly but because everything was so horrible.

"Nay," said the King, "you loosed me from the tree: you glided before me like a snake last night in the wood and took Puzzle: and you, Eustace, killed your man. But you are too young to share in such a bloody end as we others must meet tonight or, it may be, three days hence. I entreat you—nay, I command you—to return to your own place. I should be put to shame if I let such young warriors fall in battle on my side."

"No, no, no," said Jill (very white when she began speaking and then suddenly very red and then white again). "We won't, I don't care what you say. We're going to stick with you whatever happens, aren't we, Eustace?"

"Yes, but there's no need to get so worked up about it," said Eustace who had stuck his hands in his pockets (forgetting how very odd that looks when you are wearing a mail shirt). "Because, you see, we haven't any choice. What's the good of talking about our going back! How? We've got no magic for doing it!"

This was very good sense but, at the moment, Jill hated Eustace for saying it. He was fond of being dreadfully matter-of-fact when other people got excited.

When Tirian realized that the two strangers could not get home (unless Aslan suddenly whisked them away), he next wanted them to go across the Southern mountains into Archenland where they might possibly be safe. But they didn't know their way and there was no one to send with them. Also, as Poggin said, once the Calormenes had Narnia they would certainly take Archenland in the next week or so: The Tisroc had always wanted to have these Northern countries for his own. In the end Eustace and Jill begged so hard that Tirian said they could come with him and take their chance—or, as he much more sensibly called it, "the adventure that Aslan would send them."

—*The Last Battle*

Why do you think Jill is so resistant to returning home? And why does she hate Eustace for a moment for pointing out that they cannot return home? Would you want to return to safety or to stay for the adventure that Aslan would send them?

Grown-Up Silliness

CHILDREN HAVE ONE KIND OF SILLINESS, as you know, and grown-ups have another kind. At this moment Uncle Andrew was beginning to be silly in a very grown-up way. Now that the Witch was no longer in the same room with him he was quickly forgetting how she had frightened him and thinking more and more of her wonderful beauty. He kept on saying to himself, "A dem fine woman, sir, a dem fine woman. A superb creature." He had also somehow managed to forget that it was the children who had got hold of this "superb creature": he felt as if he himself by his Magic had called her out of unknown worlds.

"Andrew, my boy," he said to himself as he looked in the glass, "you're a devilish well-preserved fellow for your age. A distinguished-looking man, sir."

You see, the foolish old man was actually beginning to imagine the Witch would fall in love with him. The two drinks probably had something to do with it, and so had his best clothes. But he was, in any case, as vain as a peacock; that was why he had become a Magician.

—*The Magician's Nephew*

What is Uncle Andrew's particular brand of grown-up silliness? How have you been guilty of this foolishness?

Our Last Night on Earth

Tirian, with his head against Jewel's flank, slept as soundly as if he were in his royal bed at Cair Paravel, till the sound of a gong beating awoke him and he sat up and saw that there was firelight on the far side of the stable and knew that the hour had come.

"Kiss me, Jewel," he said. "For certainly this is our last night on earth. And if ever I offended against you in any matter great or small, forgive me now."

"Dear King," said the Unicorn, "I could almost wish you had, so that I might forgive it. Farewell. We have known great joys together. If Aslan gave me my choice I would choose no other life than the life I have had and no other death than the one we go to."

—*The Last Battle*

What do Tirian's and Jewel's words to each other reveal about them? What would you say to your loved ones if you believed it your last night on earth?

The Sunrise

SLOWLY THE DOOR OPENED AGAIN and out there came a figure as tall and straight as the girl's but not so slender. It carried no light but light seemed to come from it. As it came nearer, Lucy saw that it was like an old man. His silver beard came down to his bare feet in front and his silver hair hung down to his heels behind and his robe appeared to be made from the fleece of silver sheep. He looked so mild and grave that once more all the travelers rose to their feet and stood in silence.

But the old man came on without speaking to the travelers and stood on the other side of the table opposite to his daughter. Then both of them held up their arms before them and turned to face the east. In that position they began to sing. I wish I could write down the song, but no one who was present could remember it. Lucy said afterward that it was high, almost shrill, but very beautiful, "A cold kind of song, an early morning kind of song." And as they sang, the grey clouds lifted from the eastern sky and the white patches grew bigger and bigger till it was all white, and the sea began to shine like silver. And long afterward (but those two sang all the time) the east began to turn red and at last, unclouded, the sun came up out of the sea and its long level ray shot down the length of the table on the gold and silver and on the Stone Knife.

Once or twice before, the Narnians had wondered whether the sun at its rising did not look bigger in these seas than it had looked at home. This time they were certain. There was no mistaking it. And the brightness of its rays on the dew and on the table was far beyond any morning brightness they had ever seen. And as Edmund said afterward, "Though lots of things happened on that trip which *sound* more exciting, that moment was really the most exciting." For now they knew that they had truly come to the beginning of the End of the World.

—*The Voyage of the* Dawn Treader

Why would this moment of seeing the sunrise be the most exciting of their journey?

A Terrible Journey

[T]HE WITCH AND EDMUND drove out under the archway and on and away into the darkness and the cold. This was a terrible journey for Edmund, who had no coat. Before they had been going quarter of an hour all the front of him was covered with snow—he soon stopped trying to shake it off because, as quickly as he did that, a new lot gathered, and he was so tired. Soon he was wet to the skin. And oh, how miserable he was! It didn't look now as if the Witch intended to make him a King. All the things he had said to make himself believe that she was good and kind and that her side was really the right side sounded to him silly now. He would have given anything to meet the others at this moment—even Peter! The only way to comfort himself now was to try to believe that the whole thing was a dream and that he might wake up at any moment. And as they went on, hour after hour, it did come to seem like a dream.

—The Lion, the Witch, and the Wardrobe

Which do you think are worse for Edmund—the physical discomforts of the journey or his miserable thoughts?

Tash

I N THE SHADOW OF THE TREES on the far side of the clearing something was moving. It was gliding very slowly Northward. At a first glance you might have mistaken it for smoke, for it was grey and you could see things through it. But the deathly smell was not the smell of smoke. Also, this thing kept its shape instead of billowing and curling as smoke would have done. It was roughly the shape of a man but it had the head of a bird; some bird of prey with a cruel, curved beak. It had four arms which it held high above its head, stretching them out Northward as if it wanted to snatch all Narnia in its grip; and its fingers—all twenty of them—were curved like its beak and had long, pointed, bird-like claws instead of nails. It floated on the grass instead of walking, and the grass seemed to wither beneath it.

After one look at it Puzzle gave a screaming bray and darted into the Tower. And Jill (who was no coward, as you know) hid her face in her hands to shut out the sight of it. The others watched it for perhaps a minute, until it streamed away into the thicker trees on their right and disappeared. Then the sun came out again, and the birds once more began to sing.

Everyone started breathing properly again and moved. They had all been still as statues while it was in sight.

"What was it?" said Eustace in a whisper.

"I have seen it once before," said Tirian. "But that time it was carved in stone and overlaid with gold and had solid diamonds for eyes. It was when I was no older than thou, and had gone as a guest to The Tisroc's court in Tashbaan. He took me into the great temple of Tash. There I saw it, carved above the altar."

"Then that—that thing—was Tash?" said Eustace.

But instead of answering him Tirian slipped his arm behind Jill's shoulders and said, "How is it with you, Lady?"

"A-all right," said Jill, taking her hands away from her pale face and trying to smile. "I'm all right. It only made me feel a little sick for a moment."

"It seems, then," said the Unicorn, "that there is a real Tash, after all."

"Yes," said the Dwarf. "And this fool of an Ape, who didn't believe in Tash, will get more than he bargained for! He called for Tash: Tash has come."

"Where has it—he—the Thing—gone to?" said Jill.

"North into the heart of Narnia," said Tirian. "It has come to dwell among us. They have called it and it has come."

—*The Last Battle*

How are the group's feelings upon seeing Tash different from when they first met Aslan?

As They Were Before

"WHEN WILL THE SPELL WORK?" asked Lucy. "Will the Duffers be visible again at once?"

"Oh yes, they're visible now. But they're probably all asleep still; they always take a rest in the middle of the day."

"And now that they're visible, are you going to let them off being ugly? Will you make them as they were before?"

"Well, that's rather a delicate question," said the Magician. "You see, it's only *they* who think they were so nice to look at before. They say they've been uglified, but that isn't what I called it. Many people might say the change was for the better."

—*The Voyage of the* **Dawn Treader**

Do you think it would matter to the Duffers that other people thought they looked just fine before, if they didn't feel that way? When people compliment your appearance, do you tend to believe them? Whose opinion about your appearance matters most to you?

New Faces

Let us now proceed to the coronation of King Frank of Narnia and Helen his Queen."

The children now noticed these two for the first time. They were dressed in strange and beautiful clothes, and from their shoulders rich robes flowed out behind them to where four dwarfs held up the King's train and four river-nymphs the Queen's. Their heads were bare; but Helen had let her hair down and it made a great improvement in her appearance. But it was neither hair nor clothes that made them look so different from their old selves. Their faces had a new expression, especially the King's. All the sharpness and cunning and quarrelsomeness which he had picked up as a London cabby seemed to have been washed away, and the courage and kindness which he had always had were easier to see. Perhaps it was the air of the young world that had done it, or talking with Aslan, or both.

"Upon my word," whispered Fledge to Polly. "My old master's been changed nearly as much as I have! Why, he's a real master now."

—*The Magician's Nephew*

Why does Narnia bring out the best in the new king and queen and the worst in others, such as the Witch and Uncle Andrew?

DECEMBER

The Falling of the Stars

THEN THE GREAT GIANT raised a horn to his mouth. They could see this by the change of the black shape he made against the stars. After that—quite a bit later, because sound travels so slowly—they heard the sound of the horn: high and terrible, yet of a strange, deadly beauty.

Immediately the sky became full of shooting stars. Even one shooting star is a fine thing to see; but these were dozens, and then scores, and then hundreds, till it was like silver rain: and it went on and on. And when it had gone on for some while, one or two of them began to think that there was another dark shape against the sky as well as the giant's. It was in a different place, right overhead, up in the very roof of the sky as you might call it. "Perhaps it is a cloud," thought Edmund. At any rate, there were no stars there: just blackness. But all around, the downpour of stars went on. And then the starless patch began to grow, spreading further and further out from the center of the sky. And presently a quarter of the whole sky was black, and then a half, and at last the rain of shooting stars was going on only low down near the horizon.

With a thrill of wonder (and there was some terror in it too) they all suddenly realized what was happening. The spreading blackness was not a cloud at all: it was simply emptiness. The black part of the sky was the part in which there were no stars left. All the stars were falling: Aslan had called them home.

—*The Last Battle*

What must it have felt like to watch the sky overtaken by emptiness? Does emptiness frighten you? Why or why not? What do you think it means to be called home by Aslan?

Hope Rises

WHAT LOVELY GRAPES!" came Aunt Letty's voice. "I'm sure if anything could do her good these would. But poor, dear little Mabel! I'm afraid it would need fruit from the land of youth to help her now. Nothing in *this* world will do much." Then they both lowered their voices and said a lot more that he could not hear.

If [Digory] had heard that bit about the land of youth a few days ago he would have thought Aunt Letty was just talking without meaning anything in particular, the way grown-ups do, and it wouldn't have interested him. He almost thought so now. But suddenly it flashed upon his mind that he now knew (even if Aunt Letty didn't) that there really were other worlds and that he himself had been in one of them. At that rate there might be a real Land of Youth somewhere. There might be almost anything. There might be fruit in some other world that would really cure his mother! And oh, oh—Well, you know how it feels if you begin hoping for something that you want desperately badly; you almost fight against the hope because it is too good to be true; you've been disappointed so often before. That was how Digory felt. But it was no good trying to throttle this hope. It might—really, really, it just might be true. So many odd things had happened already. And he had the magic rings. There must be worlds you could get to through every pool in the wood. He could hunt through them all. And then—*Mother well again.* Everything right again. He forgot all about watching for the Witch. His hand was already going into the pocket where he kept the yellow ring, when all at once he heard a sound of galloping.

—The Magician's Nephew

Why is this particular hope so hard for Digory to suppress? What would happen to us if we ceased to hope?

Oughtn't Something to Be Done?

"AND I THINK, PERHAPS," said Shasta, "someone ought to be told that there's an army of savage Calormenes attacking Anvard at this very moment."

"You don't say so!" answered the Hedgehog. "Well, think of that. And they do say that Calormen is hundreds and thousands of miles away, right at the world's end, across a great sea of sand."

"It's not nearly as far as you think," said Shasta. "And oughtn't something to be done about this attack on Anvard? Oughtn't your High King to be told?"

"Certain sure, something ought to be done about it," said the Hedgehog. "But you see I'm just on my way to bed for a good day's sleep. Hullo, neighbor!"

The last words were addressed to an immense biscuit-colored rabbit whose head had just popped up from somewhere beside the path. The Hedgehog immediately told the Rabbit what it had just learned from Shasta. The Rabbit agreed that this was very remarkable news and that somebody ought to tell someone about it with a view to doing something.

And so it went on. Every few minutes they were joined by other creatures, some from the branches overhead and some from little underground houses at their feet, till the party consisted of five rabbits, a squirrel, two magpies, a goat-foot faun, and a mouse, who all talked at the same time and all agreed with the Hedgehog. For the truth was that in that golden age when the Witch and the Winter had gone and Peter the High King ruled at Cair Paravel, the smaller woodland people of Narnia were so safe and happy that they were getting a little careless.

—*The Horse and His Boy*

Why do you think the creatures prefer to tell others the news rather than to take action immediately? When have you ever felt so safe and happy that you became a little careless? What were the results?

Can't You See Him?

LOOKING DOWN, she could see a steep and narrow path going slantwise down into the gorge between rocks, and Aslan descending it. He turned and looked at her with his happy eyes. Lucy clapped her hands and began to scramble down after him. From behind her she heard the voices of the others shouting, "Hi! Lucy! Look out, for goodness' sake. You're right on the edge of the gorge. Come back—". . .

Half-way down the path Edmund caught up with her.

"Look!" he said in great excitement. "Look! What's that shadow crawling down in front of us?"

"It's *his* shadow," said Lucy.

"I do believe you're right, Lu," said Edmund. "I can't think how I didn't see it before. But where is he?"

"With his shadow, of course. Can't you see him?"

"Well, I almost thought I did—for a moment. It's such a rum light.". . .

In a few minutes they were at the bottom, and the roaring of water filled their ears. Treading delicately, like a cat, Aslan stepped from stone to stone across the stream. In the middle he stopped, bent down to drink, and as he raised his shaggy head, dripping from the water, he turned to face them again. This time Edmund saw him. "Oh, Aslan!" he cried, darting forward. But the Lion whisked round and began padding up the slope on the far side of the Rush.

"Peter, Peter," cried Edmund. "Did you see?"

"I saw something," said Peter. "But it's so tricky in this moonlight. On we go, though, and three cheers for Lucy. I don't feel half so tired now, either."

Aslan without hesitation led them to their left, farther up the gorge. The whole journey was odd and dream-like—the roaring stream, the wet grey grass, the glimmering cliffs which they were approaching, and always the glorious, silently pacing beast ahead. Everyone except Susan and the Dwarf could see him now.

—*Prince Caspian*

What does it take for the others to be able to see Aslan, as Lucy always could?

Tears for King Caspian

THEN ASLAN STOPPED, and the children looked into the stream. And there, on the golden gravel of the bed of the stream, lay King Caspian, dead, with the water flowing over him like liquid glass. His long white beard swayed in it like water-weed. And all three stood and wept. Even the Lion wept: great Lion-tears, each tear more precious than the Earth would be if it was a single solid diamond. And Jill noticed that Eustace looked neither like a child crying, nor like a boy crying and wanting to hide it, but like a grown-up crying. At least, that is the nearest she could get to it; but really, as she said, people don't seem to have any particular ages on that mountain.

—*The Silver Chair*

What does it mean to cry like a grown-up? Why is it appropriate to cry at the end of Caspian's life?

The Capture of the Dwarfs

'WARE ARROWS," said Poggin suddenly.

Everyone ducked and pulled his helmet well over his nose. The Dogs crouched behind. But though a few arrows came their way it soon became clear that they were not being shot at. Griffle and his Dwarfs were at their archery again. This time they were coolly shooting at the Calormenes.

"Keep it up, boys!" came Griffle's voice. "All together. Carefully. We don't want Darkies any more than we want Monkeys—or Lions—or Kings. The Dwarfs are for the Dwarfs."

Whatever else you may say about Dwarfs, no one can say they aren't brave. They could easily have got away to some safe place. They preferred to stay and kill as many of both sides as they could, except when both sides were kind enough to save them trouble by killing one another. They wanted Narnia for their own.

What perhaps they had not taken into account was that the Calormenes were mail-clad and the Horses had had no protection. Also the Calormenes had a leader. Rishda Tarkaan's voice cried out:

"Thirty of you keep watch on those fools by the white rock. The rest, after me, that we may teach these sons of earth a lesson."

Tirian and his friends, still panting from their fight and thankful for a few minutes' rest, stood and looked on while the Tarkaan led his men against the Dwarfs. It was a strange scene by now. The fire had sunk lower: the light it gave was now less and of a darker red. As far as one could see, the whole place of assembly was now empty except for the Dwarfs and the Calormenes. In that light one couldn't make out much of what was happening. It sounded as if the Dwarfs were putting up a good fight. Tirian could hear Griffle using dreadful language, and every now and then the Tarkaan calling, "Take all you can alive! Take them alive!"

Whatever that fight may have been like, it did not last long. The noise of it died away. Then Jill saw the Tarkaan coming back to the stable: eleven men followed him, dragging eleven bound Dwarfs. (Whether the others had all been killed, or whether some of them had got away, was never known.)

"Throw them into the shrine of Tash," said Rishda Tarkaan.

And when the eleven Dwarfs, one after the other, had been flung or kicked into that dark doorway and the door had been shut again, he bowed low to the stable and said:

"These also are for thy burnt offering, Lord Tash."

And all the Calormenes banged the flats of their swords on their shields and shouted, "Tash! Tash! The great god Tash! Inexorable Tash!" (There was no nonsense about "Tashlan" now.)

—*The Last Battle*

How can looking out for only your kind lead to destruction?

The Happy Land of Narnia

THE HORSE HAD LIFTED ITS HEAD. Shasta stroked its smooth-as-satin nose and said, "I wish *you* could talk, old fellow."

And then for a second he thought he was dreaming, for quite distinctly, though in a low voice, the Horse said, "But I can."

Shasta stared into its great eyes and his own grew almost as big, with astonishment.

"How ever did *you* learn to talk?"

"Hush! Not so loud," replied the Horse. "Where I come from, nearly all the animals talk."

"Wherever is that?" asked Shasta.

"Narnia," answered the Horse. "The happy land of Narnia—Narnia of the heathery mountains and the thymy downs, Narnia of the many rivers, the plashing glens, the mossy caverns and the deep forests ringing with the hammers of the Dwarfs. Oh the sweet air of Narnia! An hour's life there is better than a thousand years in Calormen." It ended with a whinny that sounded very like a sigh.

"How did you get here?" said Shasta.

"Kidnapped," said the Horse. "Or stolen, or captured—whichever you like to call it. I was only a foal at the time. My mother warned me not to range the Southern slopes, into Archenland and beyond, but I wouldn't heed her. And by the Lion's Mane I have paid for my folly. All these years I have been a slave to humans, hiding my true nature and pretending to be dumb and witless like *their* horses."

"Why didn't you tell them who you were?"

"Not such a fool, that's why. If they'd once found out I could talk they would have made a show of me at fairs and guarded me more carefully than ever. My last chance of escape would have been gone."

—***The Horse and His Boy***

Would you hide your true nature as the Horse does? How is pretending to be something you're not its own kind of slavery?

The Remains of the Castle

THEY FOUND THEMSELVES in a wide open place with walls all round it. In here there were no trees, only level grass and daisies, and ivy, and grey walls. It was a bright, secret, quiet place, and rather sad; and all four stepped out into the middle of it, glad to be able to straighten their backs and move their limbs freely.

"This wasn't a garden," said Susan presently. "It was a castle and this must have been the courtyard."

"I see what you mean," said Peter. "Yes. That is the remains of a tower. And there is what used to be a flight of steps going up to the top of the walls. And look at those other steps—the broad, shallow ones—going up to that doorway. It must have been the door into the great hall."

"Ages ago, by the look of it," said Edmund.

"Yes, ages ago," said Peter. "I wish we could find out who the people were that lived in this castle; and how long ago."

"It gives me a strange feeling," said Lucy.

"Does it, Lu?" said Peter, turning and looking hard at her. "Because it does the same to me. It is the queerest thing that has happened this queer day. I wonder where we are and what it all means?"

—*Prince Caspian*

Why might a place give them a strange feeling? When has a place made you feel strange? Afterward, were you able to discern any reason for your feeling?

The Seven Kings and Queens

AND TIRIAN TURNED TO SEE who had spoken. And what he saw then set his heart beating as it had never beaten in any fight.

Seven Kings and Queens stood before him, all with crowns on their heads and all in glittering clothes, but the Kings wore fine mail as well and had their swords drawn in their hands. Tirian bowed courteously and was about to speak when the youngest of the Queens laughed. He stared hard at her face, and then gasped with amazement, for he knew her. It was Jill: but not Jill as he had last seen her, with her face all dirt and tears and an old drill dress half slipping off one shoulder. Now she looked cool and fresh, as fresh as if she had just come from bathing. And at first he thought she looked older, but then didn't, and he could never make up his mind on that point. And then he saw that the youngest of the Kings was Eustace: but he also was changed as Jill was changed.

Tirian suddenly felt awkward about coming among these people with the blood and dust and sweat of a battle still on him. Next moment he realized that he was not in that state at all. He was fresh and cool and clean, and dressed in such clothes as he would have worn for a great feast at Cair Paravel. (But in Narnia your good clothes were never your uncomfortable ones. They knew how to make things that felt beautiful as well as looking beautiful in Narnia: and there was no such thing as starch or flannel or elastic to be found from one end of the country to the other.)

"Sire," said Jill, coming forward and making a beautiful curtsey, "let me make you known to Peter the High King over all Kings in Narnia."

Tirian had no need to ask which was the High King, for he remembered his face (though here it was far nobler) from his dream. He stepped forward, sank on one knee and kissed Peter's hand.

"High King," he said. "You are welcome to me."

And the High King raised him and kissed him on both cheeks as a High King should. Then he led him to the eldest of the Queens—but even she was not old, and there were no grey hairs on her head and no wrinkles on her cheek—and said, "Sir, this is that Lady Polly who came into Narnia on the First Day, when Aslan made the trees grow and the

Beasts talk." He brought him next to a man whose golden beard flowed over his breast and whose face was full of wisdom. "And this," he said, "is the Lord Digory who was with her on that day. And this is my brother, King Edmund: and this my sister, the Queen Lucy."

—*The Last Battle*

After retreating from the battle into the stable where the god Tash was, what must Tirian be feeling as he's suddenly face to face with the Kings and Queens he has read so much about, including two he has just been fighting side-by-side with? What has changed about the outward appearance of the Kings and Queens?

Return to the World Aboveground

WHAT HAD REALLY HAPPENED to Jill was this. As soon as she got her head out of the hole she found that she was looking down as if from an upstairs window, not up as if through a trap-door. She had been so long in the dark that her eyes couldn't at first take in what they were seeing: except that she was not looking at the daylit, sunny world which she so wanted to see. The air seemed to be deadly cold, and the light was pale and blue. There was also a good deal of noise going on and a lot of white objects flying about in the air. It was at that moment that she had shouted down to Puddleglum to let her stand on his shoulders.

When she had done this, she could see and hear a good deal better. The noises she had been hearing turned out to be two kinds: the rhythmical thump of several feet, and the music of four fiddles, three flutes, and a drum. She also got her own position clear. She was looking out of a hole in a steep bank which sloped down and reached the level about fourteen feet below her. Everything was very white. A lot of people were moving about. Then she gasped! The people were trim little Fauns, and Dryads with leaf-crowned hair floating behind them. For a second they looked as if they were moving anyhow; then she saw that they were really doing a dance—a dance with so many complicated steps and figures that it took you some time to understand it. Then it came over her like a thunderclap that the pale, blue light was moonlight, and the white stuff on the ground was really snow. And of course! There were the stars staring in a black frosty sky overhead. And the tall black things behind the dancers were trees. They had not only got out into the upper world at last, but had come out in the heart of Narnia. Jill felt she could have fainted with delight; and the music—the wild music, intensely sweet and yet just the least bit eerie too, and full of good magic as the Witch's thrumming had been full of bad magic—made her feel it all the more.

—*The Silver Chair*

Having just come up from the Underworld, Jill takes awhile to make out even familiar sights aboveground. How can adventures allow you to come back and see your old world with new eyes?

Aslan Learns of Edmund's Betrayal

WELCOME, PETER, Son of Adam," said Aslan. "Welcome, Susan and Lucy, Daughters of Eve. Welcome He-Beaver and She-Beaver."

His voice was deep and rich and somehow took the fidgets out of them. They now felt glad and quiet and it didn't seem awkward to them to stand and say nothing.

"But where is the fourth?" asked Aslan.

"He has tried to betray them and joined the White Witch, O Aslan," said Mr. Beaver. And then something made Peter say,

"That was partly my fault, Aslan. I was angry with him and I think that helped him to go wrong."

And Aslan said nothing either to excuse Peter or to blame him but merely stood looking at him with his great unchanging eyes. And it seemed to all of them that there was nothing to be said.

"Please—Aslan," said Lucy, "can anything be done to save Edmund?"

"All shall be done," said Aslan. "But it may be harder than you think." And then he was silent again for some time. Up to that moment Lucy had been thinking how royal and strong and peaceful his face looked; now it suddenly came into her head that he looked sad as well.

—The Lion, the Witch, and the Wardrobe

Why do you think Aslan reacts the way he does to the news of Edmund's betrayal and Peter's subsequent confession? At what times in your life have you felt there was nothing to be said?

No Son of Yours

[Said the Tarkaan,] "This boy is manifestly no son of yours, for your cheek is as dark as mine but the boy is fair and white like the accursed but beautiful barbarians who inhabit the remote North."

"How well it was said," answered the fisherman, "that Swords can be kept off with shields but the Eye of Wisdom pierces through every defense! Know then, O my formidable guest, that because of my extreme poverty I have never married and have no child. But in that same year in which the Tisroc (may he live forever) began his august and beneficent reign, on a night when the moon was at her full, it pleased the gods to deprive me of my sleep. Therefore I arose from my bed in this hovel and went forth to the beach to refresh myself with looking upon the water and the moon and breathing the cool air. And presently I heard a noise as of oars coming to me across the water and then, as it were, a weak cry. And shortly after, the tide brought to the land a little boat in which there was nothing but a man lean with extreme hunger and thirst who seemed to have died but a few moments before (for he was still warm), and an empty waterskin, and a child, still living. 'Doubtless,' said I, 'these unfortunates have escaped from the wreck of a great ship, but by the admirable designs of the gods, the elder has starved himself to keep the child alive and has perished in sight of land.' Accordingly, remembering how the gods never fail to reward those who befriend the destitute, and being moved by compassion (for your servant is a man of tender heart)—"

"Leave out all these idle words in your own praise," interrupted the Tarkaan. "It is enough to know that you took the child—and have had ten times the worth of his daily bread out of him in labor, as anyone can see. And now tell me at once what price you put on him, for I am wearied with your loquacity.". . .

At this point Shasta got up and tiptoed away. He had heard all he wanted, for he had often listened when men were bargaining in the village and knew how it was done. He was quite certain that Arsheesh would sell him in the end for something much more than fifteen crescents and much less than seventy, but that he and the Tarkaan would take hours in getting to an agreement.

You must not imagine that Shasta felt at all as you and I would feel if we had just overheard our parents talking about selling us for slaves. For one thing, his life was already little better than slavery; for all he knew, the lordly stranger on the great horse might be kinder to him than Arsheesh. For another, the story about his own discovery in the boat had filled him with excitement and with a sense of relief. He had often been uneasy because, try as he might, he had never been able to love the fisherman, and he knew that a boy ought to love his father. And now, apparently, he was no relation to Arsheesh at all. That took a great weight off his mind. "Why, I might be anyone!" he thought. "I might be the son of a Tarkaan myself—or the son of the Tisroc (may he live forever)—or of a god!"

—*The Horse and His Boy*

How does hearing about his true origins bring Shasta relief? Hope?

Narnia Is No More

"SIRE," SAID THE EAGLE, "when you have heard my news you will be sorrier of my coming than of the greatest woe that ever befell you."

Tirian's heart seemed to stop beating at these words, but he set his teeth and said, "Tell on."

"Two sights have I seen," said Farsight. "One was Cair Paravel filled with dead Narnians and living Calormenes: The Tisroc's banner advanced upon your royal battlements: and your subjects flying from the city—this way and that, into the woods. Cair Paravel was taken from the sea. Twenty great ships of Calormen put in there in the dark of the night before last night."

No one could speak.

"And the other sight, five leagues nearer than Cair Paravel, was Roonwit the Centaur lying dead with a Calormene arrow in his side. I was with him in his last hour and he gave me this message to your Majesty: to remember that all worlds draw to an end and that noble death is a treasure which no one is too poor to buy."

"So," said the King, after a long silence, "Narnia is no more."

—*The Last Battle*

Upon hearing this news, would Roonwit's words about all worlds coming to an end and the importance of noble death provide you any comfort? Why or why not?

A Task Well Done

WELL DONE," said Aslan in a voice that made the earth shake. Then Digory knew that all the Narnians had heard those words and that the story of them would be handed down from father to son in that new world for hundreds of years and perhaps forever. But he was in no danger of feeling conceited for he didn't think about it at all now that he was face to face with Aslan. This time he found he could look straight into the Lion's eyes. He had forgotten his troubles and felt absolutely content.

"Well done, Son of Adam," said the Lion again. "For this fruit you have hungered and thirsted and wept. No hand but yours shall sow the seed of the tree that is to be the protection of Narnia. Throw the apple toward the river bank where the ground is soft."

Digory did as he was told. Everyone had grown so quiet that you could hear the soft thump where it fell into the mud.

"It is well thrown," said Aslan.

—The Magician's Nephew

Why might being face to face with Aslan prevent Digory from even thinking of being conceited? Whose approval in your life compares to Aslan's words of approval for Digory?

Rishda Tarkaan Is Thrown to Tash

A NEW IDEA came into Tirian's head. He dropped his sword, darted forward, in under the sweep of the Tarkaan's scimitar, seized his enemy by the belt with both hands, and jumped back into the stable, shouting:

"Come in and meet Tash yourself!"

There was a deafening noise. As when the Ape had been flung in, the earth shook and there was a blinding light.

The Calormene soldiers outside screamed, "Tash, Tash!" and banged the door. If Tash wanted their own Captain, Tash must have him. They, at any rate, did not want to meet Tash.

For a moment or two Tirian did not know where he was or even who he was. Then he steadied himself, blinked, and looked around. It was not dark inside the stable, as he had expected. He was in strong light: that was why he was blinking.

He turned to look at Rishda Tarkaan, but Rishda was not looking at him. Rishda gave a great wail and pointed; then he put his hands before his face and fell flat, face downward, on the ground. Tirian looked in the direction where the Tarkaan had pointed. And then he understood.

A terrible figure was coming toward them. It was far smaller than the shape they had seen from the Tower, though still much bigger than a man, and it was the same. It had a vulture's head and four arms. Its beak was open and its eyes blazed. A croaking voice came from its beak.

"Thou hast called me into Narnia, Rishda Tarkaan. Here I am. What hast thou to say?"

But the Tarkaan neither lifted his face from the ground nor said a word. He was shaking like a man with a bad hiccup. He was brave enough in battle: but half his courage had left him earlier that night when he first began to suspect that there might be a real Tash. The rest of it had left him now.

With a sudden jerk—like a hen stooping to pick up a worm—Tash pounced on the miserable Rishda and tucked him under the upper of his two right arms.

But immediately, from behind Tash, strong and calm as the summer sea, a voice said:

"Begone, Monster, and take your lawful prey to your own place: in the name of Aslan and Aslan's great Father the Emperor-over-the-Sea."

The hideous creature vanished, with the Tarkaan still under its arm.

—*The Last Battle*

Even though he does not believe in Tash, Rishda Tarkaan still succeeds in calling him to Narnia. What do you think it means that the Tarkaan is Tash's lawful prey?

Bother the Signs

BUT IT WAS DREADFUL TO be out on top again. Down in those narrow slits of trenches, their ears had almost begun to thaw. They had been able to see clearly and breathe easily and hear each other speak without shouting. It was absolute misery to come back into the withering coldness. And it did seem hard when Puddleglum chose that moment for saying:

"Are you still sure of those signs, Pole? What's the one we ought to be after now?"

"Oh, come *on*! Bother the signs," said Pole. "Something about someone mentioning Aslan's name, I think. But I'm jolly well not going to give a recitation here."

As you see, she had got the order wrong. That was because she had given up saying the signs over every night. She still really knew them, if she troubled to think: but she was no longer so "pat" in her lesson as to be sure of reeling them off in the right order at a moment's notice and without thinking. Puddleglum's question annoyed her because, deep down inside her, she was already annoyed with herself for not knowing the Lion's lesson quite so well as she felt she ought to have known it. This annoyance, added to the misery of being very cold and tired, made her say, "Bother the signs." She didn't perhaps quite mean it.

"Oh, that was next, was it?" said Puddleglum. "Now I wonder, are you right? Got 'em mixed, I shouldn't wonder. It seems to me, this hill, this flat place we're on, is worth stopping to have a look at. Have you noticed—"

"Oh, Lor!" said Scrubb, "is this a time for stopping to admire the view? For goodness' sake let's get on."

"Oh, look, look, look," cried Jill and pointed. Everyone turned, and everyone saw. Some way off to the north, and a good deal higher up than the tableland on which they stood, a line of lights had appeared. This time, even more obviously than when the travelers had seen them the night before, they were windows: smaller windows that made one think deliciously of bedrooms, and larger windows that made one think of great halls with fires roaring on the hearth and hot soup or juicy sirloins smoking on the table.

"Harfang!" exclaimed Scrubb.

"That's all very well," said Puddleglum. "But what I was saying was—"

"Oh, shut up," said Jill crossly.

—*The Silver Chair*

Jill has become so distracted by the promised comforts of Harfang that she has stopped reciting the signs Aslan gave her. Why does she react so crossly when Puddleglum tries to redirect her? When have you found yourself snapping at someone who was trying to help?

Ready for War

[T]HERE CAME IN SIGHT the noblest creatures that Caspian had yet seen, the great Centaur Glenstorm and his three sons. His flanks were glossy chestnut and the beard that covered his broad chest was golden-red. He was a prophet and a star-gazer and knew what they had come about.

"Long live the King," he cried. "I and my sons are ready for war. When is the battle to be joined?"

Up till now neither Caspian nor the others had really been thinking of a war. They had some vague idea, perhaps, of an occasional raid on some Human farmstead or of attacking a party of hunters, if it ventured too far into these southern wilds. But, in the main, they had thought only of living to themselves in woods and caves and building up an attempt at Old Narnia in hiding. As soon as Glenstorm had spoken everyone felt much more serious.

"Do you mean a real war to drive Miraz out of Narnia?" asked Caspian.

"What else?" said the Centaur. "Why else does your Majesty go clad in mail and girt with sword?"

"Is it possible, Glenstorm?" said the Badger.

"The time is ripe," said Glenstorm. "I watch the skies, Badger, for it is mine to watch, as it is yours to remember. Tarva and Alambil have met in the halls of high heaven, and on earth a son of Adam has once more arisen to rule and name the creatures. The hour has struck. Our council at the Dancing Lawn must be a council of war." He spoke in such a voice that neither Caspian nor the others hesitated for a moment: it now seemed to them quite possible that they might win a war and quite certain that they must wage one.

—*Prince Caspian*

Why do you think the idea of war has not quite occurred to Caspian and his companions? Do you have anyone in your life like Glenstorm, who drives you to action?

We Have Lived Too Long

"WELL," SAID THE KING AT LAST, "we must go on and take the adventure that comes to us."

"It is the only thing left for us to do, Sire," said the Unicorn. He did not see at the moment how foolish it was for two of them to go on alone; nor did the King. They were too angry to think clearly. But much evil came of their rashness in the end.

Suddenly the King leaned hard on his friend's neck and bowed his head.

"Jewel," he said, "what lies before us? Horrible thoughts arise in my heart. If we had died before today we should have been happy."

"Yes," said Jewel. "We have lived too long. The worst thing in the world has come upon us." They stood like that for a minute or two and then went on.

—The Last Battle

After hearing that Aslan has ordered the felling of the holy trees, King Tirian and Jewel say they wish they had died before today. What do you think they mean by this statement? Has despair ever led you to do foolish things?

Come Close to Your Own World

PLEASE, ASLAN," SAID LUCY. "Before we go, will you tell us when we can come back to Narnia again? Please. And oh, do, do, do make it soon."

"Dearest," said Aslan very gently, "you and your brother will never come back to Narnia."

"Oh, *Aslan*!!" said Edmund and Lucy both together in despairing voices.

"You are too old, children," said Aslan, "and you must begin to come close to your own world now."

—*The Voyage of the* **Dawn Treader**

Why might it be important for Lucy and Edmund to become close to their own world now that they are growing older?

In Our World

"IT ISN'T NARNIA, YOU KNOW," sobbed Lucy. "It's *you*. We shan't meet *you* there. And how can we live, never meeting you?"

"But you shall meet me, dear one," said Aslan.

"Are—are you there too, Sir?" said Edmund.

"I am," said Aslan. "But there I have another name. You must learn to know me by that name. This was the very reason why you were brought to Narnia, that by knowing me here for a little, you may know me better there."

—The Voyage of the **Dawn Treader**

What might it have been like for Lucy and Edmund to realize that Aslan has been in their world all along, but they've never noticed? Does this surprise you?

If You Like

EDMUND WAS STILL STARING after the sledge when he heard someone calling his own name, and looking round he saw Lucy coming toward him from another part of the wood.

"Oh, Edmund!" she cried. "So you've got in too! Isn't it wonderful, and now—"

"All right," said Edmund, "I see you were right and it is a magic wardrobe after all. I'll say I'm sorry if you like. But where on earth have you been all this time? I've been looking for you everywhere."

"If I'd known you had got in I'd have waited for you," said Lucy, who was too happy and excited to notice how snappishly Edmund spoke or how flushed and strange his face was. "I've been having lunch with dear Mr. Tumnus, the Faun, and he's very well and the White Witch has done nothing to him for letting me go, so he thinks she can't have found out and perhaps everything is going to be all right after all."

—*The Lion, the Witch, and the Wardrobe*

When Edmund sees Lucy, he knows he must say something about not believing her story about the land in the wardrobe. What's the difference between truly apologizing and saying, as Edmund does here, "I'll say I'm sorry if you like"? How would you feel to be on the receiving end of his words?

All Get What They Want

SON OF ADAM," said Aslan, "you have sown well. And you, Narnians, let it be your first care to guard this Tree, for it is your Shield. The Witch of whom I told you has fled far away into the North of the world; she will live on there, growing stronger in dark Magic. But while that tree flourishes she will never come down into Narnia. She dare not come within a hundred miles of the Tree, for its smell, which is joy and life and health to you, is death and horror and despair to her."

. . . Aslan suddenly swung round his head . . . and fixed his large eyes on the children. "What is it, children?" he said, for he caught them in the very act of whispering and nudging one another.

"Oh—Aslan, sir," said Digory, turning red, "I forgot to tell you. The Witch has already eaten one of those apples, one of the same kind that Tree grew from." He hadn't really said all he was thinking, but Polly at once said it for him. (Digory was always much more afraid than she of looking a fool.)

"So we thought, Aslan," she said, "that there must be some mistake, and she can't really mind the smell of those apples."

"Why do you think that, Daughter of Eve?" asked the Lion.

"Well, she ate one."

"Child," he replied, "that is why all the rest are now a horror to her. That is what happens to those who pluck and eat fruits at the wrong time and in the wrong way. The fruit is good, but they loathe it ever after."

"Oh, I see," said Polly. "And I suppose because she took it in the wrong way it won't work for her. I mean it won't make her always young and all that?"

"Alas," said Aslan, shaking his head. "It will. Things always work according to their nature. She has won her heart's desire; she has unwearying strength and endless days like a goddess. But length of days with an evil heart is only length of misery and already she begins to know it. All get what they want; they do not always like it."

—*The Magician's Nephew*

Why would getting her heart's desire turn into such a misery for the Witch?

I'm Going to Roll Anyway

BY ABOUT THE MIDDLE of the morning they were on their way. The Horses had expected that Aravis and Cor would ride, but Cor explained that except in war, where everyone must do what he can do best, no one in Narnia or Archenland ever dreamed of mounting a Talking Horse.

This reminded poor Bree again of how little he knew about Narnian customs and what dreadful mistakes he might make. So while Hwin strolled along in a happy dream, Bree got more nervous and more self-conscious with every step he took.

"Buck up, Bree," said Cor. "It's far worse for me than for you. You aren't going to be *educated*. I shall be learning reading and writing and heraldry and dancing and history and music while you'll be galloping and rolling on the hills of Narnia to your heart's content."

"But that's just the point," groaned Bree. "*Do* Talking Horses roll? Supposing they don't? I can't bear to give it up. What do you think, Hwin?"

"I'm going to roll anyway," said Hwin. "I don't suppose any of them will care two lumps of sugar whether you roll or not."

—*The Horse and His Boy*

What is at the root of the difference of opinion between Bree and Hwin? Have you ever been so concerned about whether you were doing the right thing in others' eyes that you could not enjoy yourself? In what areas are you most worried about what others think of you?

Aslan's Eyes

DIGORY NEVER SPOKE on the way back, and the others were shy of speaking to him. He was very sad and he wasn't even sure all the time that he had done the right thing; but whenever he remembered the shining tears in Aslan's eyes he became sure.

All day Fledge flew steadily with untiring wings; eastward with the river to guide him, through the mountains and over the wild wooded hills, and then over the great waterfall and down, and down, to where the woods of Narnia were darkened by the shadow of the mighty cliff, till at last, when the sky was growing red with sunset behind them, he saw a place where many creatures were gathered together by the riverside. And soon he could see Aslan himself in the midst of them. Fledge glided down, spread out his four legs, closed his wings, and landed cantering. Then he pulled up. The children dismounted. Digory saw all the animals, dwarfs, satyrs, nymphs, and other things drawing back to the left and right to make way for him. He walked up to Aslan, handed him the apple, and said:

"I've brought you the apple you wanted, sir."

—*The Magician's Nephew*

As Digory thinks through the aftermath of rejecting the Witch's offer for him to take an apple from the tree to heal his mother, he thinks back to the tears in Aslan's eyes when Digory spoke to him about his sick mother. Why do those tears make Digory so confident in him? What in your life serves as a similar touchstone to help you know or remember that you are doing the right thing or acting in the right way?

The End of Narnia

THEN ASLAN SAID, "Now make an end."
The giant . . . stretched out one arm—very black it looked, and thousands of miles long—across the sky till his hand reached the Sun. He took the Sun and squeezed it in his hand as you would squeeze an orange. And instantly there was total darkness.

Everyone except Aslan jumped back from the ice-cold air which now blew through the Doorway. Its edges were already covered with icicles.

"Peter, High King of Narnia," said Aslan. "Shut the Door."

Peter, shivering with cold, leaned out into the darkness and pulled the Door to. . . . Then, rather clumsily (for even in that moment his hands had gone numb and blue) he took out a golden key and locked it.

They had seen strange things enough through that Doorway. But it was stranger than any of them to look round and find themselves in warm daylight, the blue sky above them, flowers at their feet, and laughter in Aslan's eyes.

He turned swiftly round, crouched lower, lashed himself with his tail and shot away like a golden arrow.

"Come further in! Come further up!" he shouted over his shoulder. . . .

"So," said Peter, "night falls on Narnia. What, Lucy! You're not *crying*? With Aslan ahead, and all of us here?"

"Don't try to stop me, Peter," said Lucy, "I am sure Aslan would not. I am sure it is not wrong to mourn for Narnia. . . ."

"Yes and I *did* hope," said Jill, "that it might go on forever. I knew *our* world couldn't. I did think Narnia might."

"I saw it begin," said the Lord Digory. "I did not think I would live to see it die."

"Sirs," said Tirian. "The ladies do well to weep. See, I do so myself. I have seen my mother's death. What world but Narnia have I ever known? It were no virtue, but great discourtesy, if we did not mourn."

—*The Last Battle*

Why is it discourtesy not to mourn Narnia?

We Shall Meet Again Soon

[ASLAN SAID,] "And today before sunset I must visit Trump-kin the Dwarf where he sits in the castle of Cair Paravel counting the days till his master Caspian comes home. I will tell him all your story, Lucy. Do not look so sad. We shall meet soon again."

"Please, Aslan," said Lucy, "what do you call *soon*?"

"I call all times soon," said Aslan; and instantly he was vanished away and Lucy was alone with the Magician.

"Gone!" said he, "and you and I quite crestfallen. It's always like that, you can't keep him; it's not as if he were a *tame* lion."

—*The Voyage of the* **Dawn Treader**

Why can't Aslan give Lucy a closer indication of when they will meet again? What do you think he means by "I call all times soon"?

How They Got Here

EUSTACE SAID TO KING PETER, "You haven't yet told us how you got here. You were just going to, when King Tirian turned up."

"There's not much to tell," said Peter. "Edmund and I were standing on the platform and we saw your train coming in. I remember thinking it was taking the bend far too fast. And I remember thinking how funny it was that our people were probably in the same train though Lucy didn't know about it—"

"Your people, High King?" said Tirian.

"I mean my Father and Mother—Edmund's and Lucy's and mine."

"Why were they?" asked Jill. "You don't mean to say *they* know about Narnia?"

"Oh no, it had nothing to do with Narnia. They were on their way to Bristol. I'd only heard they were going that morning. But Edmund said they'd be bound to be going by that train.". . .

"And what happened then?" said Jill.

"Well, it's not very easy to describe, is it, Edmund?" said the High King.

"Not very," said Edmund. "It wasn't at all like that other time when we were pulled out of our own world by Magic. There was a frightful roar and something hit me with a bang, but it didn't hurt. And I felt not so much scared as—well, excited. Oh—and this is one queer thing. I'd had a rather sore knee, from a hack at rugger. I noticed it had suddenly gone. And I felt very light. And then—here we were."

"It was much the same for us in the railway carriage," said the Lord Digory. . . . "Only I think you and I, Polly, chiefly felt that we'd been un-stiffened. You youngsters won't understand. But we stopped feeling old."

—*The Last Battle*

What was so different about this journey than their other trips to Narnia? What changes in your own body would you hope would result from being transported to this place?

Those Who Have Died

SON OF ADAM," said Aslan, "go into that thicket and pluck the thorn that you will find there, and bring it to me."

Eustace obeyed. The thorn was a foot long and sharp as a rapier.

"Drive it into my paw, Son of Adam," said Aslan, holding up his right fore-paw and spreading out the great pad toward Eustace.

"Must I?" said Eustace.

"Yes," said Aslan.

Then Eustace set his teeth and drove the thorn into the Lion's pad. And there came out a great drop of blood, redder than all redness that you have ever seen or imagined. And it splashed into the stream over the dead body of the King. At the same moment the doleful music stopped. And the dead King began to be changed. His white beard turned to grey, and from grey to yellow, and got shorter and vanished altogether; and his sunken cheeks grew round and fresh, and the wrinkles were smoothed, and his eyes opened, and his eyes and lips both laughed, and suddenly he leaped up and stood before them—a very young man, or a boy. (But Jill couldn't say which, because of people having no particular ages in Aslan's country. Even in this world, of course, it is the stupidest children who are the most childish and the stupidest grown-ups who are the most grown-up.) And he rushed to Aslan and flung his arms as far as they would go round the huge neck; and he gave Aslan the strong kisses of a King, and Aslan gave him the wild kisses of a Lion.

At last Caspian turned to the others. He gave a great laugh of astonished joy.

"Why! Eustace!" he said. "Eustace! So you did reach the end of the world after all. What about my second-best sword that you broke on the sea-serpent?"

Eustace made a step toward him with both hands held out, but then drew back with a startled expression.

"Look here! I say," he stammered. "It's all very well. But aren't you—? I mean, didn't you—?"

"Oh, don't be such an ass," said Caspian.

"But," said Eustace, looking at Aslan. "Hasn't he—er—died?"

"Yes," said the Lion in a very quiet voice, almost (Jill thought) as if he were laughing. "He has died. Most people have, you know. Even I have. There are very few who haven't."

—*The Silver Chair*

Why would Eustace's question make Aslan sound almost as if he were laughing? How does this passage match up with or differ from your ideas about death?

Home at Last

"PETER," SAID LUCY, "where is this, do you suppose?". . .
"If you ask me," said Edmund, "it's like somewhere in the Narnian world. Look at those mountains ahead—and the big ice-mountains beyond them. Surely they're rather like the mountains we used to see from Narnia, the ones up Westward beyond the Waterfall?". . .

"And yet they're not like," said Lucy. "They're different. They have more colors on them and they look further away than I remembered and they're more . . . more . . . oh, I don't know . . ."

"More like the real thing," said the Lord Digory softly. . . .

"But how can it be?" said Peter. "For Aslan told us older ones that we should never return to Narnia, and here we are."

"Yes," said Eustace. "And we saw it all destroyed and the sun put out."

"And it's all so different," said Lucy.

"The Eagle is right," said the Lord Digory. "Listen, Peter. When Aslan said you could never go back to Narnia, he meant the Narnia you were thinking of. But that was not the real Narnia. That had a beginning and an end. It was only a shadow or a copy of the real Narnia which has always been here and always will be here: just as our own world, England and all, is only a shadow or copy of something in Aslan's real world. You need not mourn over Narnia, Lucy. All of the old Narnia that mattered, all the dear creatures, have been drawn into the real Narnia through the Door. And of course it is different; as different as a real thing is from a shadow or as waking life is from a dream." His voice stirred everyone like a trumpet as he spoke these words: but when he added under his breath "It's all in Plato, all in Plato: bless me, what *do* they teach them at these schools!" the older ones laughed. It was so exactly like the sort of thing they had heard him say long ago in that other world where his beard was grey instead of golden. He knew why they were laughing and joined in the laugh himself. But very quickly they all became grave again: for, as you know, there is a kind of happiness and wonder that makes you serious. It is too good to waste on jokes. . . .

It was the Unicorn who summed up what everyone was feeling. He stamped his right fore-hoof on the ground and neighed, and then cried:

"I have come home at last! This is my real country! I belong here. This is the land I have been looking for all my life, though I never knew it till now. The reason why we loved the old Narnia is that it sometimes looked a little like this. Bree-hee-hee! Come further up, come further in!"

—*The Last Battle*

What do you think the Unicorn means when he says that the reason they loved the old Narnia is that sometimes it looked a little like this? When have you caught a glimpse of something more, something better in your world?

Narnia Within Narnia

ABOUT HALF AN HOUR LATER—or it might have been half a hundred years later, for time there is not like time here—Lucy stood with her dear friend, her oldest Narnian friend, the Faun Tumnus, looking down over the wall of that garden, and seeing all Narnia spread out below. But when you looked down you found that this hill was much higher than you had thought: it sank down with shining cliffs, thousands of feet below them and trees in that lower world looked no bigger than grains of green salt. Then she turned inward again and stood with her back to the wall and looked at the garden.

"I see," she said at last, thoughtfully. "I see now. This garden is like the stable. It is far bigger inside than it was outside."

"Of course, Daughter of Eve," said the Faun. "The further up and the further in you go, the bigger everything gets. The inside is larger than the outside."

Lucy looked hard at the garden and saw that it was not really a garden but a whole world, with its own rivers and woods and sea and mountains. But they were not strange: she knew them all.

"I see," she said. "This is still Narnia, and more real and more beautiful than the Narnia down below, just as *it* was more real and more beautiful than the Narnia outside the stable door! I see . . . world within world, Narnia within Narnia. . . ."

"Yes," said Mr. Tumnus, "like an onion: except that as you continue to go in and in, each circle is larger than the last."

—*The Last Battle*

What do you think the Faun means by saying that the further up and the further in you get the bigger everything gets? What else in life has an inside bigger than its outside?

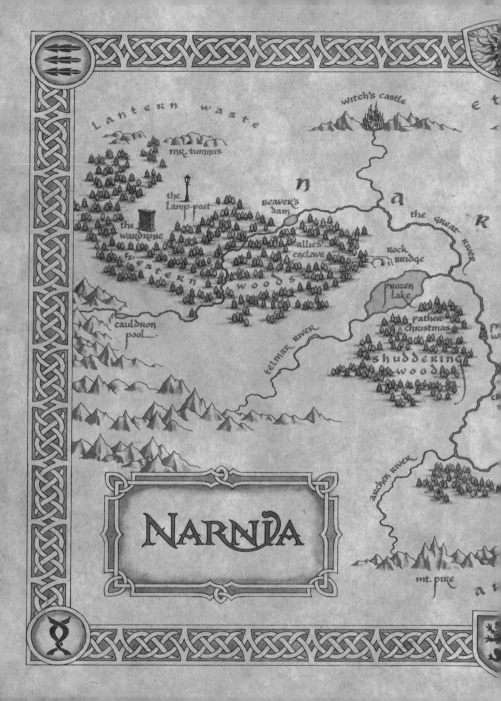